REFRESHED ◆ REVISED ◆ UPDATED

Hachette CHILDREN'S Yearbook & Infopedia 2025

hachette INDIA

First published in 2024 by Hachette India
(Registered name: Hachette Book Publishing India Pvt Ltd)
An Hachette UK company
www.hachetteindia.com

1

IMAGE COPYRIGHT INFORMATION: FRONT COVER: SUNIL CHHETRI: Wikimedia Commons: GODL-India: Press Information Bureau on behalf of President's Secretariat, Government of India under the ID 171473 and CNR 151932; TAYLOR SWIFT 2019: CC SA 4.0 International license/ © Glenn Francis, www.PacificProDigital.com; PRIME MINISTER SIR KEIR STARMER OFFICIAL PORTRAIT: the United Kingdom Open Government Licence v3.0: https://www.nationalarchives.gov.uk/doc/open-government-licence/version/3/; SONAM WANGCHUK: CC BY-SA 2.0 Generic: Sonam Wangchuk; ROHIT SHARMA, VIRAT KOHLI and NARENDRA MODI: Wikimedia Commons: GODL-India: PIB on behalf of Prime Minster's Office; SUNITA WILLIAMS: NASA: http://www.jsc.nasa.gov/Bios/htmlbios/williams-s.html; P.V. SINDHU: Wikimedia Commons: GODL-India: PIB on behalf of Prime Minister's office; NEERAJ CHOPRA: CC CC0 1.0 Universal Public Domain Dedication/ Lakyanaik; GAGANYAAN CREW AT RUSSIA: Indian Space Research Organisation; RAM JANMABHOOMI MANDIR: Wikimedia Commons: GODL-India: PIB on behalf of Prime Minister's Office; MANIKA BATRA: CC BY-SA 4.0 International license: Author: Government of Odisa; PIXABAY: Olympic rings, elephant, AI; **BACK COVER:** MANU BHAKER: CC BY-SA 4.0 International license: Author: Government of Odisa; RLV-TD LEX-02 Landing Experiment: ISRO. The remaining photographs and illustrations are sourced from the public domain.

The copyright details and credits for the photographs in the book are on page 224, which is to be considered as an extension of the copyright page.

RESEARCH AND CONTENT WRITING: Anadya Narain, Lakshika Ahuja, Umikha Hemant Rathod, Navaneethakkrishnan, Charvi Solanki, Mouli Joshi

ISBN 978-93-5731-914-0

Hachette Book Publishing India Pvt. Ltd
4th & 5th Floors, Corporate Centre
Plot No. 94, Sector 44, Gurugram 122003, India

MIX
Paper | Supporting responsible forestry
FSC™ C043100
www.fsc.org

Typeset and design by Syed Salahuddin

Printed and bound in India
by Manipal Technologies Limited

CONTENTS

NEWS

The Year Ahead

UPDATES

LITERATURE

COUNTRIES

EARTH

SPACE

HISTORY

CONTENTS

INDIAN STATES AND UNION TERRITORIES

SCIENCE AND TECHNOLOGY

SPORTS

1 NEWS

INDIA

OCTOBER 2023

AI-powered chest X-ray application launched on the Raj-Silicosis portal

To facilitate the silicosis certification procedure on the new Silicosis Portal at the District Pneumoconiosis Board level, Dr Samit Sharma, secretary to the government of Rajasthan, announced the development of an Artificial Intelligence (AI)–based application. Social Justice and Empowerment Minister Tikaram Juli of Rajasthan inaugurated the application. By enabling early disease detection, the application aims to allow for prompt intervention and treatment, potentially preventing disease progression.

Agroha set to become a global city

Urban Local Bodies Minister Dr Kamal Gupta announced a plan to develop Agroha as a global city within a radius of 25 kilometers. This development aims to give Agroha a distinctive identity, similar to Singapore and Mauritius. Dr Gupta mentioned that a large museum, modelled after Rakhigarhi, is intended to be developed by the Haryana government. The Excavation Branch of the Survey of India and the Haryana State Archaeology Department will collaborate on the excavation of the Agroha archaeological site.

NOVEMBER 2023

Cancer patients will receive financial assistance akin to Old Age Respect Allowance

Third- and fourth-stage cancer patients will receive monthly financial assistance to help cover living expenses, basic necessities, medical costs, indirect costs, out-of-pocket expenses and other needs. The proposal to offer this monthly financial help to cancer patients, modelled after the Old Age Samman stipend plan, was approved at the Cabinet meeting on 27 November 2023, presided over by Haryana Chief Minister Manohar Lal.

JANUARY 2024

PRITHvi VIgyan Scheme

The scheme aims to enhance Earth System Sciences and offer essential services for societal, environmental and economic well-being. This project consists of five sub-schemes.

- ACROSS: Atmosphere & Climate Research Modelling Observing

Systems & Services.

- O-SMART: Ocean Services, Modelling Application, Resources and Technology.
- Polar Science and Cryosphere Research, or PACER.
- SAGE (Seismology and Geosciences): Its goal is to improve research on the solid components of Earth and earthquake monitoring.
- Research, Education, Training and Outreach is known as REACHOUT.

The scheme promotes the development of technology for maritime resource exploration and sustainable exploitation. In order to enable quick and efficient disaster management, PRITHvi offers advanced warning services for natural disasters such as cyclones, floods, heat waves and earthquakes.

Ayodhya Ram Mandir inaugurated

On 22 January, 2024, PM Narendra Modi conducted the 'Pran Pratishtha' ceremonies in the Ram Mandir at Ayodhya, revealing the visage of Ram Lalla, the infant Lord Ram. The inauguration ceremony was attended by numerous dignitaries, religious leaders and thousands of devotees from across the country, marking a significant moment in the history of the temple.

Vantara: World's largest animal rehabilitation centre

Vantara, which translates to 'Star of the Forest', is the biggest rehabilitation centre for animals in the world. The project established by Anant Ambani, the younger son of Reliance Industries Chairman Mukesh Ambani, aims at providing a natural environment to preserve and nurture endangered animals. The shelter comprises a one-of-its-kind hospital to rescue and tend to elephants who are generally poached for their ivory tusks. With state-of-the-art technology and facilities, Vantara is set to turn into a successful global biodiversity project and reflects a significant step towards sustainable wildlife conservation.

India's first underwater metro now open

Covering a distance of 4.8 kilometres, the first underwater metro of

India is located in Kolkata. The metro service is a part of the new Green line and goes from Howrah Maidan to Esplanade stations under the Hooghly river. The service is open for public use from 7 a.m. to 9.45 p.m. Prime Minister Narendra Modi inaugurated the new metro stations on 6 March, marking a significant milestone in India's transportation infrastructure. The underwater metro project is a marvel of modern engineering, designed to ease traffic congestion and provide a faster, more efficient mode of transportation for the city's residents.

RLV-LEX-02 launched successfully by ISRO

ISRO successfully conducted the second landing experiment using its Reusable Launch Vehicle (RLV) technology, named RLV-LEX-02. The mission took place at the Aeronautical Test Range in Chitradurga, Karnataka. The winged vehicle, named Pushpak, was carried by an Indian Air Force helicopter and released mid-air to demonstrate autonomous landing capabilities.

This test is a significant milestone in ISRO's efforts to develop reusable space launch technology aimed at reducing the cost of access to space. The Pushpak vehicle was designed to simulate the final approach phase of a reusable space vehicle's return to Earth. After being released from the helicopter, Pushpak autonomously glided and executed a precise landing on a designated runway, demonstrating its robust navigation and control systems. RLV-LEX-03, scheduled for June, the goal of which is to check the sink rate and hopefully lower it to lessen the weight impact.

Kodaikanal Solar Observatory completed 125 years

Established by the British East India Company in 1899, the Kodaikanal Solar Observatory marks its 125th anniversary as a unique astronomical site in the world. Located in Tamil Nadu, this observatory has played a pivotal role in advancing Indian astronomy through a series of significant observations. Over the years, it has contributed immensely to solar research, making key discoveries and laying the foundational groundwork for Indian astronomy. Its strategic location provides ideal conditions for studying the sun and other celestial phenomena. The observatory continues to be a vital hub for

scientific research, attracting astronomers and researchers from around the globe.

Sonam Wangchuk ends 21-day-long hunger strike

Sonam Wangchuk, the prominent Leh-based engineer and climate activist, concluded his 21-day-long hunger strike aimed at drawing attention to the deteriorating condition of the Himalayan ecosystem and advocating for statehood for Ladakh. His hunger strike highlighted the urgent need for environmental conservation in the fragile Himalayan region. In continuation of his efforts, a peaceful 'border march' took place on 7 April to raise awareness about the challenges faced by the Himalayan peaks.

APRIL 2024

Bindyarani Devi bags a bronze medal in IWF World Cup 2024

Bindyarani Devi, a weightlifter from Manipur bagged the third position in women's 59-kilogram event in Phuket, Thailand. She lifted a total weight of 196 kilograms and was beaten by North Korea's Kang Hyon Gyong, who lifted 234 kilograms, and Romania's Cambei Mihaela-Valentina, who lifted 201 kilograms, claiming the first and second positions, respectively. Bindyarani Devi also earned the silver medal in the clean and jerk category with a lift of 113 kilograms. Her achievement at the World Cup underscores her dedication and talent in weightlifting, bringing pride to India on the international stage.

MAY 2024

BHISHM portable hospital launched

The Aarogya Maitri Aid Cube hospital, part of India's Bharat Health Initiative for Sahyog Hita and Maitri (BHISHM) initiative, is a groundbreaking 'flatpack' field hospital swiftly deployable via helicopter to disaster zones. Comprising 72 compact, waterproof cubes each weighing under 15 kilograms, it's equipped with ventilators, portable X-ray and ultrasound devices, mini-ICU units and an operating theatre. Powered by generators and solar panels, it includes cooking facilities and water. Launched by Prime Minister Narendra Modi, it aims to aid global disaster response with rapid deployment capabilities and advanced medical tools. Recently, two units bolstered medical preparedness at the Ayodhya Pran Prathistha ceremony, exemplifying its pivotal role in emergency healthcare.

KKR dominates IPL 2024

Kolkata Knight Riders (KKR) defeated Sunrisers Hyderabad (SRH) in the Tata Indian Premier League IPL 2024 final match that was held on 27 May. They secured the title by dominating SRH's batting line-up. It was the bowlers that clinched the title this time. Mitchel Starc, the Player of the Match, led the bowlers. KKR managed to chase down 50 runs within 5 overs and got past 100 runs inside 9 overs. This is KKR's third claim on the title in the past 15 years. Captained by Shreyas Iyer, KKR had 9 wins from 14 games this season. Iyer's boys demolished their opponents by 8 wickets and 57 balls to spare, making this match the shortest final ever played. Shah Rukh Khan, the co-owner of the team, was present at the event, and received congratulatory wishes from several celebrities. This win was particularly significant because Gautam Gambhir, the former international cricketer and ex-captain of KKR, returned as a mentor to the team, inspiring resolution and reminiscence for another win.

INDIAN PREMIER LEAGUE®

Major heatwave grips nation

India experienced its most intense heatwaves in recent years, with temperatures soaring well above normal across several states. The heatwave resulted in increased cases of heatstroke and dehydration, prompting authorities to issue warnings and advise citizens to stay indoors during peak hours. The extreme weather has affected agriculture, with reports of crop damage and water scarcity adding to the challenges. Meteorologists attributed the heatwave to prolonged dry spells and climatic factors exacerbated by global warming.

JUNE 2024

Indian cricket team wins ICC T20 World Cup

India's cricket team secured a historic triumph in the ICC T20 World Cup, defeating their opponents in a thrilling final match. Held in a packed stadium, the team showcased exceptional skill and teamwork, clinching the coveted trophy amidst jubilant celebrations.

Captain Rohit Sharma led the charge with exemplary leadership, while a standout performance from Suryakumar Yadav contributed to the team's success. The victory marks a significant achievement for Indian cricket, igniting nationwide pride and joy among fans. The team's resilience and determination throughout the tournament underscore their status as champions on the global stage.

JULY 2024

Gautam Gambhir appointed head coach of India men's cricket team

Following Rahul Dravid's decision to step away as head coach to the men's cricket team, India's cricket board appointed Gautam Gambhir as his successor. His first appearance as coach of the national team was the white-ball tour of Sri Lanka in late July.

Gautam Gambhir is the only Indian cricketer – and one of four international cricketers, which includes Jacques Kallis, Mohammad Yousuf and Don Bradman – to have scored centuries in five successive Test matches. He has also scored more than 10,000 international runs during his 13-year-long international career for India since his ODI debut in 2003.

STOP PRESS

Sunita Williams stuck in space

NASA astronaut Sunita Williams and Butch Wilmore have been stuck on the International Space Station since 5 June 2024 due to software issues, helium leaks and thruster anomalies detected in the Starliner capsule, which brought them to space. It is speculated that they may be stuck there till February 2025.

SUNITA WILLIAMS

Vinesh Phogat announces retirement

Olympic wrestler Vinesh Phogat announced her retirement from the sport after being disqualified from the finals match for exceeding the stipulated weight limit. She has been professionally competing since young, and representing the country in international competitions since 2013. She is one of the most decorated Indian wrestlers, having won multiple medals at the Commonwealth Games, the Asian Games and the World Wrestling Championships. She has been urged to reverse this decision by her supporters.

VINESH PHOGAT

India House at Olympic Village

Reliance Foundation, in partnership with the Indian Olympic Association (IOA), presented the India House, the representative Olympic hospitality house of India. The India House was the conceptualization of the country's culture, history and practices. From yoga sessions to live performances by renowned dancers and singers, from a bazaar for traditional textiles, craftsmanship and artworks, to food from all around the nation, India House had it all.

NOVEMBER 2023

World's first overseas flight using 100% green fuels

A first-of-its-kind 100 per cent sustainable aviation flight called 'Flight100' was launched by Virgin Atlantic. The flight took off from London's Heathrow Airport and landed safely at John F. Kennedy International Airport, New York. Richard Branson, the founder of Virgin Atlantic, CEO Shai Weiss and UK Transport Minister Mark Harper were the passengers on board. The replacement of traditional jet fuel with 'green fuel' aims to reduce the net carbon emissions of the aviation industry and is a milestone achievement in the field.

4th ASEAN India Grassroots Innovation Forum

Through Science, Technology and Innovation (STI), the fourth edition of ASEAN India Grassroots Innovation Forum (AIGIF) aimed to strengthen the relationship between India and ASEAN Member States. Malaysia's Minister of Science, Technology and Innovation Y.B. Chang Lih Kang inaugurated AIGIF 2023 and established its principles. Seventeen student innovators formed the Indian delegation and around 200 participants from eleven countries attended the conference.

DECEMBER 2023

Chinese ship drills Earth's mantle

Mengxiang became the first ship launched by China to excavate into the Earth's upper mantle. With a length of 179 metres and a cargo capacity of 33,000 tonnes, the vessel can traverse 15,000 nautical miles in 120 days. The expedition revealed vital information related to the mantle's energy sources, deep sea organisms and plate tectonics, among other things. The ship is equipped with advanced drilling technology and sensors, allowing scientists to gather new data on Earth's internal processes and composition.

Resolution on Gaza ceasefire is vetoed by the US

The United Nations Security Council (UNSC) passed a resolution on the Gaza ceasefire with 153 nations in favour, 10 against and 23 abstaining. Despite being supported by the majority, the resolution failed as the US used its veto power in Israel's favour. The five permanent members of the UNSC, also known as the P5 (the United States, the United Kingdom, France, China and Russia), can exercise their veto powers to block any resolution. Many member states have criticized the power enjoyed by the P5 members.

JANUARY 2024

Bhutan elections won by PDP

With a clear majority of 30 out of 47 seats, the People's Democratic Party (PDP) was declared as the winner of Bhutan elections 2024. The remainder 17 seats were won by the Bhutan Tendrel Party, which emerged as the opposition party. The PDP's campaign focused on infrastructure development and the growth of the private sector, whereas the Bhutan Tendrel Party stressed on innovation and local empowerment. This election marked the fourth edition of the National Assembly election of Bhutan. However, the voter turnout reduced considerably from 2018.

FEBRUARY 2024

Indian Ocean Conference held in Perth

With an aim to protect the Indian Ocean region from geopolitical, economic and other security threats, the Indian Ocean Conference was established and held in Singapore in 2006 for the first time. Since its debut the conference has played an important role in bringing together countries to discuss prospects of regional cooperation and ensure maritime security and safety. After the sixth edition in 2023 in Bangladesh, the seventh and most recent edition was held in Perth, Australia. Some of the key concerns of the conference are piracy, terrorism and rapid climate change. The theme of this year was 'Towards a Stable and Sustainable Indian Ocean'.

AI-generated robocalls banned in US

The US Federal Communications Commission (FCC) has banned robocalls generated by AI after a surge in voice cloning scams. AI can easily fake a human's voice and tone, convincing the receivers to believe that they are speaking to their acquaintance. Many fraudulent cases have reported such calls demanding for sensitive information or money. The FCC has warned people against AI robocalls as well as banned companies from using them immediately.

MARCH 2024

EU passes world's first regulation on AI

On 13 March, the European Parliament passed the European AI Act, the world's first comprehensive regulation on AI by a major regulator anywhere. The Act adopts a risk-based approach, banning AI systems deemed to pose 'unacceptable' risks and regulating others based on their risk levels. The responsibilities mainly fall on AI developers. The Act prohibits AI models that manipulate human behaviour or exploit vulnerabilities related to race, religion or sexual orientation. Low-risk systems, like spam filters, are minimally regulated. The legislation covers AI across various sectors, excluding military, national security, research and non-professional uses. Amnesty International, an NGO focused on human rights, criticized the Act for not banning real-time facial recognition and the export of harmful AI technologies, warning of potential threats to human rights and civil liberties.

APRIL 2024

Dubai floods highlight climate change

Dubai experienced severe flooding in April 2024 following unprecedented rainfall, the heaviest in 75 years. The torrential downpour, which exceeded the city's annual rainfall in just a few hours, caused widespread disruption. Major highways were submerged and Dubai International Airport, a key global travel hub, faced significant delays as flights were diverted. Authorities issued a stay-at-home order, urging residents to avoid travel. Many schools and businesses were temporarily closed. The government allocated significant resources to address the damage. The flood highlights the challenges of climate change, but despite this the infrastructure and spirit of the people of Dubai helped in the recovery of the city.

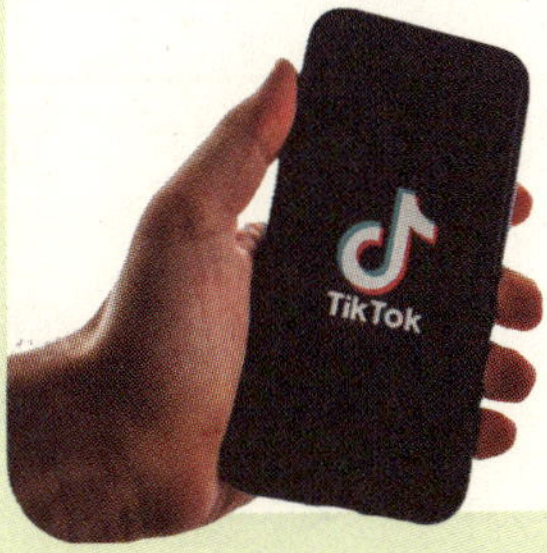

TikTok faces US ban

TikTok, the popular social media app, owned by Chinese company ByteDance, has faced scrutiny over data breach and privacy concerns. The US senate approved a bill that could force a sale of TikTok by its Chinese owner or ban it outright in the United States. Lawmakers argued that

TikTok posed a risk to user data, potentially allowing the Chinese government to access sensitive information on American citizens. The ban sparked significant debate around free speech and digital rights. The bill has posed resistance from Beijing, and TikTok plans to challenge the bill in court. It could take a while before the app gets banned.

The great solar storm frenzy

In May, Earth faced its most intense solar storm in 20 years, driven by a series of powerful solar flares and coronal mass ejections (CMEs). The sun, a massive ball of electrically charged hot gas, undergoes an 11-year cycle where its magnetic field flips, influencing solar activity such as sunspots and flares. This storm's CMEs sent billions of tonnes of solar plasma towards Earth, swelling the upper atmosphere and causing the magnetic field to vibrate. The resulting geomagnetic storm created spectacular auroras visible even in low latitudes like the southern United States and northern India. However, the storm also posed significant risks to global infrastructure, potentially disrupting satellites, internet cables and power grids. India's Centre of Excellence in Space Sciences issued a severe space weather notice, urging ISRO to protect space assets. If the bombardment was strong enough, it may have caused a geomagnetic storm that would have blown satellites out of orbit, cut off the underwater cables that connect the Internet and caused widespread blackouts due to failed power grids.

The first US president to be convicted of a crime

Donald Trump became the first US president to be convicted of a crime on 30 May, when a New York jury found him guilty of falsifying documents to cover up a payment to silence an actress ahead of the 2016 election. After two days of deliberation, the 12-member jury pronounced Trump guilty on all 34 felony counts he faced. The prosecution argued that Trump falsified business records to hide a $130,000 payment to Stormy Daniels, which was intended to influence the outcome of the 2016 presidential election. This payment was deemed an illegal campaign contribution as it exceeded the $2,700 individual contribution cap. Prosecutors asserted that the falsifications were intended to cover up violations of New York state election law, which criminalizes promoting a candidate's election through unlawful means.

Ebrahim Raisi passes away in a helicopter crash

Iran's president Ebrahim Raisi was declared dead on 19 May after the helicopter he was travelling in crashed in East Azerbaijan province. The helicopter, carrying Raisi, Foreign Minister Hossein Amir-Abdollahian and six others, went down in blizzard conditions. Initially, it was reported that the helicopter made a hard landing in foggy conditions but later its charred wreckage were found. According to local reports, Raisi had been visiting the area near the Azerbaijan border to open the Qiz Qalasi and Khoda-Afarin dams and had met with President Ilham Aliyev. The Iranian Red Crescent confirmed the recovery of all bodies. Raisi, considered a successor to Supreme Leader Ali Khamenei, was elected president in 2021.

JUNE 2024

Thailand passes equal marriage law

In June 2024, Thailand made a historic decision by passing a law granting equal marriage rights to same-sex couples. This landmark legislation allows people of the same gender to marry legally, giving them the same rights as everyone else. The new law was approved by the Thai parliament after years of advocacy and campaigning by activists and supporters of equal human rights. Thailand is now the first Southeast Asian country to legalize same-sex marriage, joining over 30 countries worldwide in recognizing marriage equality. This significant move reflects Thailand's commitment to promoting equality and human rights, and it has been widely celebrated by the LGBTQ+ community and its allies.

NEWS: WORLD

JULY 2024

Labour Party wins the UK general elections

The United Kingdom held its highly anticipated general elections in July. The two main parties were the Conservatives, led by Prime Minister Rishi Sunak, and the Labour Party, led by Keir Starmer. After months of intense campaigning, the election saw a high voter turnout, reflecting the public's keen interest choosing their next leaders. The Labour Party emerged victorious, gaining a majority in the House of Commons. This victory marked a significant change in British politics, making Keir Starmer the new prime minister of the UK. The key issues discussed in the campaigns were the growth of the economy, better healthcare and focus on climate change. The Labour Party promised to spend more money on hospitals and schools and to make big changes to help green policies.

Global IT Outage: Blue Screen of Death

On 19 July, Crowdstrike, a cybersecurity software, initiated an update which resulted in a global IT outage. The software usually comes integrated with Windows, and its update affected the working of all Microsoft Office 365 apps and services, bringing major tech firms and systems to a sudden halt. The 'Falcon Sensor' software caused the operating system to crash and display the 'Blue Screen of Death'. Users and services affected ranged from individuals, businesses in the UK, the USA, India, Australia and Germany, to international airports such as Tokyo, Amsterdam, Berlin, London and Delhi. The total number of computers affected around the world is said to be 8.5 million.

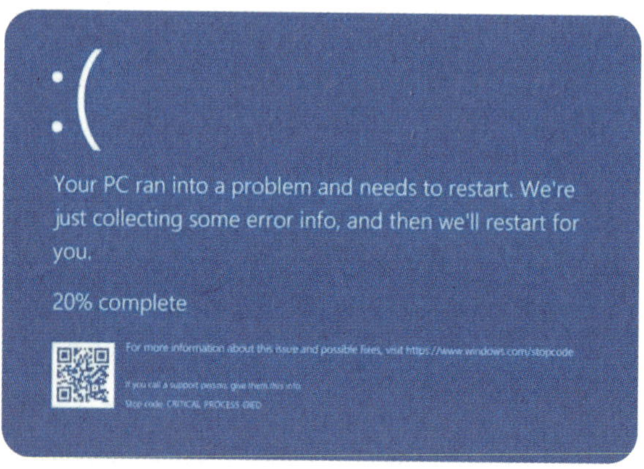

Earthquake in Japan

A 7.1 magnitude 'megaquake' shook southwestern Japan on 8 August, triggering tsunami warnings for multiple islands off the country's coast. According to Japan's meteorological agency, the earthquake hit the Miyazaki Prefecture at a depth of around 29 kilometres, at 4.42 p.m. local time. Another earthquake of 5.3 magnitude hit Tokyo and surrounding areas the next day, increasing concerns amongst citizens and neighbouring countries. Japan thus issued a first-of-its- kind 'megaquake advisory' warning of higher probabilities of huge earthquakes and tsunamis that may incur losses up to US $1.5 trillion.

Bangladesh student protests

Bangladesh was embroiled in nationwide protests following a controversial quota system for government jobs being reinstated by a high court. The quota system had been scrapped by the Sheikh Hasina government in 2018; this system allowed for a reservation of up to 30 per cent for families of war veterans who fought in Bangladesh's war for independence in 1971. Peaceful student protests that started from mid-July onwards turned violent after clashes with the police, resulting in an estimated death count of more than 200. Though the Supreme Court overturned the decision, the protestors demanded the dismissal of Sheikh Hasina and her supporters from the government, and instilled an interim government, currently headed by Nobel laureate Muhammad Yunus.

Kamala Harris becomes the new face of US presidential elections

Kamala Harris is the 49th vice president of the US, the first female vice president, as well as the first African American and Asian American official in the history of the United States. A member of the Democratic Party, she is currently the highest-ranking female official in US history. She is also the party's nominee for the 2024 US presidential election. Her campaign promises include abortion access, gun law reform, and increasing minimum wage.

PEOPLE TO REMEMBER

MICHAEL GAMBON (19 October 1940–27 September 2023): The Olivier Award–winning actor, best known for playing Harry Potter's Albus Dumbledore in major motion pictures, passed away at the age of 83.

M.S. SWAMINATHAN (7 August 1925–28 September 2023): The eminent Indian scientist, who played a pivotal role in the Green Revolution, passed away at the venerable age of 98.

BISHAN SINGH BEDI (25 September 1946–23 October 2023): The cricketing legend, and former captain of the Indian cricket team, passed away at the age of 77. During his career, Bedi represented India in 67 Test matches, leaving a lasting impact with his remarkable performances.

MATTHEW PERRY (19 August 1969–28 October 2023): Actor Matthew Langford Perry was a Canadian American born in the United States. He became well-known throughout the world for his role as Chandler Bing in the sitcom *Friends* on NBC.

JUSTICE FATHIMA BEEVI (30 April 1927–23 November 2023): The first female judge of Supreme Court and former Governor of Tamil Nadu passed away at the age of 96.

ANDRE BRAUGHER (1 July 1962–11 December 2023): The two-time Emmy winning–actor who debuted on screen in the Civil War drama *Glory* (1989), Andre was renowned for his role as Raymond Holt on *Brooklyn Nine-Nine*. He passed away at the age of 61.

PANKAJ UDHAS (17 May 1951–26 February 2024): The famous Indian ghazal and playback singer and recipient of Padma Shri passed away at the age of 72 due to a prolonged illness.

AZIZ QURESHI (24 April 1941–1 March 2024): Former governor of Uttar Pradesh and senior Congress leader Aziz Qureshi passed away after a prolonged illness. He had also served as governor of Uttarakhand, Uttar Pradesh and Mizoram.

BERNARD HILL (17 December 1944–5 May 2024): The actor who played the doomed King of Rohan in the Lord of the Rings franchise and Capt. Edward J. Smith in *Titanic* – one of the only characters in the film based on a real person – passed away at the age of 79.

DAVID WILLIAM SANBORN (30 July 1945–12 May 2024): The saxophonist who earned six Grammy Awards, eight gold albums and one platinum album died on Sunday in Tarrytown, New York. He was 78.

WILLIAM RUSSELL (19 November 1924–3 June 2024): Best known for playing Ian Chesterton in *Doctor Who*, this English actor passed away at the age of 99.

CHERUKURI RAMOJI RAO (16 November 1936–8 June 2024): A businessman, media proprietor and film producer, he was the head of the Ramoji Group which owns the world's largest film production facility, Ramoji Film City, in Hyderabad.

PADMA SHRI

Art: Khalil Ahamad, M. Badrappan, Kaluram Bamniya, Rezwana Chaudhary Bannya, Naseem Bano, Ram Lal Bareth, Gita Ray Barman, Som Datt Battu, Takdira Begum, Drono Bhuyan, Ashok Kumar Biswas, Smriti Rekha Chakma, Velu Anandachari, Ghulam Nabi Dar, Mahabir Singh Guddu, Anupama Hoskere, Janki Lal Bhand, Ratan Kahar, Dasari Kondappa, Jordan Lepcha, Binod Maharana, Daliparthi Umamaheswari, Ram Kumar Mallick, Surendra Mohan Mishra (Posthumous), Ali Mohammed and Ghani Mohammed (Duo), Kiran Nadar, Narayanan E.P., Bhagabat Padhan, Sanatan Rudra Pal, Binod Kumar Pasayat, Silbi Passah, Shanti Devi Paswan and Shivan Paswan (Duo), Romalo Ram, Nirmal Rishi, Pran Sabharwal, Gaddam Sammaiah, Machihan Sasa, Omprakash Sharma, Godawari Singh, Seshampatti T. Sivalingam, Urmila Srivastava, Nepal Chandra Sutradhar (Posthumous), Gopinath Swain, Laxman Bhatt Tailang, Jagdish Trivedi, Balakrishnan Sadanam Puthiyaveetil, Babu Ram Yadav

Literature and Education: Raghuveer Chaudhari, R.N. Joe D'Cruz, Pierre Sylvain Filliozat, Rajaram Jain, Yashwant Singh Kathoch, Zahir I. Kazi, Sridhar Makam Krishnamurthy, Pakaravur Chithran Namboodiripad (Posthumous), Harish Nayak (Posthumous), Fred Negrit, Muni Narayana Prasad, Bhagwatilal Rajpurohit, Navjivan Rastogi, Kethavath Somlal, Gouri Lakshmi Bayi Thampuratty, Kurella Vittalacharya

Literature and Education (Journalism): Surendra Kishore

Medicine: Prema Dhanraj, Radha Krishan Dhiman, Manohar Krishna Dole, Yazdi Maneksha Italia, Hemchand Manjhi, Chandrashekhar Mahadeorao Meshram, G. Natchiar, Radhey Shyam Pareek, Dayal Mavjibhai Parmar, C.R. Chandrashekar

Public Affairs: Sasindran Muthuvel

Science and Engineering: Narayan Chakraborty, Ram Chet Chaudhary, Shailesh Nayak, Hari Om, Eklabya Sharma, Ram Chander Sihag, Ravi Prakash Singh

Social Work: Parbati Barua, Dukhu Majhi, Chami Murmu, Shankar Baba Pundlikarao Papalkar, K.S. Rajanna, Sangthankima, Gurvinder Singh, Somanna, Maya Tandon, Sano Vamuzo, Jageshwar Yadav

Sports: Rohan Machanda Bopanna, Joshana Chinappa, Uday Vishwanath Deshpande, Gaurav Khanna, Satendra Singh Lohia, Purnima Mahato, Harbinder Singh

Trade and Industry: Kalpana Morparia, Shashi Soni

Others: Agriculture: Sarbeswar Basumatary, Sathyanarayana Beleri, K. Chellammal, Yanung Jamoh Lego, Sanjay Anant Patil

Yoga: Charlotte Chopin, Kiran Vyas

Spiritualism: Chitta Ranjan Debbarma

PADMA VIBHUSHAN

Art: Vyjayantimala Bali, Konidela Chiranjeevi, Padma Subrahmanyam
Public Affairs: M. Venkaiah Naidu
Social Work: Bindeshwar Pathak (Posthumous)

PADMA BHUSHAN

Art: Mithun Chakraborty, Dattatray Ambadas Mayaloo alias Rajdutt, Pyarelal Sharma, Usha Uthup, Vijayakant (Posthumous)
Literature and Education (Journalism): Hormusji N. Cama, Kundan Vyas
Social Work: Sitaram Jindal
Trade and Industry: Young Liu
Public Affairs: M. Fathima Beevi (Posthumous), Satyabrata Mookherjee (Posthumous), Ram Naik, Olanchery Rajagopal
Medicine: Ashwin Balachand Mehta, Tejas Madhusudan Patel, Chandreshwar Prasad Thakur
Spiritualism: Togdan Rinpoche (Posthumous)

GRAMMY AWARDS 2024

Record of the year: *Flowers* by Miley Cyrus
Album of the year: *Midnights* by Taylor Swift
Song of the year: 'What Was I Made For?' by Billie Eilish and Finneas
Best New Artist: Victoria Monét
Best Pop Vocal Album: *Midnights* by Taylor Swift
Best Country Album: *Bell Bottom Country* by Lainey Wilson
Best Folk Album: *Joni Mitchell at Newport* by Joni Mitchell
Best Rap Album: *Michael* by Killer Mike
Best Rock Album: *This Is Why* by Paramore
Best Progressive R&B Album: *SOS* by SZA

96TH ACADEMY AWARDS (OSCARS)

Best Picture: *Oppenheimer*
Best Director: Christopher Nolan, *Oppenheimer*
Actor in a Leading Role: Cillian Murphy for *Oppenheimer*
Actress in a Leading Role: Emma Stone for *Poor Things*
Actor in a Supporting Role: Robert Downey Jr. for *Oppenheimer*
Actress in a Supporting Role: Da'Vine Joy Randolph for *The Holdovers*
Animated Feature Film: *The Boy and the Heron*, Hayao Miyazaki and Toshio Suzuki
Cinematography: *Oppenheimer*, Hoyte van Hoytema
Costume Design: Holly Waddington for *Poor Things*
Directing: Christopher Nolan for *Oppenheimer*
Documentary (Feature Film): Mstyslav Chernov, Michelle Mizner and Raney Aronson-Rath for *20 Days in Mariupol*
Documentary (Short Film): Ben Proudfoot and Kris Bowers for *The Last Repair Shop*
Film Editing: Jennifer Lame for *Oppenheimer*
International Feature Film: *The Zone of Interest* (UK) directed by Jonathan Glazer
Production Design: *Poor Things*: James Price and Shona Heath for Production Design; Zsuzsa Mihalek for Set Decoration
Short Film (Animated): Dave Mullins and Brad Booker for *War is Over!*
Short Film (Live Action): Wes Anderson and Steven Rales for *The Wonderful Story of Henry Sugar*
Best Original Screenplay: Justine Triet and Arthur Harari for *Anatomy of a Fall*
Best Adapted Screenplay: Cord Jefferson for *American Fiction*

PULITZER PRIZES

Public Service: ProPublica

Breaking News Reporting: Staff of Lookout Santa Cruz, California

Investigative Reporting: Hannah Dreier of *The New York Times*

Explanatory Reporting: Sarah Stillman of *The New Yorker*

Local Reporting: Sarah Conway of City Bureau and Trina Reynolds-Tyler of the Invisible Institute

National Reporting: Staff of Reuters and Staff of *The Washington Post*

International Reporting: Staff of *The New York Times*

Feature Writing: Katie Engelhart, contributing writer, *The New York Times*

Commentary: Vladimir Kara-Murza, contributor, *The Washington Post*

Criticism: Justin Chang of the *Los Angeles Times*

Editorial Writing: David E. Hoffman of *The Washington Post*

Illustrated Reporting and Commentary: Medar de la Cruz, contributor, *The New Yorker*

Breaking News Photography: Photography Staff of Reuters

Feature Photography: Photography Staff of Associated Press

Audio Reporting: Staffs of the Invisible Institute and USG Audio

BOOKS, DRAMA AND MUSIC

Fiction: *Night Watch* by Jayne Anne Phillips

Drama: *Primary Trust* by Eboni Booth

History: *No Right to an Honest Living: The Struggles of Boston's Black Workers in the Civil War Era* by Jacqueline Jones

Biography: *King: A Life* by Jonathan Eig and *Master Slave Husband Wife: An Epic Journey from Slavery to Freedom* by Ilyon Woo

Memoir or Autobiography: *Liliana's Invincible Summer: A Sister's Search for Justice* by Cristina Rivera Garza

Poetry: *Tripas: Poems* by Brandon Som

General Nonfiction: *A Day in the Life of Abed Salama: Anatomy of a Jerusalem Tragedy* by Nathan Thrall

Music: *Adagio (For Wadada Leo Smith)* by Tyshawn Sorey

SAHITYA AKADEMI BAL PURASKAR 2024

Assamese: *Biponna Bismoi Khel* (Novel) by Ranju Hazarika

Bengali: *Mahidadur Antidote* (Novel) by Dipanwita Roy

Bodo: *Buhuma Boynibw* (Poetry) by Virgin Jekova Machahary

Dogri: *Kukdu Kadoon* (Poetry) by Bishan Singh 'Dardi'

English: *The Blue Horse and Other Amazing Animals from Indian History* (Historical Fiction) by Nandini Sengupta

BY HACHETTE INDIA

Gujarati: *Hasati Haveli* (Stories) by Gira Pinakin Bhatt

Hindi: *51 Baal Kahaniyan* (Stories) by Devender Kumar

Kannada: *Choomantrayyana Kathegalu* (Short Stories) by Krishnamurthy Biligere

Kashmiri: *Sone Gobrew* (Poetry) by Muzaffar Hussain Dilbar

Konkani: *Ek Ashil'lem Bayul* (Novel) by Harsha Sadguru Shetye

Maithili: *Anar* (Short Stories) by Narayanjee

Malayalam: *Algorithangalude Nadu* (Novel) by Unni Ammayambalam

Manipuri: *Malem Atiya* (Novel) by Kshetrimayum Subadani

Marathi: *Samsher Aani Bhootbangala* (Novel) by Bharat Sasane

Nepali: *Desh Ra Fuchhey* (Poetry) by Basanta Thapa

Odia: *Gapa Kalika* (Short Stories) by Manas Ranjan Samal

Punjabi: *Mai Jalianwala Bagh Bolda Haan* (Play) by Kuldeep Singh Deep

Rajasthani: *Mhari Dhani* (Poetry) by Prahlad Singh 'Jhorda'

Sanskrit: *Bubhukshitah Kakah* (Short Stories) by Harshdev Madhav

Santali: *Miru Arang* (Poetry) by Dugai Tudu

Sindhi: *Dostan ji Dosti* (Stories) by Lal Hotchandani 'Lachaar'

Tamil: *Thanviyin Piranthanal* (Stories) by Yuma Vasuki

Telugu: *Maya Lokam* (Novel) by P. Chandrashekhar Azad

Urdu: *Barf Ka Des Antarctica* (Short Stories) by Shamsul Islam Farooqi

NATIONAL CREATORS AWARD 2024

- **New India Champion:** Abhi and Niyu
  YouTube: @AbhiandNiyu
- **Best Storyteller:** Keerthika Govindhasamy
  YouTube: @Keerthihistory
- **Disruptor of the Year:** Ranveer Allahbadia
  YouTube: @RanveerAllahbadia
- **Green Champion A:** Pankti Pandey
  Instagram: @zerowasteadda
- **Best Creative for Social Change:** Jaya Kishori
  YouTube: @Iamjayakishori
- **Most Impactful Agri Creator:** Lakshya Dabas
  YouTube: @OrganicAcre
- **Cultural Ambassador of the Year:** Maithili Thakur
  YouTube: @maithilithakur
- **Best International Creator:** Drew Hicks, Kili Paul, Cassandra Mae Spittmann
  Instagram: @indiadrew77, @cassmaeofficial
  YouTube: @OfficialKiliPaul
- **Best Travel Creator:** Kamiya Jani
  YouTube: @curlytalesdigital
- **Tech Creator:** Gaurav Chaudhary
  YouTube: @TechnicalGuruji
- **Swachhata Ambassador:** Malhar Kalambe
  Instagram: @kalambemalhar
- **Heritage Fashion Icon:** Jahnvi Singh
  Instagram: @janhvsingh
- **Best Creative Creator:** **(Female):** Shraddha Jain
  Instagram: @aiyyoshraddha
- **Best Creative Creator:** **(Male):** RJ Raunac
  Instagram: @rjraunac
- **Best Creator in Food Category:** Kabita's Kitchen
  YouTube: @KabitasKitchen
- **Best Creator in Education Category:** Naman Deshmukh
  YouTube: @NamanDeshmukhvlogs
- **Best Health and Fitness Creator:** Ankit Baiyanpuria
  YouTube: @Ankitbaiyanpuria
- **Gaming Creator:** Nischay
  YouTube: @triggeredinsaan
- **Best Micro Creator:** Aridaman
  YouTube: @vedic_siddhanta5376
- **Best Nano Creator:** Piyush Purohit
  Instagram: @aboyfrompahad
- **Best Celebrity Creator:** Aman Gupta (Founder and CEO of boAT)
  Instagram: @boatxaman

ANTIM PANGHAL

In the news for: **Being named United World Wrestling (UWW) Rising Star of the Year 2023 in the women's section;**
Where: **India**

The eighteen-year-old freestyle wrestler from Haryana created history by winning India's first-ever gold medal at the 2022 World U20 Wrestling Championships. She went on

to consolidate her legacy by winning the Asian Wrestling Championships in Astana and a bronze medal at the Asian Games in Hangzhou in 2023. Her remarkable achievements earned her the title of Rising Star of the Year in the women's section by UWW. Antim Panghal was born on 31 August 2004 in Bhagana village of Hisar district in Haryana. She is the youngest daughter of five children born to Ram Niwas Panghal and Krishna Kumari. Antim's elder sister Sarita, a national-level kabaddi player, turned her to wrestling when she was just ten years old.

ARUNDHATI ROY

In the news for: **Winning the PEN Pinter Prize; Where:** **UK**

Indian author and activist Arundhati Roy has been honoured with this year's PEN Pinter Prize for her unwavering and fearless writings that dive deep into the harsh truths of our societies. The award ceremony will take place at the British Library in London on 10 October 2024. During the event, Roy will also announce the recipient of the Writer of Courage award, selected by her from a shortlist. According to PEN International, Roy is a 'luminous voice of freedom and justice', and her literary contributions, beginning with her acclaimed debut novel, *The God of Small Things*, have served as a guiding light during global crises and times of darkness. The award recognizes not only the integrity of her body of work but also the relevance and depth of her insights, arriving precisely when they are most needed.

BILLIE EILISH

In the news for: **Breaking an eighty-seven-year-old record as the youngest person to win two Academy Awards; Where: USA**

Billie Eilish, along with her brother Finneas, became the youngest-ever two-time winner of an Oscar, upon winning the Original Song trophy. The siblings won the trophy for 'What Was I Made For ?' from *Barbie*. The duo and they broke an eighty-seven-year-old record held by actress Luise Rainer, who was twenty-eight when she won her second Best Actress Oscar. The sibling duo keep creating and producing original songs with lyrics that seem to win the hearts of audiences by making them felt seen.

BLUE ORIGIN

In the news for: Sending six people up just past the edge of space; Where: USA

Blue Origin, a space tourism venture founded by Amazon's Jeff Bezos, achieved success with its May 2024 launch after a failed attempt in 2022. This time, the mission was a success, and all passengers returned safely to Earth. Among them, Ed Dwight, at ninety years old, made history as the oldest person to travel to space.

CLAUDIA SHEINBAUM

In the news for: Being elected Mexico's first woman president; Where: Mexico

In her historic election victory on 2 June 2024, Claudia Sheinbaum, the sixty-one-year-old former mayor of Mexico City, made headlines globally as she became Mexico's first woman president. Winning an impressive 59.35 per cent of the votes in the general elections, Sheinbaum's triumph marked a significant milestone for gender equality in Mexican politics. Sheinbaum, known for her progressive policies and dedication to public service, vowed to lead with integrity and inclusivity, promising to address pressing issues such as social inequality, environmental sustainability and economic prosperity.

DEEPTI SHARMA

In the news for: Winning WPL 2024 Most Valuable Player Award; **Where:** India

Deepti Sharma's remarkable performance at the Women's Premier League 2024 not only made her the first Indian to achieve a hat-trick in the tournament but also solidified her reputation as a versatile and impactful cricketer. Playing for UP Warriorz, she not only displayed her prowess with the ball by taking 4 wickets for just 19 runs but also showcased her batting skills with a crucial half-century. Her achievement underscores the growing influence of women in cricket.

GABRIEL ATTAL

In the news for: Becoming the youngest prime minister of France; **Where:** France

Gabriel Attal's appointment as France's new prime minister in January 2024 marked a significant moment in the country's political landscape. At just thirty-two years old, Attal not only became the youngest person to hold the position but also made history as France's first openly gay prime minister. His rise to power symbolizes a progressive shift towards greater inclusivity and diversity in French politics.

As he assumes office, Attal faces a range of challenges, including navigating economic reforms and addressing social inequalities, and steering France through a complex geopolitical landscape. His tenure is expected to be closely watched both domestically and internationally, as he seeks to implement policies that resonate with President Emmanuel Macron's vision for a forward-looking and united France.

GRETA GERWIG

In the news for: Writing and directing the *Barbie* movie; **Where:** USA

Greta Gerwig sparked a cultural sensation with her blockbuster film *Barbie*. Audiences embraced the movie with enthusiasm, often dressing in pink as they flocked to theatres where 'Hi Barbie!' became a popular greeting. The film's debut week saw impressive global earnings of US$420 million, establishing it as a commercial powerhouse.

In addition to its financial success, *Barbie* received the Golden Globe in the inaugural Cinematic and Box Office Achievement category. The accolade marked the film's impact on both popular culture and the entertainment industry, solidifying Gerwig's reputation as a visionary filmmaker.

DOMMARAJU GUKESH

In the news for: **Becoming the youngest challenger for the World Chess Champion title; Where: India**

Gukesh D.'s meteoric rise in the world of chess is nothing short of extraordinary. Hailing from Chennai, he made headlines globally when he achieved the title of Grandmaster at the incredibly young age of twelve, showcasing exceptional talent and dedication to the game. In April 2024, Gukesh achieved another milestone by becoming the youngest-ever challenger for the World Chess Championship, surpassing the record set decades ago by the legendary Russian player Garry Kasparov in 1984. This achievement not only highlights Gukesh's exceptional skill but also positions him as a formidable contender in the world of competitive chess. The World Chess Championship tournament holds immense significance for Gukesh as he prepares to compete against the world's best chess players.

HANA-RAWHITI MAIPI-CLARKE

In the news for: **Performing the native Māori community 'war cry' in Parliament; Where: New Zealand**

New Zealand's youngest MP made a memorable entrance into Parliament, garnering attention for her powerful display of the traditional Māori war dance, known as the 'haka'. This bold gesture not only celebrated her indigenous heritage but

also symbolized her deep commitment to advocating for the rights of New Zealand's native tribes and communities. In Parliament, she continues to champion policies that promote inclusivity, diversity and social justice, reflecting a progressive vision for her country's future. Her embrace of the haka as a symbol of strength and identity resonates widely, reinforcing the importance of cultural pride in New Zealand's political landscape.

JENNY ERPENBECK

In the news for: Winning the 2024 International Booker Prize;
Where: UK

Jenny Erpenbeck and Michael Hofmann won the 2024 International Booker prize for Erpenbeck's personal and political novel *Kairos*, translated from the German by Hofmann. Jenny Erpenbeck was born in East Berlin in 1967 and is also a playwright and, opera director. *Kairos* novel is set in an unnerving time in Europe and follows the heartbreaking journey of two lovers through the ruins of their relationship. In an interview with The Booker Prizes website, Jenny Erpenbeck said, 'It's a private story of a big love and its decay, but it's also a story of the dissolution of a whole political system. Simply put, how can something that seems right in the beginning turn into something wrong?'

HAYAO MIYAZAKI

In the news for: Winning the Academy Award for Best Animated Feature Film;
Where: Japan

Hayao Miyazaki stands as a titan in the realm of animation, renowned globally for his profound influence and visionary storytelling. His latest masterpiece, *The Boy and the Heron*, recently garnered him an Oscar for Animated Feature Film, marking Miyazaki's second Academy Award win. He broke records as the oldest director ever nominated for the prestigious category and became the oldest winner by over two decades, cementing his legacy as a cinematic icon.

MARGRETHE II OF DENMARK

In the news for: Being the first Danish monarch to voluntarily relinquish the throne in nearly 900 years; **Where:** Denmark

On 31 December 2023, Queen Margrethe II of Denmark delivered a poignant speech to her nation, announcing her decision to abdicate the throne effective 14 January 2024, due to health reasons. This historic moment marked the first voluntary abdication by a Danish monarch in approximately 900 years. Upon her abdication, Queen Margrethe was succeeded by her older son, who ascended to the throne as King Frederik X.

MIRA ERDA

In the news for: Being the first Indian woman to win internationally in Formula 4; Where: India

Mira Erda, a young racer from Vadodara, Gujarat, became the first Indian woman to win internationally in the Formula 4 racing category after achieving a podium finish in the South East Asia championship held in Malaysia in 2019. She has already accumulated a number of titles to her name; including becoming the youngest female LGB Formula 4 competitor in 2014 and being the first Indian woman to race in the Euro JK category in 2017. She is also India's first and youngest female Formula 4 BMW driver.

The 2000 born racer had a passion for racing from an early age, having started from her family-owned track in Vadodara and moving up to international leagues. She won a race in the Formula LGB 1300 category of the MRF MMSC FMSCI Indian National Car Racing Championship, a category dominated by male drivers, on 19 August 2024.

PAYAL KAPADIA

In the news for: Becoming the first person from India to win the Grand Prix at the Cannes Film Festival; Where: France

The Cannes Film Festival, a prestigious event held annually in Cannes, France, showcases a wide array of films from various genres and countries, including documentaries. At the 77th Cannes Film Festival, Payal Kapadia received the Grand Prix for her film *All We Imagine as Light*. Kapadia's film is a compelling drama centred around two Malayali nurses who have relocated to Mumbai. The narrative explores themes of life, love and sisterhood, providing a poignant portrayal of the experiences and challenges in a bustling urban environment. Winning the Grand Prix at Cannes is a significant achievement that highlights Kapadia's directorial talent and the film's impactful storytelling. *All We Imagine as Light* captivated audiences and critics alike resonating with its emotional depth and exploration of complex relationships against the backdrop of modern-day Mumbai.

ROHIT SHARMA

In the news for: Winning the 2024 T20 World Cup; Where: Barbados

The Indian cricket team clinched the T20 World Cup with a historic victory over South Africa in a thrilling final held in Barbados. This triumph marked their first title in thirteen years and has significant implications for the team's future. The win was particularly poignant as it coincided with the retirement announcements of key players like Rohit Sharma, Virat Kohli, and Ravindra Jadeja from T20 internationals, although they will continue playing other formats of cricket. Furthermore, the victory signalled the end of Rahul Dravid's tenure as head coach of the Indian team. His departure marks the beginning of a new era in Indian cricket, focusing on nurturing the next generation of players. This coaching transition is expected to bring about substantial changes in the team's strategy and development approach moving forward.

SABYASACHI MUKHERJEE

In the news for: Being the first Indian designer at the Met Gala; Where: USA

On 6 May 2024, Sabyasachi Mukherjee made history as the first Indian fashion designer to attend the Met Gala held at New York's Metropolitan Museum of Art. Renowned for

his meticulous craftsmanship and love for intricate details, Sabyasachi's designs reflect a majestic elegance that pays homage to India's cultural richness. In addition to gracing the event, he curated actor Alia Bhatt's attire, displaying the timeless beauty of the sari in a creation that blended traditional artistry with contemporary flair. A dedicated team of 163 skilled artisans, including craftsmen, embroiderers, artists and dyers, invested a total of 1,965 hours to bring this masterpiece to life.

NEWSMAKERS

S.S. RAJAMOULI

In the news for: Making *Time* magazine's list of 100 most influential people of 2023; Where: India

S.S. Rajamouli, director of the *RRR* and *Baahubali* movies, has been named one of *Time* magazine's 100 most influential people of 2023, alongside Bollywood star Shah Rukh Khan. They are the only two Indians on the list. Shah Rukh Khan returned to the big screen after nearly four years with the blockbuster movie *Pathaan* in January this year. The film, made with a budget of about ₹250 crore, shattered box office records, earning ₹543.09 crore in India and a total of Rs 1,050.05 crore worldwide, including ₹392.55 crore from overseas markets.

SONAM WANGCHUK

In the news for: Sitting on a twenty-one-day fast demanding statehood and Sixth Schedule implementation for Ladakh; Where: India

Sonam Wangchuk, an engineer and advocate for education reform in Ladakh, has been at the forefront of innovative approaches to sustainable development in the region. His efforts have garnered attention for their impact on both education and environmental conservation. Recently, Wangchuk has been actively involved in a protest urging Prime Minister Narendra Modi and Home Minister Amit Shah to take action to protect the fragile Himalayan ecosystem. This initiative also supports the Kargil Democratic Alliance in its call for statehood and the safeguarding of rights for the majority tribal population in the region under the Sixth Schedule of the Constitution.

SUNITA WILLIAMS

In the news for: Being the first woman pilot to lead a fully crewed mission to space; Where: USA

Sunita Williams has once again made history in space! She achieved a major milestone by becoming the first woman pilot to lead a fully crewed mission aboard the inaugural flight of Boeing Starliner. This spacecraft, designed for human travel, launched from Cape Canaveral in Florida and safely docked at the International Space Station. Williams, who is of Indian origin and fifty-eight years old, piloted the capsule on 5 June alongside mission commander Butch Wilmore. This mission is significant as it marks Starliner's debut in transporting astronauts, following SpaceX's Crew Dragon. The mission is part of NASA's Commercial Crew Program aimed at enhancing space travel capabilities.

NEWSMAKERS

TAYLOR SWIFT **In the news for:** Being named *Time*'s Person of the Year 2023; **Where:** USA

Taylor Swift's impact on the entertainment industry has reached unprecedented heights in recent years. Following the immense success of her sixth world tour, 'The Eras Tour', which shattered records by becoming the highest-grossing tour of all time, Swift was named *Time* magazine's Person of the Year. This milestone was further solidified as the tour crossed the monumental US $1 billion mark in earnings. *Forbes* also recognized Swift's influence, ranking her as the most powerful woman in the entertainment industry and the fifth most powerful overall. This accolade highlights Swift's exceptional talent, business acumen and enduring appeal to global audiences.

VIKRANT MASSEY **In the news for:** Acting in the movie *12th Fail*, which hit a silver jubilee; **Where:** India

Vikrant Massey, starring in *12th Fail*, recently celebrated a remarkable achievement as the film completed twenty-five weeks in theatres, marking its silver jubilee. The poignant story of IPS officer Manoj Kumar resonated deeply with audiences, touching the hearts of many across India. The film's success extended beyond its theatrical run, as it was selected as India's official entry for the 2024 Oscars. This recognition emphasiz *12th Fail*'s captivating storytelling and Massey's compelling portrayal of the protagonist. With its enduring popularity and critical acclaim, *12th Fail* has not only entertained audiences but also highlighted important societal issues through the lens of its narrative. Massey's performance and the film's success further solidifies its place in Indian cinema as a significant and memorable achievement.

Caricatures by Mistunee Chowdhury

8 January **90th birth anniversary of ELVIS PRESLEY**
(8 January 1935–16 August 1977)

Elvis was an American singer and actor, known as the 'King of Rock and Roll'. Presley was one of the first celebrities in the era of mass communication, and he is regarded as one of the most significant cultural figures of the twentieth century. He is one of the best-selling music artistes in history, with worldwide sales of 500 million records. His name, image and voice are instantly recognizable worldwide. He has inspired so many imitators that being an Elvis impersonator could be a professional job!

'...the image is one thing, and the human being is another... it's very hard to live up to an image'

17 January **205th birth anniversary of ANNE BRONTË**
(17 January 1820–28 May 1849)

The lesser-known writer of the Brontë sisters, Anne Brontë was an English poet and author. Her work was more provocative than that of her sisters and so she was subject to criticism. She published two novels, *Agnes Grey* and *The Tenant of Wildfell Hall*. Overshadowed by her sisters, Anne's work never garnered any acclaim. Her writing was often called a 'pale imitation' of her sisters' novels.

'But he who dares not grasp the thorn should never crave the rose.'

28 January **160th birth anniversary of LALA LAJPAT RAI**
(28 January 1865–17 November 1928)

An Indian politician, author, revolutionary, and one of the most revered freedom fighters of India, Lala Lajpat Rai was known as one of the extremists of the Indian independence movement. He was popularly known as 'Punjab Kesari', and was one of the three in the Lal, Bal, Pal trio – Lala Lajpat Rai of Punjab, Bal Gangadhar Tilak of Maharashtra, and Bipin Chandra Pal of Bengal. He advocated against untouchability and British imperialism. In the protest against the Simon Commission, Rai was assaulted by the police, sustaining injuries that led to his untimely death. Some of his important writings are *The Story of My Deportation*, *Arya Samaj* and *The United States of America: A Hindu's Impression*.

'The strength of a nation lies in the character of its people.'

30 January **112th birth anniversary of AMRITA SHER-GIL**
(30 January 1913–December 1941)

A pioneer of the modern Indian art movement, and an avant-garde painter who is often placed at the same level of brilliance as the artists of the Bengal Renaissance, Amrita Sher-Gil was influenced by the wall paintings of the Ajanta Caves in western India. She also drew inspiration from seventeenth-century Mughal miniatures. Her art was often contrasted with that of her contemporaries from the Bengal school, which she considered stagnant and retrograde. She also drew inspiration from 17th-century Mughal miniatures. Her paintings are bid at the highest of prices. In 2023, her painting *The Storyteller* was sold for over ₹60 crore.

6 March **550th birth anniversary of MICHELANGELO**
(6 March 1475–18 February 1564)

Italian poet, painter, sculptor and architect of the High Renaissance, Michelangelo di Lodovico Buonarroti Simoni, popularly known as Michelangelo, was born in Florence. Initially gaining fame as a fraud for selling a fake ancient sculpture to a dealer, the artistic skill he displayed in the same sculpture earned him his first commission to carve the *Pieta*. Although he worked on marble sculptures his whole life, it is his frescoes, paintings done rapidly in watercolour on wet plaster, on the ceilings of the Sistine Chapel in the Vatican Palace that are most celebrated. Other famous works of his are the *David* and *Apollo*, and the sculptures at the Medici Chapel.

24 March **120th death anniversary of JULES VERNE**
(8 February 1828–24 March 1905)

Jules Gabriel Verne was a French writer who is famous for pioneering the science fiction genre. He has been ranked as the second-most translated author in the world since 1979. He is said to have made a strong influence on the avant-garde and surrealist literary movements. His most famous works are *Around the World in 80 Days*, *Twenty Thousand Leagues Under the Sea*, *Journey to the Center of the Earth* and *The Mysterious Island*, among many others. He is often lauded as a prophet of scientific progress as the strange, futuristic technology in his books have become our reality.

19 May 100th birth anniversary of MALCOLM X (19 May 1925–24 February 1965)

An American civil rights activist and advocate for Black empowerment within the African American community, Malcolm is considered as USA's most resolute proponent of Black nationalism. Born Malcolm Little, he later adopted the name Malcolm X to signify the loss of his African heritage. He was a powerful orator, a captivating figure and an unwavering activist who captured the repressed rage, dissatisfaction and resentment of African Americans throughout the pivotal period of the civil rights movement from 1955 to 1965. He delivered speeches at prestigious campuses like Harvard and Oxford and preached in the neighbourhoods of Harlem, a predominantly Black area in New York. He was an enthusiastic radical with a sharp mind, sharp humour and powerful criticisms of American civilization.

'A man who stands for nothing will fall for anything.'

8 June 400th birth anniversary of GIOVANNI DOMENICO CASSINI (8 June 1625–14 September 1712)

Known for discovering the dark gap between the rings A and B of Saturn, four of Saturn's moons and being the first to record observations of the zodiacal lights, as well contributing to the discovery of the Cassini Division, this French-born, Italian scientist's theories and discoveries made him one of the most important astronomers of the seventeenth and eighteenth centuries. Cassini was the first to succeed at measuring longitudes using the method outlined by Galileo. He was also the first to observe the differential rotation in Jupiter's atmosphere.

13 June 160th birth anniversary of WILLIAM BUTLER YEATS (13 June 1865–28 January 1939)

William Butler Yeats was one of the greatest poets of the twentieth century. His poems were extensively influenced by Irish folklore and mythology. His poems and prose reflected the political environment of Ireland and the rest of Europe, paralleled against the growing resentment among the masses. He was awarded the Nobel Prize for Literature in 1923. Some of his most famous poems are *Sailing to Byzantium*, *The Tower*, *The Second Coming* and *Leda and the Swan*. Yeats co-founded the Abbey Theatre in Dublin, which became an important venue for Irish literary and dramatic works.

27 June 145th birth anniversary of HELEN KELLER (27 June 1880–1 June 1968)

Helen Keller was a twentieth-century humanitarian, educator and writer who was afflicted with an illness at the age of seven that left her deaf and blind. Her exceptional journey of overcoming her limitations earned her fame, and her life was chronicled in newspapers and books. She advocated for women's suffrage and the differently abled, and co-founded the American Civil Liberties Union. She has written several books, namely *The Story of My Life*, *The World I Live in* and *My Religion*, among others.

'The best and most beautiful things in the world cannot be seen or even touched – they must be felt with the heart.'

5 August 95th birth anniversary of NEIL ARMSTRONG (5 August 1930–25 August 2012)

The first man to set foot on the moon was research pilot, aeronautical engineer and NASA astronaut Neil Armstrong, as a part of the Apollo 11 mission. He was a member of the Presidential Commission on the Space Shuttle Challenger Accident, which was established in 1986 to examine the safety flaws in the Challenger accident, as well as the National Commission on Space, which established the programme's objectives. Armstrong was awarded the Presidential Medal of Freedom in 1969, the Congressional Space Medal of Honor in 1978 and the Congressional Gold Medal in 2009.

'That's one small step for man, one giant leap for mankind.'

12 August 106th birth anniversary of VIKRAM SARABHAI (12 August 1919–30 December 1971)

An Indian physicist and industrialist, Vikram Sarabhai is considered the Father of the Indian Space Programme. He initiated research into the fields of space and nuclear power in India, establishing the Indian

National Committee for Space Research in 1962 that was later renamed the Indian Space Research Organisation. He also initiated programmes to make education accessible to remote villages through satellite communication and advocated for peaceful uses of nuclear power for defence purposes. He planned to apply space technology in the fields of geology, forestry, cartography, agriculture and oceanography to benefit the world.

2 November 270th birth anniversary of MARIE ANTOINETTE (2 November 1755–16 October 1793)

An Austrian princess and the wife of King Louis XVI, Marie Antoinette was one of the most iconic characters in the rich history of Versailles and the French court. Crowned during the most tumultuous period of the French monarchy, she is said to have played an influential role in its ultimate downfall. Her bold tastes and libertine ways were criticized and highlighted in her trial before her subsequent execution. She has been depicted as ignorant and indifferent to the conditions of the poor and her subjects. Yet, evidence suggests that as a woman with power, she may have just been a victim of politics and circumstance.

16 December 250th birth anniversary of JANE AUSTEN (16 December 1775–18 July 1817)

An author of everlasting classic books that have remained popular for over two centuries, Jane Austen was an English writer who decidedly introduced modern characters to the novel. The unwavering popularity of her books is reflected in their varied screen adaptations and parodies. Her writing inspired the possibility of domestic novels, novels of manners and sentimental novels that centre around women and their journeys of self discovery. Some of her most renowned novels are *Pride and Prejudice*, *Sense and Sensibility*, *Persuasion* and *Emma*.

30 December 160th birth anniversary of RUDYARD KIPLING (30 December 1865–18 January 1936)

One of the best known late Victorian poets and novelists, Rudyard Kipling realistically portrayed the colloquial speech of soldiers and sailors. He garnered admiration for his work in children's literature. Some of his most notable works are *The Jungle Book*, *Kim*, *The Seven Seas* and *Just So Stories*. He not only received the Nobel Prize for Literature in 1907 but was also the recipient of the Gold Medal of the Royal Society of Literature in 1926, of which only a few have been deemed worthy.

HERE'S MORE IN 2024

- **JAN** 100th anniversary of the WINTER OLYMPICS on 25 January
- **FEB** 140th anniversary of the publication of the OXFORD ENGLISH DICTIONARY on 1 February
- **MAR** 135th anniversary of the EIFFEL TOWER OPENING on 31 March
- **APR** 75th anniversary of NATO, founded on 4 April
- **MAY** 95th anniversary of the ACADEMY AWARDS on 16 May
- **JUN** 80th anniversary of D-DAY, which was initiated on 6 June
- **JUL** 55th anniversary of MAN WALKING ON THE MOON on 20 July
- **AUG** 110th anniversary of the FIRST WORLD WAR, which began on 1 August
- **SEP** 75th anniversary of the BERLIN AIRLIFT, which ended on 30 September
- **OCT** 120th anniversary of the NEW YORK CITY SUBWAY OPENING on 27 October
- **NOV** 165th anniversary of THE PUBLICATION OF THE *ORIGIN OF SPECIES* on 24 November
- **DEC** 110th anniversary of the CHRISTMAS TRUCE on 25 December

WHAT ALL DO YOU KNOW ABOUT CRICKET?

The term 'cricket' is believed to come from '*criquet*,' an Old French word meaning stick, goal or post. Some also think it might have stemmed from '*kricke*,' a Dutch/Flemish word from the Middle Ages for stick or staff.

The origins of cricket are a bit uncertain, with some saying that shepherds were the ones who came up with the game. These shepherds supposedly created the game as a way to entertain themselves while looking after their sheep. In the sixteenth century, kids in the Weald region of south-east England started playing cricket in the streets. At first, they used a tree stump as wickets, and later they even used a gate from a sheep pen as wickets, with a crossbar on top acting as a bail.

The first reference to cricket being played as an adult sport was in 1611.

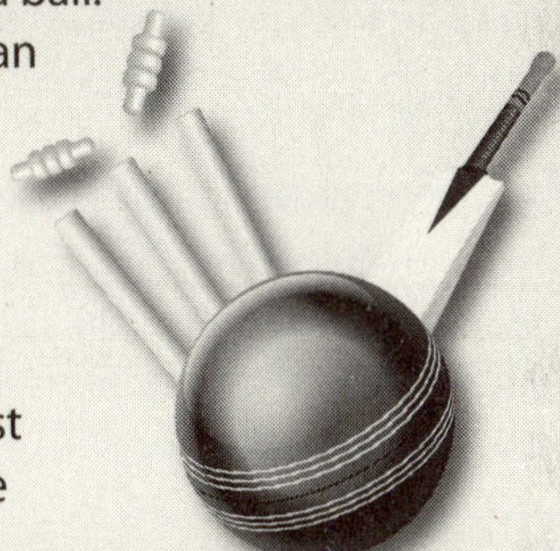

Village cricket had developed by the middle of the seventeenth century and the first English 'county teams' were formed in the second half of the century, when 'local experts' from village cricket were employed as the earliest professionals. The first known game in which the teams used county names was in 1709.

Cricket had various forms for centuries, but in 1788, the Marylebone Cricket Club (MCC) created the initial set of rules. These laws outlined the fundamental regulations regarding the bat, ball, wicket size, pitch dimensions, overs and the different ways a batsman could get out.

The first ever international cricket game was played between the USA and Canada in 1844 at the St George's Cricket Club in New York.

Cricket formats

There are three formats of cricket played at the international level – Test matches, One Day Internationals and Twenty20 Internationals. These matches are played under the rules and regulations approved by the International Cricket Council (ICC), which also provides match officials for them.

- Played since 1877, Test cricket is the traditional form of the game. It has now settled in a five-day format and consists of two innings each.

It is considered the pinnacle form of the game as the teams are tested over a longer period of time and are required to exhibit endurance, technique and temperament to perform well in this format.

- One Day Internationals, commonly known as ODIs, are a pacier format of the game. Although started in 1971, they gained popularity in the 1980s. An ODI consists of one-inning matches of 50 overs per side in which teams with a blend of technique, speed and skill are expected to perform well. ICC's pinnacle event, the ICC Cricked World Cup, is contested in this format every four years.
- Twenty20 Internationals are the newest, shortest and the fasted format of the game. Comprising 20 overs per side, the format marked its beginning in 2005 and has been a prominent part of the game ever since. The match generally lasts three hours and is hugely popular worldwide for its skilful bowling, huge hitting and amazing fielding.

THE ICC CHAMPIONS TROPHY

History

Originally referred to as the ICC KnockOut when it took place in 1998 in Dhaka, Bangladesh, and in 2000 in Nairobi, Kenya, the competition underwent a name change to the ICC Champions Trophy in 2002. The ICC KnockOut Trophy was held with the goal of generating funds to support ICC associate nations.

It used to be held every two years until 2009, (with the exception of 2008, in Pakistan, where it was cancelled and rescheduled for South Africa in 2009). Subsequently, the tournament shifted to a four-year cycle and includes the top eight teams in the ICC one-day rankings. The initial stage of the tournament consists of two groups of four teams each, with the top two from each group advancing to the semi-finals and the winners then competing in the final match. The competition is known for being brief, intense and highly competitive. It is, therefore, also known as the Mini World Cup.

A much-awaited comeback

The ICC Champions Trophy 2025 is going to be the ninth edition of the event. It's a comeback after seven years, with the last event being held in 2017.

The Champions Trophy was stopped in 2017 because it was becoming less important in the Future Tours Programme (FTP) and due to the rise of the T20 World Cup as another major tournament alongside the ODI World Cup.

Past Tournaments and Winners

HOST COUNTRY	YEAR	WINNER
Bangladesh	1998	South Africa
Kenya	2000	New Zealand
Sri Lanka	2002	India and Sri Lanka (Shared)
England	2004	West Indies
India	2006	Australia
South Africa	2009	Australia
England	2013	India
England	2017	Pakistan

What to expect?

The ninth edition is set to take place in Pakistan in February 2025.

The 2025 competition will follow the same structure as the 2017 tournament, featuring eight teams divided into two groups of four. Each team will face the others in their group once, with the top two teams from each group progressing to the semi-finals.

The top eight teams of the ODI World Cup 2023 qualified for the ICC Champions Trophy 2025: India, South Africa, Australia and New Zealand – the top four teams that made it to the semi-finals of the 2023 World Cup – along with Pakistan as the host and Afghanistan in sixth place. Bangladesh, ranked eighth with four points, also qualified for the competition.

TEAM	PLAYED	WON	LOST	POINTS	NET RUN RATE
1. India	9	9	0	18	+2.570
2. South Africa	9	7	2	14	+1.261
3. Australia	9	7	2	14	+0.841
4. New Zealand	9	5	4	10	+0.743
5. Pakistan	9	4	5	8	-0.199
6. Afghanistan	9	4	5	8	-0.336
7. England	9	3	6	6	-0.572
8. Bangladesh	9	2	7	4	-1.084
9. Sri Lanka	9	2	7	4	-1.419
10. Netherlands	9	2	7	4	-1.825

Karachi, Lahore and Rawalpindi are the three locations where the Pakistan Cricket Board (PCB) intends to hold the two-week Champions Trophy.

Pakistan will host an ODI tri-series with New Zealand and South Africa in preparation for the ICC Champions Trophy 2025.

The PCB's plan for the 2025 Champions Trophy might involve having India stay in one city throughout the tournament, as they try to make arrangements for what could be India's first trip to Pakistan in almost seventeen years. This decision is being made to steer clear of any safety issues.

Record holders

Most Runs Scored

PLAYER	PLAYING SPAN	MATCHES PLAYED	RUNS SCORED
C.H. Gayle (WI)	2002–2013	17	791
D.P.M.D. Jayawardene (SL)	2000–2013	22	742
S. Dhawan (IND)	2013–2017	10	701
K.C. Sangakkara (SL)	2000–2013	22	683
S.C. Ganguly (IND)	1998–2004	13	665

Highest Team Totals

TEAM	SCORE	RUN RATE	OPPOSITION	MATCH DATE
New Zealand	347/4	6.94	v USA	10 Sep 2004
Pakistan	338/4	6.76	v India	18 Jun 2017
India	331/7	6.62	v South Africa	6 Jun 2013
England	323/8	6.46	v South Africa	27 Sep 2009
Sri Lanka	322/3	6.61	v India	8 Jun 2017

Most Wickets

PLAYER	SPAN	MATCHES	BALLS	WICKETS
K.D. Mills (NZ)	2002–2013	15	675	28
S.L. Malinga (SL)	2006–2017	16	864	25
M. Muralidaran (SL)	1998–2009	17	805	24
B. Lee (AUS)	2000–2009	16	739	22
G.D. McGrath (AUS)	2000–2006	12	612	21

Most Sixes

PLAYER	SPAN	MATCHES	SIXES
S.C. Ganguly (IND)	1998–2004	13	17
C.H. Gayle (WI)	2002–2013	17	15
E.J.G. Morgan (ENG)	2009–2017	13	14
S.R. Watson (AUS)	2002–2013	17	12
P.D. Collingwood (ENG)	2004–2009	11	11

Most Centuries

PLAYER	SPAN	MATCHES	RUNS	100
S. Dhawan (IND)	2013–2017	10	701	3
H.H. Gibbs (SA)	2002–2009	10	460	3
S.C. Ganguly (IND)	1998–2004	13	665	3
C.H. Gayle (WI)	2002–2013	17	791	3
Saeed Anwar (PAK)	2000–2002	4	289	2

Decision pending

The much-anticipated verdict is still pending regarding India's involvement in the ICC Champions Trophy 2025. With Pakistan set to host the event, India's participation remains uncertain due to the strained relations between the two countries.

Previously, the PCB had suggested that India should compete in all matches in Lahore. In response, Board of Control for Cricket in India (BCCI) Vice President Rajeev Shukla mentioned that the Indian squad would only visit Pakistan with approval from the central government. However, the ICC has not officially announced the timetable, and there are strong doubts that India will receive government clearance to travel to Pakistan for this significant tournament.

BCCI President Jay Shah has stated that India's senior players will be part of the 2025 Champions Trophy, but it remains unclear whether this involves travelling to Pakistan.

Some interesting facts

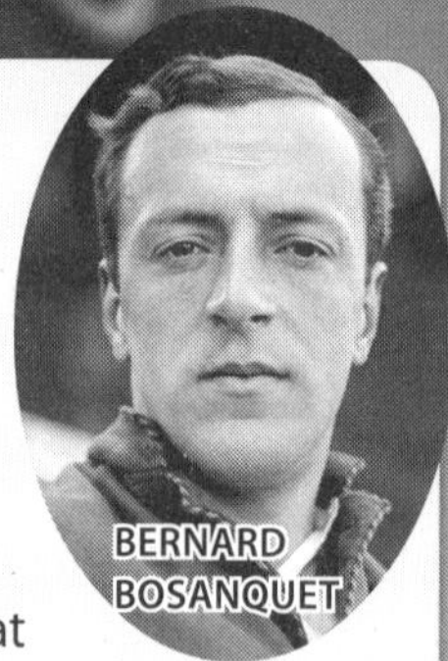

- The youngest cricketer to play for England was Rehan Ahmed aged 18 years and 149 days. But the youngest player in cricketing history was Pakistan's Hasan Raza. He was aged 14 years and 227 days when he made his international debut for Pakistan in 1996.
- The googly, which is a leg spinner's classic delivery that goes the other way with a leg-spin grip to deceive the batsman, was invented by English leg spinner Bernard Bosanquet. He first used the googly to trick the batsman on 20 July 1900.
- The Ashes series in 1971 saw a bizarre dismissal. English pacer John Snow struck Aussie batsman Terry Jenner on the head with a bouncer. Jenner's helmet flew off and landed on the stumps, dislodging a bail, and the umpire declared that Jenner was out.

- Kepler Wessels became the first cricketer to play for two countries in ODI history. He represented Australia from 1982 to 1985 and then went on to join the South African team in 1991.
- A strike rate of over 80 in Test cricket? It is unbelievable but true, as former Indian batsman Virender Sehwag played 104 international Tests for India and scored 8,586 runs with a strike rate of more than 80. He is the only cricketer to have played over a hundred Tests with a strike rate of over 80.
- The first Test of the 2013–14 tour of India to South Africa saw a remarkable incident. In the Test match played at Johannesburg, M.S. Dhoni and A.B. de Villiers became the first pair of wicketkeepers to bowl in the same Test match in cricketing history.
- Ex-Australian fast bowler Jeff Thomson set a new world record for the fastest delivery in cricket in 1983. Thomson had bowled at a speed of 160.45 km/hr.
- A.B. de Villiers holds the record for the fastest century in ODI cricket. In 2015, he smashed a century in just 31 balls against the West Indies.
- The Test match between England and the West Indies in Antigua in 2009 was the shortest match in the history of cricket with only 10 balls being bowled.
- The year 1939 witnessed the longest cricket match in the history of the game between England and South Africa. This match lasted for an astonishing ten days.

ELECTIONS IN INDIA

When India became a republic in 1950, it adopted universal suffrage (or universal adult franchise), which ensures the right to vote for as many people bound by a government's laws as possible, as supported by the 'one person, one vote' principle. Initially, anyone above the age of 21 could cast their vote in the Lok Sabha, Vidhan Sabha and local body elections, and in 1988, it the voting age was lowered to 18.

The country is divided into a number of constituencies – of Lok Sabha and Vidhan Sabha – that were decided by dividing the total population of the various provinces of the country into electoral constituencies of roughly equal demographic value.

Constituencies tend to have roughly the same number of people, though the territory covered would be very small in densely populated areas and vice versa. Periodic adjustments of constituencies are made taking into account population changes reflected in the latest census, under a Delimitation Commission. Four such commissions have been constituted so far, in 1952, 1963, 1973 and 2002, with the next one scheduled for after 2026.

FIRST GENERAL ELECTION

The first-ever elections in the country were organized during 1951–52, with a total of 401 constituencies. The Indian National Congress witnessed a landslide victory and formed the government.

Elections in India are planned and supervised by the Election Commission of India (ECI), set up in 1950 with the Representation of the People Act. The Chief Election Commissioner (CEC), who presided over the Commission, used to enjoy a broad range of powers in deciding the timing and way the elections were to be held in the country. Now, however, the ECI consists of a CEC and two Election Commissioners, and the CEC does not have overruling powers, and any decision is taken by the opinion of the majority among the three.

The ECI made an important change in the 1990s to the voting process with the introduction of the electronic voting machines. It deterred certain electoral malpractices that had been present until its introduction.

Candidates contesting in an election may either be affiliated to a political

FIRST USE OF INDELIBLE INK

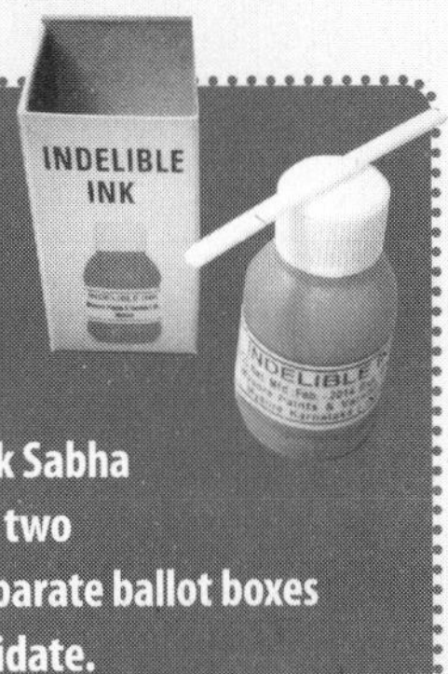

Indelible ink, more commonly known as the election ink, was first used in the third Lok Sabha elections in 1962. In the two elections before that separate ballot boxes were kept for each candidate.

party, or be independent. Normally, an independent candidate would play no significant role except for being in contention, but, when a party falls short of majority, independents play a crucial role in government formation, by joining (or leaving) a political combination. Further, like-minded politicians have run first as independents and only upon being elected gone on to form regional parties.

A brief guide to the 2024 Lok Sabha elections (aka general elections)

- The 2024 Indian general election was held in seven phases between 19 April and 1 June, spanning forty-four days to elect the eighteenth Lok Sabha. The results were declared on 4 June 2024 and Narendra Modi was re-elected as the prime minister of India on 9 June 2024.
- Elections to the Lok Sabha need to be held every five years, as required by Article 83 of the Constitution of India.
- The Lok Sabha, or the House of the People, is the Lower House of India's Parliament. Currently, the House has 543 seats.
- The members are elected using 'first-past-the-post' voting where voters cast a vote for a single candidate, and the candidate with the highest (and here, a minimum of 272) votes wins the election.
- Of the 272 seats required for a majority in the Lok Sabha, the Bharatiya Janata Party (BJP), led by Modi, secured a total of 240 seats, short of the majority marker of 272, and formed the National Democratic Alliance (NDA); adding up the seats won by the allies, the NDA secured a majority of 292 seats.
- The Indian National Congress (INC) won 99 seats and the Congress-led Indian National Developmental Inclusive Alliance (INDIA) bloc won 234 seats.
- Approximately 1.4 billion people were eligible to vote this year and the voter turnout was 65.79 per cent.
- On 9 June 2024, Modi began his third consecutive tenure as prime minister of India after his swearing-in ceremony earlier that day.
- The average age of MPs elected to the eighteenth Lok Sabha is 56 years, a slight decrease from 59 years in the seventeenth Lok Sabha.

FIRST NOTA

The 2014 general elections were the first to offer the option of choosing 'None of the Above' (NOTA). It provides a neutral vote to those who do not wish to vote for any candidate from the electoral ballot.

Portfolios:

Narendra Modi 		**Prime Minister** and also in-charge of: Ministry of Personnel, Public Grievances and Pensions, Department of Atomic Energy, Department of Space, All important policy issues, All other portfolios not allocated to any minister
Cabinet Ministers		
1	Rajnath Singh	Minister of Defence
2	Amit Shah	Minister of Home Affairs Minister of Cooperation
3	Nitin Jairam Gadkari	Minister of Road Transport and Highways
4	Jagat Prakash Nadda	Minister of Health and Family Welfare Minister of Chemicals and Fertilisers
5	Shivraj Singh Chouhan	Minister of Agriculture and Farmers Welfare Minister of Rural Development
6	Nirmala Sitharaman	Minister of Finance Minister of Corporate Affairs
7	Dr Subrahmanyam Jaishankar	Minister of External Affairs
8	Manohar Lal	Minister of Housing and Urban Affairs Minister of Power
9	H.D. Kumaraswamy	Minister of Heavy Industries Minister of Steel
10	Piyush Goyal	Minister of Commerce and Industry
11	Dharmendra Pradhan	Minister of Education
12	Jitan Ram Manjhi	Minister of Micro, Small and Medium Enterprises
13	Rajiv Ranjan Singh alias Lalan Singh	Minister of Panchayati Raj Minister of Fisheries, Animal Husbandry and Dairying
14	Sarbananda Sonowal	Minister of Ports, Shipping and Waterways
15	Dr Virendra Kumar	Minister of Social Justice and Empowerment
16	Kinjarapu Ram Mohan Naidu	Minister of Civil Aviation
17	Pralhad Joshi	Minister of Consumer Affairs, Food and Public Distribution Minister of New and Renewable Energy
18	Jual Oram	Minister of Tribal Affairs
19	Giriraj Singh	Minister of Textiles

20	Ashwini Vaishnaw	Minister of Railways Minister of Information and Broadcasting Minister of Electronics and Information Technology
21	Jyotiraditya M. Scindia	Minister of Communications Minister of Development of North Eastern Region
22	Bhupender Yadav	Minister of Environment, Forest and Climate Change
23	Gajendra Singh Shekhawat	Minister of Culture Minister of Tourism
24	Annpurna Devi	Minister of Women and Child Development
25	Kiren Rijiju	Minister of Parliamentary Affairs Minister of Minority Affairs
26	Hardeep Singh Puri	Minister of Petroleum and Natural Gas
27	Dr Mansukh Mandaviya	Minister of Labour and Employment Minister of Youth Affairs and Sports
28	G. Kishan Reddy	Minister of Coal Minister of Mines
29	Chirag Paswan	Minister of Food Processing Industries
30	C.R. Patil	Minister of Jal Shakti
Ministers of State (Independent Charge)		
1	Rao Inderjit Singh	Minister of State (Independent Charge) of the Ministry of Statistics and Programme Implementation Minister of State (Independent Charge) of the Ministry of Planning Minister of State in the Ministry of Culture
2	Dr Jitendra Singh	Minister of State (Independent Charge) of the Ministry of Science and Technology Minister of State (Independent Charge) of the Ministry of Earth Sciences Minister of State in the Prime Minister's Office Minister of State in the Ministry of Personnel, Public Grievances and Pensions Minister of State in the Department of Atomic Energy Minister of State in the Department of Space
3	Arjun Ram Meghwal	Minister of State (Independent Charge) of the Ministry of Law and Justice Minister of State in the Ministry of Parliamentary Affairs
4	Prataprao Ganpatrao Jadhav	Minister of State (Independent Charge) of the Ministry of Ayush Minister of State in the Ministry of Health and Family Welfare

5	Jayant Chaudhary	Minister of State (Independent Charge) of the Ministry of Skill Development and Entrepreneurship Minister of State in the Ministry of Education
Ministers of State		
1	Jitin Prasada	Minister of State in the Ministry of Commerce and Industry Minister of State in the Ministry of Electronics and Information Technology
2	Shripad Yesso Naik	Minister of State in the Ministry of Power Minister of State in the Ministry of New and Renewable Energy
3	Pankaj Chaudhary	Minister of State in the Ministry of Finance
4	Krishan Pal	Minister of State in the Ministry of Cooperation
5	Ramdas Athawale	Minister of State in the Ministry of Social Justice and Empowerment
6	Ram Nath Thakur	Minister of State in the Ministry of Agriculture and Farmers Welfare
7	Nityanand Rai	Minister of State in the Ministry of Home Affairs
8	Anupriya Patel	Minister of State in the Ministry of Health and Family Welfare Minister of State in the Ministry of Chemicals and Fertilizers
9	V. Somanna	Minister of State in the Ministry of Jal Shakti Minister of State in the Ministry of Railways
10	Dr Chandra Sekhar Pemmasani	Minister of State in the Ministry of Rural Development Minister of State in the Ministry of Communications
11	Prof. S.P. Singh Baghel	Minister of State in the Ministry of Fisheries, Animal Husbandry and Dairying Minister of State in the Ministry of Panchayati Raj
12	Shobha Karandlaje	Minister of State in the Ministry of Micro, Small and Medium Enterprises Minister of State in the Ministry of Labour and Employment
13	Kirti Vardhan Singh	Minister of State in the Ministry of Environment, Forest and Climate Change Minister of State in the Ministry of External Affairs
14	B.L. Verma	Minister of State in the Ministry of Consumer Affairs, Food and Public Distribution Minister of State in the Ministry of Social Justice and Empowerment

15	Shantanu Thakur	Minister of State in the Ministry of Ports, Shipping and Waterways
16	Suresh Gopi	Minister of State in the Ministry of Petroleum and Natural Gas Minister of State in the Ministry of Tourism
17	Dr L. Murugan	Minister of State in the Ministry of Information and Broadcasting Minister of State in the Ministry of Parliamentary Affairs
18	Ajay Tamta	Minister of State in the Ministry of Road Transport and Highways
19	Bandi Sanjay Kumar	Minister of State in the Ministry of Home Affairs
20	Kamlesh Paswan	Minister of State in the Ministry of Rural Development
21	Bhagirath Choudhary	Minister of State in the Ministry of Agriculture and Farmers Welfare
22	Satish Chandra Dubey	Minister of State in the Ministry of Coal Minister of State in the Ministry of Mines
23	Sanjay Seth	Minister of State in the Ministry of Defence
24	Ravneet Singh	Minister of State in the Ministry of Food Processing Industries Minister of State in the Ministry of Railways
25	Durgadas Uikey	Minister of State in the Ministry of Tribal Affairs
26	Raksha Nikhil Khadse	Minister of State in the Ministry of Youth Affairs and Sports
27	Sukanta Majumdar	Minister of State in the Ministry of Education Minister of State in the Ministry of Development of North Eastern Region
28	Savitri Thakur	Minister of State in the Ministry of Women and Child Development
29	Tokhan Sahu	Minister of State in the Ministry of Housing and Urban Affairs
30	Raj Bhushan Choudhary	Minister of State in the Ministry of Jal Shakti
31	Bhupathi Raju Srinivasa Varma	Minister of State in the Ministry of Heavy Industries; and Minister of State in the Ministry of Steel
32	Harsh Malhotra	Minister of State in the Ministry of Corporate Affairs Minister of State in the Ministry of Road Transport and Highways
33	Nimuben Jayantibhai Bambhaniya	Minister of State in the Ministry of Consumer Affairs, Food and Public Distribution

34	Murlidhar Mohol	Minister of State in the Ministry of Cooperation Minister of State in the Ministry of Civil Aviation
35	George Kurian	Minister of State in the Ministry of Minority Affairs Minister of State in the Ministry of Fisheries, Animal Husbandry and Dairying
36	Pabitra Margherita	Minister of State in the Ministry of External Affairs; and Minister of State in the Ministry of Textiles

Top stats and facts

Largest electorate (world record): The number of voters in the 2024 general election was 1.4 billion, making India the largest (most populous) democracy in the world.

2019 GENERAL ELECTIONS	2024 GENERAL ELECTIONS
₹550 billion is estimated to have been spent during the 2019 Lok Sabha elections. At the time, this was a world record.	Breaking the old record, ₹1.35 trillion is estimated to have been spent in the 2024 elections, which is roughly a 145 per cent increase from the previous one.
The 2019 general election had a voter turnout of 613 million – about 67.1 per cent of the total electorate.	The 2024 general election had the largest voter turnout, with 642 million – about 66.3 per cent of the total electorate.
The 2019 elections registered 723 female candidates.	The 2024 elections registered the largest number of female candidates at 797.
Seventy-eight women were elected in the 2019 elections, making it the election with the most number of successful female candidates in the country.	Seventy-four women were elected in the 2024 elections.
Four independent candidates won in the 2019 elections.	Seven independent candidates won in the 2024 elections.

State with the largest electorate: Uttar Pradesh emerged as the state with the largest electorate in the 2024 elections, with a total of 154,103,670 eligible voters.

State/UT with the smallest electorate: Lakshadweep emerged as the UT with the smallest electorate in the 2024 elections, with a total of 57,784 eligible voters.

Most NOTA votes: Indore, a city in Madhya Pradesh, registered the highest number of NOTA ('None of the Above') votes ever – 202,212.

Uncontested candidate declared winner ahead of the rest: BJP candidate Mukesh Dalal was declared the uncontested winner from Surat after all other eight candidates withdrew after the rejection of Congress nominee Nilesh Kumbhani's nomination the day before.

Lowest margin victory: Ravindra Dattaram Waikar won by the lowest margin in the 2024 Lok Sabha election. He defeated Amol Gajanan Kirtikar by just 48 votes in Mumbai North West constituency. Waikar secured 452,644 votes, while Kirtikar got 452,596 votes.

Jammu and Kashmir's highest poll participation in 35 years: The union territory witnessed its highest poll participation in the last 35 years. The combined voter turnout at the polling stations for the entire UT (five Lok Sabha seats) was 58.46 per cent in the 2024 elections. (It was 44.37 per cent in 2019.)

Home voting for eligible voters for the first time in 2024 elections: Facility for voting from the comfort of home for senior citizens above 85 years of age and persons with disabilities with 40 per cent benchmark disability was extended for the first time across India in the 2024 elections.

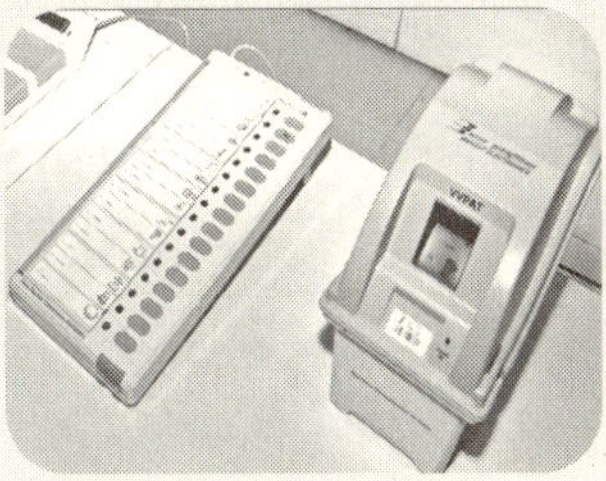

Largest margin victory against a candidate: Rakibul Hussain from Assam's Dhubri secured a historic victory by a vote margin of 1,012,476 votes. Hussain bagged 1,471,885 votes while Mohammed Badruddin Ajmal secured 459,409 votes.

Largest margin victory against NOTA: Sanjay Lalwani had the biggest victory margin in the 2024 election. His victory margin of 1,175,092 votes came against his closest rival Sanjay Solanki who got 51,659 votes in Madhya Pradesh's Indore constituency. However, the NOTA option got 218,674 votes in Indore, making it the runner up in the constituency.

PARIS OLYMPICS RECAP

The 2024 Olympics took place from 26 July to 11 August in Paris, France. This marked the third time that France has hosted the Olympics. The first time was in 1900, the second was in 1924, which was also the first year that women were allowed to participate. After a century, France once again had the honour of hosting the Olympics.

OLYMPICS	XXXIII
Host	Paris, France
Dates	26 July to 11 August
Mascot	Phryge
Total Sports	32
Total Medal Events	329
Debut Sport	Breaking (Break dancing)
Athletes	10,500
Volunteers	45,000
Venues	35

DID YOU KNOW?
The 2024 Olympics had a flame that didn't involve fire! Instead of the traditional fiery flame, Paris opted for a set-up where the flame was placed in a massive cauldron, featuring 40 LED spotlights and 200 misting nozzles. This cauldron was connected to a huge hot-air balloon that rose into the sky every night of the Games.

Opening ceremony

- The ceremony began with the athletes sailing in on boats in a parade down the Seine, making it the first time in history that the opening ceremony hasn't taken place in a stadium.
- The ceremony commenced at various iconic Parisian sites, structured into different symbolic segments named after French terms like *'Synchronicité', 'Liberté'* and *'Egalité.'*
- Rafael Nadal, Serena Williams, Carl Lewis and Nadia Comăneci each had a chance to carry the Olympic torch before it arrived at the cauldron.
- France seized the opportunity to exhibit one of its forte – fashion – in a runway event, coinciding with the athletes' parade. Emerging designers showcased their creations on diverse models during this event.

2024 Olympics highlights

- **USA** topped the charts with a total of 126 medals, including 40 gold, 44 silver and 42 bronze. **China** secured the second spot with 91 medals – 40 gold, 27 silver and 24 bronze. **Japan** with a total of 45 medals, including 20 gold, came third.
- **Léon Marchand** won a total of five medals, including four gold

and one bronze. He became the first male swimmer since Michael Phelps to win four gold medals in the same Olympics. The twenty-two-year-old also broke two Olympic records.

ARSHAD NADEEM

- **Arshad Nadeem** clinched a remarkable gold in the men's javelin throw, setting a new Olympic Record with his outstanding throw of 92.97m. This makes him the first Pakistani athlete to secure an individual medal in athletics. This also makes it Pakistan's first Olympic medal since Barcelona 1992.
- Boxer **Cindy Ngamba** made history by winning the first-ever medal for the International Olympic Committee (IOC) Refugee Olympic Team.
- Four countries won their first-ever gold medal at the 2024 Olympics – Saint Lucia, Botswana, Dominica and Guatemala.
- **Philip Kim**, known as Phil Wizard, from Canada and **Ami Yuasa** from Japan won gold in Olympics debut sport – breaking.
- **Novak Djokovic** added an Olympic gold to his tally of 24 grand slams by defeating Carlos Alcaraz in men's singles final at the 2024 Olympics.

SIMONE BILES

- **Simone Biles** had an outstanding performance at the Olympics, winning a total of four medals – three gold and one silver. With these additional medals, Biles now stands as the second most decorated female gymnast in Olympic history, with an impressive total of 11 medals. Her remarkable collection includes seven gold, two silver and two bronze medals. This also makes her the most decorated American gymnast in history.
- **Mondo Duplantis** won a gold medal in men's pole vault and surpassed his own world record of 6.24m by setting a new record of 6.25m. This also marks the ninth time he has broken the world record.
- **Yusuf Dikeç** from Turkey gained attention at the 2024 Olympics for winning a silver medal in the 10m air pistol event. He stood out not only for his impressive athletic abilities but also for competing without traditional protective gear like earplugs or shooting glasses, which sparked a viral sensation online.

India at 2024 Olympics

- At the Paris 2024 Olympics, the Indian contingent was composed of **117** athletes across 16 sports disciplines, with 70 men and 47 women.

They competed in 69 events, aiming for a total of 95 medals.

- India won six medals (one silver and five bronze) at the Paris 2024 Olympics.
- **Manu Bhaker** won two bronze medals. She clinched her first medal in women's **10m air pistol** and second in mixed team **10m air pistol** by teaming up with **Sarabjot Singh**. She made history by becoming the first Indian athlete (after Independence) to secure more than one medal in a single Olympics. Her victory also made her the first Indian woman to win a medal in shooting.

MANU BHAKER

- **Neeraj Chopra** won the silver medal in **men's javelin** at the Olympics with a throw of 89.45m. The first position was awarded to Arshad Nadeem from Pakistan, who threw 92.97m and set a new record. Grenada's Anderson Peters secured bronze with 88.54m.

NEERAJ CHOPRA

- **Aman Sehrawat** clinched a bronze medal in **men's 57kg freestyle division**. He became the youngest Indian Olympic medallist at 21 years and 24 days old, surpassing P.V. Sindhu's record of 21 years and one month when she won silver at the Rio 2016 Olympics.
- **Swapnil Kusale** clinched the bronze medal in the **men's 50m rifle three positions** final. This marked India's first-ever Olympic shooting medal in the 50m 3P event and the third medal in rifle shooting following Abhinav Bindra's gold in men's 10m air rifle at Beijing 2008 and Gagan Narang's bronze in the same event at London 2012.
- The Indian **men's hockey team** secured the bronze medal at the Paris 2024 Olympics.
- **Vinesh Phogat** made it to the final of the **women's 50kg weight** category. Despite being on track to be the first Indian woman to reach an Olympic wrestling final, Vinesh's hopes were crushed when she couldn't meet the weight requirement on the day of the gold medal match against Sarah Hildebrandt from the US. Although an appeal was made to the Court of Arbitration for Sport (CAS) for a joint-silver medal, it was dismissed.

VINESH PHOGAT

- **P.V. Sindhu** was unable to advance beyond pre-quarterfinals in women's singles and, therefore, missed the chance of becoming the first Indian athlete to win three medals in the Olympics.

- **Dhiraj Bommadevara** and **Ankita Bhakat** came in fourth place in the mixed team event, achieving India's highest-ever result in archery at the Olympics.
- **Lakshya Sen** made history by becoming the first Indian badminton player to advance to the semi-finals in a **men's badminton** event at the Olympics.
- **Manika Batra** became the first Indian table **tennis player** to reach the pre-quarterfinals of the Olympic Games.

MANIKA BATRA

Indian Medal Winners at 2024 Paris Olympics

NO.	ATHLETE	EVENT	SPORT	MEDAL
1	Manu Bhaker	Women's 10m air pistol	Shooting	Bronze
2	Manu Bhaker–Sarabjot Singh	Mixed team 10m air pistol	Shooting	Bronze
3	Swapnil Kusale	Men's 50m rifle 3 positions	Shooting	Bronze
4	Team India	Men's event	Hockey	Bronze
5	Neeraj Chopra	Men's javelin throw	Athletics	Silver
6	Aman Sehrawat	Men's freestyle 57kg	Wrestling	Bronze

India's Olympics tally

SPORT	FIRST WON	LAST WON	GOLD	SILVER	BRONZE	TOTAL
Field Hockey	Amsterdam 1928	Paris 2024	8	1	4	13
Wrestling	Helsinki 1952	Paris 2024	0	2	6	8
Shooting	Athens 2004	Paris 2024	1	2	4	7
Athletics	Paris 1900	Paris 1924	1	3	0	4
Badminton	London 2012	Tokyo 2020	0	1	2	3
Boxing	Beijing 2008	Tokyo 2020	0	0	3	3
Weightlifting	Sydney 2000	Tokyo 2020	0	1	1	2
Tennis	Atlanta 1996		0	0	1	1
Total			**10**	**10**	**21**	**41**

Medal Tally/Rankings

RANK	COUNTRY	GOLD	SILVER	BRONZE	TOTAL
1.	United States of America	40	44	42	126
2.	People's Republic of China	40	27	24	91
3.	Japan	20	12	13	45
4.	Australia	18	19	16	53
5.	France	16	26	22	64
6.	Netherlands	15	7	12	34
7.	Great Britain	14	22	29	65
8.	Republic of Korea	13	9	10	32
9.	Italy	12	13	15	40
10.	Germany	12	13	8	33

Top Medallists

MEDALLIST	COUNTRY	GOLD	SILVER	BRONZE	TOTAL
Zhang Yufei	China	0	1	5	6
Léon Marchand	France	4	0	1	5
Torri Huske	United States of America	3	2	0	5
Mollie O'Callaghan	Australia	3	1	1	5
Regan Smith	United States of America	2	3	0	5
Kaylee McKeown	Australia	2	1	2	5
Summer McIntosh	Canada	3	1	0	4
Simone Biles	United States of America	3	1	0	4
Shinnosuke Oka	Japan	3	0	1	4
Ariarne Titmus	Australia	2	2	0	4

DID YOU KNOW?
The 2024 Olympics marked a historic moment as the first Games to prioritize gender equality, achieved through ensuring equal participation across all sports. Additionally, there was a balanced representation of male and female volunteers, with a 50–50 split.

Green Olympics

- Instead of installing air conditioning, the organizers of the Olympic village for the 2024 Games in Paris opted for a geothermal system that circulates cool water under the floors.
- The beds in the athletes' village at 2020 Tokyo Olympics were made from recycled cardboard. The cardboard beds made a return at this year's Olympics. The mattresses too were made from recycled fishnets.
- Paris relied on renewable energy sources such as geothermal and solar power.
- All the Olympic sites were easily accessible by public transportation. Paris also introduced special services to make travel easier for visitors.
- The city also established 1,000 kilometres of dedicated bike lanes and provided 3,000 bikes for rent during the Games.
- Paris 2024 aimed to promote plant-based, locally-sourced and sustainable food choices.
- Instead of building new structures, Paris utilized existing buildings or temporary installations for 95 per cent of its Olympic competitions.

World Records at 2024 Olympics

SPORTS	CATEGORY	OLD RECORD		NEW RECORD	
		RECORD HOLDER	RECORD	RECORD HOLDER	RECORD
Swimming	Men's 100m freestyle	Pan Zhanle	46.80	Pan Zhanle	46.40
	Mixed 4x100m medley relay	Great Britain	3:37.58	USA	3:37.43
	Men's 1500m freestyle	Sun Yang	14:31.02	Bobby Finke	14:30.67
	Women's 4x100m medley relay	USA	3:50.40	USA	3:49.63
Athletics	4x400m mixed relay	USA	3:08.80	USA	3:07.41
	Pole vault	Armand Duplantis	6.24m	Armand Duplantis	6.25m
	Women's 400m hurdles	Sydney McLaughlin-Levrone	50.65	Sydney McLaughlin-Levrone	50.37
Archery	Women's 70m 72 arrows round	Kang Chae-young	692	Lim Si-hyeon	694
Track Cycling	Women's team sprint	Great Britain	45.338	Great Britain	45.186
	Men's team sprint	Netherlands	41.191	Netherlands	40.949
	Men's team pursuit	Italy	3:42.032	Australia	3:40.730
	Men's 200m flying start	Matthew Richardson	9.091	Harrie Lavreysen	9.088
	Women's sprint	Ellesse Andrews	10.108	Lea Friedrich	10.029

UPDATES

SPORTS	CATEGORY	OLD RECORD		NEW RECORD	
		RECORD HOLDER	RECORD	RECORD HOLDER	RECORD
Sport Climbing	Women's speed climbing	Aleksandra Mirosław	6.21	Aleksandra Mirosław	6.06
	Men's speed	Tom Watson	4.75	Tom Watson	4.74
Weightlifting	Men's 89kg	Karlos Nasar	213kg	Karlos Nasar	224kg
	Men's 89kg	Li Dayin	396kg	Karlos Nasar	404kg
Canoe Sprint	Women's canoe single 200m			Katie Vincent	44.12
Modern Pentathlon	Laser run	Martin Vlach	9:44.80, 716 points	Emiliano Hernández	9:40.80, 720 points
	Overall points	Csaba Bohm	1551 points	Ahmed Elgendy	1555 points
	Overall points	Alice Sotero	1443 points	Michelle Gulyás	1461 points

Closing ceremony

- The closing ceremony took place at the Stade de France, where the track and field events were held, contrasting with the opening ceremony that took place on the River Seine.
- **Manu Bhaker** and **P.R. Sreejesh** carried the national flags for India, joining athletes from all nations who walked in the ceremony.
- The last medal ceremony of Paris 2024 was for the women's marathon, serving as a highly symbolic way to conclude the first-ever Olympic Games with full gender parity.

DID YOU KNOW?
The medals for the 2024 Olympics and Paralympic Games in Paris included recycled metal from the Eiffel Tower. The metal is shaped like a hexagon, symbolizing France, often referred to as L'Hexagone because of its hexagonal shape.

- Paris bid farewell to the Olympics by emphasizing the significance of protecting the essence of the games in a world filled with uncertainty and conflict.
- French closing ceremony flagbearer Antoine Dupont, who won gold with the men's rugby sevens team, handed the French national flag to the French Paralympic team.
- The Olympic Flag has been transferred from Paris Mayor Anne Hidalgo to IOC President Thomas Bach, and then to Los Angeles Mayor Karen Bass. The 2028 Olympics are set to take place in Los Angeles.

3 LITERATURE

The word 'literature' means 'acquaintance with letters', from the Latin 'lettera' or letter. Literature is broadly divided into two categories: fiction, which is imaginary, and non-fiction, which is factual. Here are the common types of literature:

Autobiography: A narration of a person's life that they tell themselves.

Biography: A factual narration of a person's life, told by somebody else.

Drama: A piece of writing, with dialogue and action, meant to be performed on stage.

Essay: A written discussion of a topic from an individual's viewpoint.

Fable: A moral story in which the characters are typically animals.

Fairy tale: A fictional story with central themes of fantasy and magic.

Folk tale: Traditional stories, circulated orally among people of a specific community, region or country.

Journal or Diary: The day-to-day recordings of someone's life, usually autobiographical in nature, but often fictional too.

Legend: A story about an important individual or event popularly regarded as historical although not verifiable.

Memoir: An autobiographical account of the writer's memories, emotions and views.

Myth: An ancient religious, spiritual or traditional story describing how the world or humankind came to be.

Novel: A full-length piece of fiction, written in prose. A **novella** is a short novel.

Poetry: A piece written in verse, in which lines may or may not rhyme or stick to a specific meter.

Short story: A narrative in prose, much shorter than a novel, and usually, but not always, about the size of a chapter in a novel.

E-literature: Electronic literature is created in digital environments. It includes conversational characters or 'chatterbots'; interactive fiction, novels in the form of emails, SMS messages or blogs; and poems and stories generated by computers. An e-book is an electronic version of a print book, to be read on a computer or a device such as a tablet, a smartphone or an e-reader.

FEMOIR A MEMOIR WRITTEN BY A WELL-KNOWN FEMALE ACTOR OR COMEDIAN, EMBRACING BODY POSITIVITY, PROFESSIONAL ADVANCEMENT AND A SUPPORTIVE FEMALE COMMUNITY.

TYPES OF FICTION

Fiction includes novels, short stories, fables, folk tales, fairy tales, plays, poetry and comic books. Here are the main types of fiction genres.

Campus novel: A novel in which the main action takes place around the campus of a university, college or school.

Children's: A book written primarily for children is listed in this genre. This includes fiction written in many formats, such as picture books, graphic fiction, short stories and full-length novels. A category higher than children's fiction is young adult (YA) fiction. It broadly includes books for adolescents and young adults in the age group of 14 to 19 years.

Comedy: Fiction that intends to amuse readers and provoke laughter.

Crime: Fiction written about crime and detection. There are several subgenres, such as detective fiction, legal thrillers and courtroom drama.

Fantasy: This genre looks at magic and other forms of the supernatural as its primary inspiration. 'Fantastic' elements may be hidden in a semi-real-world setting (like the Harry Potter series) or they may occur in a fantastical world.

MAGICAL REALISM IS A GENRE IN WHICH MAGICAL EVENTS ARE A PART OF ORDINARY LIFE.

Graphic fiction: This genre covers a huge range from picture books and comic books to graphic novels and manga, in which a series of images and word or speech balloons convey a narrative.

Horror: Fiction that primarily aims to scare and incite fear in the reader. Although they largely use supernatural elements, books with gruesome, frightening or suspenseful themes are also part of the genre.

Romance: Novels in this genre are centred on a romantic relationship. This genre extends from classics to Mills & Boon romances.

Spy: Born of the political climate in Europe prior to the First World War, spy fiction began around the time the first modern intelligence services were formed and swiftly became popular through the Second World War.

Thriller: This eventful genre involves suspense and exciting action. It typically follows a hero pitted against a villain who aims to destroy the hero, his country or even the world.

Satire: When an author ridicules or derides a vice or a folly through humour and wit, it is called satire. It is marked by irony, sarcasm, parody and exaggeration.

Wild West Fiction: This genre originated in the American Wild West, cowboy heroism and Native American life.

TYPES OF POETRY

Here are the main forms of poetry:

Acrostic: The first letter, syllable or word of each line or stanza spells out a word/message.

Ballad: A poem that tells a story similar to a folk tale or legend.

Blank/free verse: A poem that does not rhyme, or follow a meter.

Burlesque poetry: In this a serious subject is treated with humour.

Couplet: A poem of two consecutive lines that rhyme.

Elegy: A sad poetic reflection about the death of a person.

Epic: A long serious poem, telling the story of a heroic figure.

Epitaph: A commemorative poem praising the deceased.

Haiku: A Japanese poem of three unrhymed lines of five, seven and five syllables, usually with a reference to a 'season'.

Limerick: A short, humorous five-line poem.

Lyric: A poem that expresses the thoughts/feelings of the poet.

Narrative: A poem that tells a story.

Ode: A long meditative lyric, with a formal stanzaic structure.

Pastoral: It depicts rural life.

Rhyme: This repeats same or similar sounds in words at the end of lines.

Romantic: Poetry of nature and love.

Shape: A poem written in the shape of an object.

Sonnet: A lyric fourteen-line poem, with a formal rhyme scheme.

TYPES OF DRAMA

Drama is a work of fiction that is meant to be performed on stage, or acted out.

Epic: A long poem about heroism and events significant for a culture or nation. Oral or primary epics are handed down through the spoken word and written down after centuries. Examples are Greek epics, such as *The Iliad* and Indian epics like the Mahabharata. Literary epics are modern works such as John Milton's *Paradise Lost*.

Romance: Also known as chivalric romance, this deals with the courageous quests and adventures of a heroic individual, often a brave knight.

Tragicomedy: This describes work that blends elements of tragedy and comedy. Black (or serious/dark) comedy is also part of it.

Comedy: This includes parody, satire, burlesque, clowning and romantic comedy, among other types of comedy.

Tragedy: Coming from the poetic and religious traditions of ancient Greece, tragedy takes its inspiration from human suffering. Shakespeare's *Hamlet* and Sophocles's *Antigone* are examples.

CLI-FI OR CLIMATE FICTION IS A SUBGENRE OF SCIENCE FICTION THAT DEALS WITH THE GROWING CONCERN OVER GLOBAL WARMING.

BOOKS TO SCREEN

Coming soon to a screen, all these films and shows are based on fabulous books!

- ***A Good Girl's Guide to Murder* (2024):** The young adult sleuthing summer is back again with a new crime detective on the block – Pip played by Emma Mayers. *A Good Girl's Guide to Murder* is a BBC series adapted by Poppy Cogan from Holly Jackson's 2019 bestseller by the same name.
- ***Harold and the Purple Crayon* (2024):** *Harold and the Purple Crayon*, a beloved children's picture book since its 1950s debut, tells the story of a four-year-old boy who discovers a magical purple crayon, enabling him to bring his imaginative creations to life.
- ***The Spiderwick Chronicles* (2024):** This American fantasy series is partially based on Tony DiTerlizzi and Holly Black's *The Spiderwick Chronicles*. The show centres on the Grace family as they move into their ancestral home and solve a sinister mystery surrounding their great-uncle's discovery of the parallel and secret realm of fairies.
- ***The Wild Robot (Wild Robot Series #1)* (2024):** *The Wild Robot* is an American animated science fiction survival drama film based on the book series of the same name by Peter Brown, produced by DreamWorks Animation and distributed by Universal Pictures.
- ***Uglies* (2024):** Set in a society where a compulsory procedure at age sixteen eliminates physical distinctions to enforce a singular beauty ideal, the story follows protagonist Tally Youngblood as she confronts decisions that will reshape her destiny.
- ***Charlie and the Great Glass Elevator* (2025):** *Charlie and the Great Glass Elevator* is a children's book by British author Roald Dahl. It is the sequel to *Charlie and the Chocolate Factory*, continuing the story of young Charlie Bucket and chocolatier Willy Wonka as they travel in the Great Glass Elevator. The book was published in 1972.
- ***Frankenstein* (2025):** *Frankenstein* is an upcoming American science fiction horror film written and directed by Guillermo del Toro, based on the 1818 novel of the same name by Mary Shelley. The film stars Oscar Isaac, Jacob Elordi, Mia Goth and Lars Mikkelsen.
- ***The Twits* (2025):** Netflix is expanding the roster of Roald Dahl adaptations with an animated version of *The Twits*, a children's novel from 1980. This story revolves around a mischievous couple who delight in playing elaborate practical jokes on others for their own entertainment. Other Dahl classics that have been adapted multiple times are the Willy Wonka films, *Fantastic Mr. Fox* and *Matilda*.

4 COUNTRIES

Important International Organizations

- **ACP:** African, Caribbean and Pacific Group of States
- **ADB:** Asian Development Bank
- **AI:** Amnesty International
- **APEC:** Asia-Pacific Economic Cooperation
- **ASEAN:** Association of Southeast Asian Nations
- **EU:** European Union
- **IFAD:** International Fund for Agricultural Development
- **IFRC:** International Federation of Red Cross and Red Crescent Societies
- **IMSO:** International Mobile Satellite Organization
- **INTERPOL:** International Criminal Police Organization
- **IOC:** International Olympic Committee
- **ISO:** International Organization for Standardization
- **ITSO:** International Telecommunications Satellite Organization
- **ITU:** International Telecommunication Union
- **NAM:** Non-Aligned Movement
- **NATO:** North Atlantic Treaty Organization
- **OECD:** Organization for Economic Co-operation and Development
- **OPEC:** Organization of the Petroleum Exporting Countries
- **SAARC:** South Asian Association for Regional Cooperation
- **WMO:** World Meteorological Organization
- **WWF:** World Wide Fund for Nature

UN: The United Nations

UN Specialized Agencies:

- **ESCAP:** Economic and Social Commission for Asia and the Pacific
- **FAO:** Food and Agricultural Organization
- **IBRD:** International Bank for Reconstruction and Development
- **IDA:** International Development Association
- **ILO:** International Labour Organization
- **IMF:** International Monetary Fund
- **UNESCO:** United Nations Educational, Scientific and Cultural Organization
- **UNICEF:** United Nations Children's Fund
- **WHO:** World Health Organization
- **WIPO:** World Intellectual Property

NOTE: Includes sovereign states in the United Nations System. Time zones are calculated from the Greenwich Mean Time (GMT) and are mentioned in hours and minutes; GDP per capita is is approximate, in US dollars and based on the last figures available; Population figures are based on each country's last national census; Life expectancy figures are in years; Internet TLD stands for Internet Top Level Domain; Flags may not match exact proportions. All information updated up to 1 July 2024.

AFGHANISTAN

LOCATION: South-central Asia

CAPITAL: Kabul

AREA: 652,230 sq. km

LANGUAGES: Pashto, Dari

MAIN RELIGION: Islam

CURRENCY: Afghani

LITERACY RATE: 37.3%

LIFE EXPECTANCY: 54.4 years

TIME ZONE: +4.30

TYPE OF GOVERNMENT: Islamic Emirate

HEAD OF STATE AND GOVT: Mullah Haibatullah Akhundzada

GDP PER CAPITA: $1,500

POPULATION: 40,121,552

ISD CODE: 93 **INTERNET TLD:** .af

Since it gained independence in 1919, Afghanistan's flag has been changed more than twenty-six times.

ALBANIA

LOCATION: South-east Europe

CAPITAL: Tirana

AREA: 28,748 sq. km

LANGUAGE: Albanian

MAIN RELIGION: Islam

CURRENCY: Lek

LITERACY RATE: 98.4%

LIFE EXPECTANCY: 79.7 years

TIME ZONE: +1

TYPE OF GOVERNMENT: Parliamentary Republic

HEAD OF STATE: President Bajram Begaj **HEAD OF GOVT:** Prime Minister Edi Rama

GDP PER CAPITA: $15,500

POPULATION: 3,107,100

ISD CODE: 355 **INTERNET TLD:** .al

Albania produces all of its electricity through hydropower or the use of water resources.

ALGERIA

LOCATION: North Africa

CAPITAL: Algiers

AREA: 2,381,740 sq. km

LANGUAGES: Arabic, French, Berber

MAIN RELIGION: Islam

CURRENCY: Algerian Dinar

LITERACY RATE: 81.4%

LIFE EXPECTANCY: 77.9 years

TIME ZONE: +1

TYPE OF GOVERNMENT: Presidential Republic

HEAD OF STATE: President Abdelmadjid Tebboune

HEAD OF GOVT: Prime Minister Nadir Larbaoui

GDP PER CAPITA: $11,200

POPULATION: 47,022,473

ISD CODE: 213 **INTERNET TLD:** .dz

In Algeria, petrol is cheaper than water.

Background: Algeria

ANDORRA

LOCATION: West Europe

CAPITAL: Andorra la Vella

AREA: 468 sq. km

LANGUAGES: Catalan, French, Castilian, Portuguese

MAIN RELIGION: Christianity

CURRENCY: Euro

LITERACY RATE: 100%

LIFE EXPECTANCY: 83.8 years

TIME ZONE: +1

TYPE OF GOVERNMENT: Parliamentary Democracy and Co-principality

HEAD OF STATE: Co-prince Emmanuel Macron and Co-prince Archbishop Joan-Enric Vives Sicilia

HEAD OF GOVT: Executive Council President Xavier Espot Zamora

GDP PER CAPITA: $49,900

POPULATION: 85,370

ISD CODE: 376

INTERNET TLD: .ad

Andorra has a small volunteer ceremonial army. Spain and France defend it with their armies.

ANGOLA

LOCATION: South-central Africa

CAPITAL: Luanda

AREA: 1,246,700 sq. km

LANGUAGES: Portuguese, Bantu, other African languages

MAIN RELIGIONS: Indigenous faiths, Christianity

CURRENCY: Kwanza

LITERACY RATE: 71.1%

LIFE EXPECTANCY: 62.9 years

TIME ZONE: +1

TYPE OF GOVERNMENT: Presidential Republic

HEAD OF STATE AND GOVT: President João Manuel Gonçalves Lourenço

GDP PER CAPITA: $5,900

POPULATION: 37,202,061

ISD CODE: 244

INTERNET TLD: .ao

After its independence from Portugal in 1975, Angola went through a civil war for twenty-seven years.

ANTIGUA AND BARBUDA

LOCATION: Central America

CAPITAL: Saint John's

AREA: 443 sq. km

LANGUAGE: English

MAIN RELIGION: Christianity

CURRENCY: East Caribbean Dollar

LITERACY RATE: 99%

LIFE EXPECTANCY: 78.3 years

TIME ZONE: –4

TYPE OF GOVERNMENT: Constitutional Monarchy and Parliamentary Democracy

HEAD OF STATE: King Charles III

HEAD OF GOVT: Prime Minister Gaston Browne

GDP PER CAPITA: $22,300

POPULATION: 102,634

ISD CODE: 1-268 **INTERNET TLD:** .ag

Antigua and Barbuda is often called the land of 365 beaches due to the beautiful and long coastline.

Background: Andorra

ARGENTINA

LOCATION: South America

CAPITAL: Buenos Aires

AREA: 2,780,400 sq. km

LANGUAGE: Spanish

MAIN RELIGION: Christianity

CURRENCY: Argentine Peso

LITERACY RATE: 99%

LIFE EXPECTANCY: 78.8 years

TIME ZONE: –3

TYPE OF GOVERNMENT: Presidential Republic

HEAD OF STATE AND GOVT: President Javier Gerardo Milei

GDP PER CAPITA: $22,500

POPULATION: 46,994,384

ISD CODE: 54 **INTERNET TLD:** .ar

The country is named after the Latin word *argentum*, which means 'silver' in English.

ARMENIA

LOCATION: South-western Asia, east of Turkiye

CAPITAL: Yerevan

AREA: 29,743 sq. km

LANGUAGE: Armenian

MAIN RELIGION: Christianity

CURRENCY: Dram

LITERACY RATE: 99.8%

LIFE EXPECTANCY: 76.7 years

TIME ZONE: +4

TYPE OF GOVERNMENT: Parliamentary Democracy

HEAD OF STATE: President Vahagn Khachaturyan **HEAD OF GOVT:** Prime Minister Nikol Pashinyan

GDP PER CAPITA: $16,100

POPULATION: 2,976,765

ISD CODE: 374 **INTERNET TLD:** .am

One of the oldest centres of civilizations, Armenia was the first country in the world to officially embrace Christianity as its religion (c. 300 BCE).

AUSTRALIA

LOCATION: Between Indian Ocean and South Pacific Ocean

CAPITAL: Canberra

AREA: 7,741,220 sq. km

LANGUAGE: English

MAIN RELIGION: Christianity

CURRENCY: Australian Dollar

LITERACY RATE: 100%

LIFE EXPECTANCY: 83.5 years

TIME ZONE: +8 to +10.30

TYPE OF GOVERNMENT: Constitutional Monarchy and Federal Parliamentary Democracy

HEAD OF STATE: King Charles III **HEAD OF GOVT:** Prime Minister Anthony Albanese

GDP PER CAPITA: $51,100

POPULATION: 26,768,598

ISD CODE: 61 **INTERNET TLD:** .au

Each year, Brisbane, a city in Australia, hosts the world championships of cockroach racing.

Background: Australia

AUSTRIA

LOCATION: Central Europe

CAPITAL: Vienna

AREA: 83,871sq. km

LANGUAGE: German

MAIN RELIGION: Christianity

CURRENCY: Euro

LITERACY RATE: 99%

LIFE EXPECTANCY: 82.7 years

TIME ZONE: +1

TYPE OF GOVERNMENT: Federal Parliamentary Republic

HEAD OF STATE: President Alexander Van der Bellen

HEAD OF GOVT: Chancellor Karl Nehammer

GDP PER CAPITA: $55,900

POPULATION: 8,967,982

ISD CODE: 43 **INTERNET TLD:** .at

The first woman to win the Nobel Peace Prize in 1905, Bertha von Suttner, was from Austria.

AZERBAIJAN

LOCATION: West Asia, bordering Caspian Sea

CAPITAL: Baku

AREA: 86,600 sq. km

LANGUAGE: Azerbaijani

MAIN RELIGION: Islam

CURRENCY: Azerbaijani Manat

LITERACY RATE: 99.8%

LIFE EXPECTANCY: 75.9 years

TIME ZONE: +4

TYPE OF GOVERNMENT: Presidential Republic

HEAD OF STATE: President Ilham Aliyev

HEAD OF GOVT: Prime Minister Ali Hidayat oglu Asadov

GDP PER CAPITA: $15,100

POPULATION: 10,650,239

ISD CODE: 994 **INTERNET TLD:** .az

The 'burning mountain' is a rare natural wonder in the Absheron Peninsula. It 'burns' all year due to natural gas escaping from the ground.

(THE) BAHAMAS

LOCATION: Central America

CAPITAL: Nassau

AREA: 13,880 sq. km

LANGUAGES: English, Creole

MAIN RELIGION: Christianity

CURRENCY: Bahamian Dollar

LITERACY RATE: 99%

LIFE EXPECTANCY: 76.7 years

TIME ZONE: –5

TYPE OF GOVERNMENT: Constitutional Monarchy and Parliamentary Democracy

HEAD OF STATE: King Charles III

HEAD OF GOVT: Prime Minister Philip Davis

GDP PER CAPITA: $34,700

POPULATION: 410,862

ISD CODE: 1-242

INTERNET TLD: .bs

The word 'Bahamas' comes from the Spanish word *bajamar*, meaning 'shallow water'. The archipelago has nearly 700 islands, with only about 30 inhabited ones.

BAHRAIN

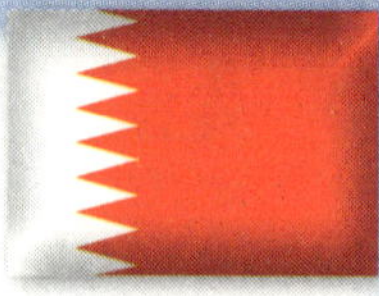

LOCATION: South-central Asia

CAPITAL: Manama

AREA: 760 sq. km

LANGUAGES: Arabic, English, Farsi, Urdu

MAIN RELIGION: Islam

CURRENCY: Bahraini Dinar

LITERACY RATE: 97.5%

LIFE EXPECTANCY: 80.4 years

TIME ZONE: +3

TYPE OF GOVERNMENT: Constitutional Monarchy

HEAD OF STATE: King Hamad bin Isa Al Khalifah **HEAD OF GOVT:** Prime Minister Salman bin Hamad Al Khalifah

GDP PER CAPITA: $51,900

POPULATION: 1,566,888

ISD CODE: 973 **INTERNET TLD:** .bh

The Bahraini Dinar is the world's second highest valued currency after the Kuwaiti Dinar.

BANGLADESH

LOCATION: South Asia

CAPITAL: Dhaka

AREA: 148,460 sq. km

LANGUAGE: Bangla (Bengali)

MAIN RELIGION: Islam

CURRENCY: Taka

LITERACY RATE: 74.9%

LIFE EXPECTANCY: 75.2 years

TIME ZONE: +6

TYPE OF GOVERNMENT: Parliamentary Republic

HEAD OF STATE: Mohammed Shahabuddin

HEAD OF GOVT: Interim chief adviser Muhammad Yunus

GDP PER CAPITA: $6,300

POPULATION: 168,697,184

ISD CODE: 880 **INTERNET TLD:** .bd

Bangladesh is blessed with deep, rich and fertile soil from the three rivers – the Ganga, the Brahmaputra and the Meghna – that form the deltaic plain upon which it sits.

BARBADOS

LOCATION: Caribbean Sea

CAPITAL: Bridgetown

AREA: 430 sq. km

LANGUAGE: English

MAIN RELIGION: Christianity

CURRENCY: Barbadian Dollar

LITERACY RATE: 99.6%

LIFE EXPECTANCY: 79 years

TIME ZONE: –4

TYPE OF GOVERNMENT: Parliamentary Republic

HEAD OF STATE: President Sandra Mason **HEAD OF GOVT:** Prime Minister Mia Mottley

GDP PER CAPITA: $15,400

POPULATION: 304,139

ISD CODE: 1-246 **INTERNET TLD:** .bb

Barbados is called 'The Land of the Flying Fish.' It comes from the island's national dish, cou-cou, and the presence of flying fish in the surrounding waters.

Background: Barbados

BELARUS

LOCATION: Eastern Europe

CAPITAL: Minsk

AREA: 207,600 sq. km

LANGUAGES: Belarusian, Russian

MAIN RELIGION: Christianity (Russian Orthodox Church)

CURRENCY: Belarusian Ruble

LITERACY RATE: 99.9%

LIFE EXPECTANCY: 74.7 years

TIME ZONE: +2

TYPE OF GOVERNMENT: Presidential Republic

HEAD OF STATE: President Alexander Lukashenko **HEAD OF GOVT:** Prime Minister Roman Golovchenko

GDP PER CAPITA: $19,100

POPULATION: 9,501,451

ISD CODE: 375 **INTERNET TLD:** .by

There are more than 20,000 rivers in Belarus.

BELGIUM

LOCATION: North-west Europe

CAPITAL: Brussels

AREA: 30,528 sq. km

LANGUAGES: Dutch, French, German

MAIN RELIGION: Christianity

CURRENCY: Euro

LITERACY RATE: 99%

LIFE EXPECTANCY: 82.3 years

TIME ZONE: +1

TYPE OF GOVERNMENT: Constitutional Monarchy and Parliamentary Democracy

HEAD OF STATE: King Philippe **HEAD OF GOVT:** Prime Minister Alexander De Croo

GDP PER CAPITA: $53,300

POPULATION: 11,977,634

ISD CODE: 32

INTERNET TLD: .be

The origin of French fries can be found in Belgium and the French people are said to have borrowed the idea.

BELIZE

LOCATION: Central America

CAPITAL: Belmopan

AREA: 22,966 sq. km

LANGUAGES: English, Creole, Spanish

MAIN RELIGION: Christianity

CURRENCY: Belize Dollar

LITERACY RATE: 82.7%

LIFE EXPECTANCY: 74.3 years

TIME ZONE: –6

TYPE OF GOVERNMENT: Constitutional Monarchy and Parliamentary Democracy

HEAD OF STATE: King Charles III **HEAD OF GOVT:** Prime Minister Johnny Briceño

GDP PER CAPITA: $8,800

POPULATION: 415,789

ISD CODE: 501 **INTERNET TLD:** .bz

The motto of the country is 'Under the shade, I flourish' due to it being covered with rainforests.

Background: Belgium

BENIN

LOCATION: West Africa

CAPITAL: Porto Novo

AREA: 112,622 sq. km

LANGUAGES: French, Fon, other African languages

MAIN RELIGIONS: Indigenous faiths, Christianity, Islam

CURRENCY: CFA Franc

LITERACY RATE: 45.8%

LIFE EXPECTANCY: 63 years

TIME ZONE: +1

TYPE OF GOVERNMENT: Presidential Republic

HEAD OF STATE AND GOVT: President Patrice Talon

GDP PER CAPITA: $3,400

POPULATION: 14,697,052

ISD CODE: 229

INTERNET TLD: .bj

Benin's name comes from a large body of water called 'The Bight of Benin'.

BHUTAN

LOCATION: South Asia

CAPITAL: Thimphu

AREA: 38,394 sq. km

LANGUAGES: Dzongkha, Sharchhopka

MAIN RELIGION: Buddhism

CURRENCY: Ngultrum

LITERACY RATE: 70.9%

LIFE EXPECTANCY: 73.7 years

TIME ZONE: +6

TYPE OF GOVERNMENT: Constitutional Monarchy

HEAD OF STATE: King Jigme Khesar Namgyel Wangchuck **HEAD OF GOVT:** Prime Minister Tshering Tobgay

GDP PER CAPITA: $10,900

POPULATION: 884,546

ISD CODE: 975 **INTERNET TLD:** .bt

Bhutan was one of the last countries to introduce television to its people. The government lifted the ban on TV in 1999.

BOLIVIA

LOCATION: Central South America

CAPITAL: La Paz

AREA: 1,098,581 sq. km

LANGUAGES: Spanish, Quechua, Aymara, Guarani

MAIN RELIGION: Christianity

CURRENCY: Boliviano

LITERACY RATE: 92.5%

LIFE EXPECTANCY: 72.5 years

TIME ZONE: –4

TYPE OF GOVERNMENT: Presidential Republic

HEAD OF STATE AND GOVT: President Luis Arce

GDP PER CAPITA: $8,200

POPULATION: 12,311,974

ISD CODE: 591 **INTERNET TLD:** .bo

Lake Titicaca in the Andes is the highest navigable lake in the world, at 3,810 m (12,500 ft) above sea level.

Background: Brazil

BOSNIA AND HERZEGOVINA

LOCATION: South-east Europe

CAPITAL: Sarajevo

AREA: 51,197 sq. km

LANGUAGES: Bosnian, Croatian, Serbian

MAIN RELIGIONS: Christianity, Islam

CURRENCY: Convertible Mark

LITERACY RATE: 98.1%

LIFE EXPECTANCY: 78.5 years

TIME ZONE: +1

TYPE OF GOVERNMENT: Parliamentary Republic

HEAD OF STATE: Chairperson of the Presidency Denis Bećirović **HEAD OF GOVT:** Chairman of Council of Ministers Borjana Krišto

GDP PER CAPITA: $16,700

POPULATION: 3,798,671

ISD CODE: 387 **INTERNET TLD:** .ba

The capital city Sarajevo was the first city in Europe with a full-time electric tram.

BOTSWANA

LOCATION: Southern Africa

CAPITAL: Gaborone

AREA: 581,730 sq. km

LANGUAGES: English, Setswana, Kalanga

MAIN RELIGION: Christianity

CURRENCY: Pula

LITERACY RATE: 88.5%

LIFE EXPECTANCY: 66.4 years

TIME ZONE: +2

TYPE OF GOVERNMENT: Parliamentary Republic

HEAD OF STATE AND GOVT: President Mokgweetsi Eric Masisi

GDP PER CAPITA: $15,500

POPULATION: 2,450,668

ISD CODE: 267

INTERNET TLD: .bw

The Okavango Delta was declared as one of the seven Natural Wonders of Africa in 2013.

BRAZIL

LOCATION: North-east South America

CAPITAL: Brasilia

AREA: 8,515,770 sq. km

LANGUAGES: Portuguese

MAIN RELIGION: Christianity

CURRENCY: Real

LITERACY RATE: 94.7%

LIFE EXPECTANCY: 76.3 years

TIME ZONE: –3

TYPE OF GOVERNMENT: Presidential Federal Republic

HEAD OF STATE AND GOVT: President Luiz Inácio Lula da Silva

GDP PER CAPITA: $15,100

POPULATION: 220,051,512

ISD CODE: 55

INTERNET TLD: .br

Brazil is home to 60 per cent of the Amazon rainforest.

BRUNEI

LOCATION: South-east Asia

CAPITAL: Bandar Seri Begawan

AREA: 5,765 sq. km

LANGUAGE: Malay

MAIN RELIGION: Islam

CURRENCY: Brunei Dollar

LITERACY RATE: 97.6%

LIFE EXPECTANCY: 78.9 years

TIME ZONE: +8

TYPE OF GOVERNMENT: Islamic Absolute Monarchy

HEAD OF STATE AND GOVT: Sultan Hassanal Bolkiah

GDP PER CAPITA: $58,700

POPULATION: 491,900

ISD CODE: 673 **INTERNET TLD:** .bn

The Istana Nurul Iman Palace in Brunei is reportedly the largest residential palace in the world, with 1,788 rooms and 257 bathrooms.

BULGARIA

LOCATION: South-east Europe

CAPITAL: Sofia

AREA: 110,879 sq. km

LANGUAGE: Bulgarian

MAIN RELIGION: Christianity

CURRENCY: Lev

LITERACY RATE: 98.4%

LIFE EXPECTANCY: 76.1 years

TIME ZONE: +2

TYPE OF GOVERNMENT: Parliamentary Republic

HEAD OF STATE: President Rumen Radev **HEAD OF GOVT:** Caretaker Prime Minister Dimitar Glavchev

GDP PER CAPITA: $27,000

POPULATION: 6,782,659

ISD CODE: 359 **INTERNET TLD:** .bg

The first Bulgarian Empire was established in 681 CE, and the name 'Bulgaria' hasn't changed since, making it the only country in Europe to never have changed its name.

BURKINA FASO

LOCATION: West Africa

CAPITAL: Ouagadougou

AREA: 274,200 sq. km

LANGUAGES: French, indigenous African languages

MAIN RELIGION: Islam

CURRENCY: CFA Franc

LITERACY RATE: 46%

LIFE EXPECTANCY: 64.2 years

TIME ZONE: 0

TYPE OF GOVERNMENT: Presidential Republic

HEAD OF STATE: President Capt. Ibrahim Traoré **HEAD OF GOVT:** Prime Minister Joachim Kyélem de Tambèla

GDP PER CAPITA: $2,200

POPULATION: 23,042,199

ISD CODE: 226

INTERNET TLD: .bf

The phrase 'Burkina Faso' means 'Land of the Honest (Incorruptible) Men.'

BURUNDI

LOCATION: Central Africa

CAPITAL: Bujumbura

AREA: 27,830 sq. km

LANGUAGES: Kirundi, French, Swahili

MAIN RELIGION: Christianity

CURRENCY: Burundi Franc

LITERACY RATE: 74.7%

LIFE EXPECTANCY: 68.1 years

TIME ZONE: +2

TYPE OF GOVERNMENT: Presidential Republic

HEAD OF STATE AND GOVT: President Évariste Ndayishimiye

GDP PER CAPITA: $700

POPULATION: 13,590,102

ISD CODE: 257 **INTERNET TLD:** .bi

The world's longest freshwater lake, Lake Tanganyika, is in Burundi. It stretches up to 673 km.

CABO VERDE

LOCATION: North Atlantic Ocean, off West Africa

CAPITAL: Praia

AREA: 4,033 sq. km

LANGUAGES: Portuguese, Creole

MAIN RELIGION: Christianity

CURRENCY: Cape Verdean Escudo

LITERACY RATE: 90.8%

LIFE EXPECTANCY: 74.3 years

TIME ZONE: –1

TYPE OF GOVERNMENT: Parliamentary Republic

HEAD OF STATE: President José Maria Neves **HEAD OF GOVT:** Prime Minister José Ulisses Correia e Silva

GDP PER CAPITA: $7,400

POPULATION: 611,014

ISD CODE: 238 **INTERNET TLD:** .cv

Only four of Cabo Verde's ten main islands support agriculture, producing over 90 per cent of the country's food.

CAMBODIA

LOCATION: South-east Asia

CAPITAL: Phnom Penh

AREA: 181,035 sq. km

LANGUAGES: Khmer, French

MAIN RELIGION: Theravada Buddhism

CURRENCY: Riel

LITERACY RATE: 83.9%

LIFE EXPECTANCY: 71.4 years

TIME ZONE: +7

TYPE OF GOVERNMENT: Parliamentary Constitutional Monarchy

HEAD OF STATE: King Norodom Sihamoni **HEAD OF GOVT:** Prime Minister Hun Manet

GDP PER CAPITA: $4,500

POPULATION: 17,063,669

ISD CODE: 855 **INTERNET TLD:** .kh

The Cambodian flag is the only flag in the world to feature a building – the Angkor Wat Temple.

Background: Cabo Verde

CAMEROON

LOCATION: Central Africa

CAPITAL: Yaounde

AREA: 475,440 sq. km

LANGUAGES: French, English, African languages

MAIN RELIGIONS: Indigenous faiths, Christianity, Islam

CURRENCY: CFA Franc

LITERACY RATE: 77.1%

LIFE EXPECTANCY: 64.2 years

TIME ZONE: +1

TYPE OF GOVERNMENT: Presidential Republic

HEAD OF STATE: President Paul Biya

HEAD OF GOVT: Prime Minister Joseph Dion Ngute

GDP PER CAPITA: $3,700

POPULATION: 30,966,105

ISD CODE: 237

INTERNET TLD: .cm

Lake Nyos, in Cameroon is the world's deadliest lake. In 1986 an explosion of CO_2 from the lake killed 1,700 people.

CANADA

LOCATION: North America

CAPITAL: Ottawa

AREA: 9,984,670 sq. km

LANGUAGES: English, French

MAIN RELIGION: Christianity

CURRENCY: Canadian Dollar

LITERACY RATE: 99%

LIFE EXPECTANCY: 84.2 years

TIME ZONE: –3.30 to –8

TYPE OF GOVERNMENT: Constitutional Monarchy and Federal Parliamentary Democracy

HEAD OF STATE: King Charles III

HEAD OF GOVT: Prime Minister Justin Trudeau

GDP PER CAPITA: $49,900

POPULATION: 38,794,813

ISD CODE: 1 **INTERNET TLD:** .ca

More than half of all the lakes in the world are located in Canada, including two of the biggest lakes in the world – Great Bear Lake and Great Slave Lake.

CENTRAL AFRICAN REPUBLIC

LOCATION: Central Africa

CAPITAL: Bangui

AREA: 622,984 sq. km

LANGUAGES: French, Sangho, Arabic, Hansa

MAIN RELIGIONS: Indigenous faiths, Christianity, Islam

CURRENCY: CFA Franc

LITERACY RATE: 37.5%

LIFE EXPECTANCY: 56.4 years

TIME ZONE: +1

TYPE OF GOVERNMENT: Presidential Republic

HEAD OF STATE: President Faustin-Archange Touadéra **HEAD OF GOVT:** Prime Minister Félix Moloua

GDP PER CAPITA: $800

POPULATION: 5,650,957

ISD CODE: 236 **INTERNET TLD:** .cf

In the 1880s, when the French colonized this area, they named it Oubangui-Chari as most of it is located in the Oubangui and Chari river basins.

Background: Chile

CHAD

LOCATION: North-central Africa

CAPITAL: N'Djamena

AREA: 1,284,000 sq. km

LANGUAGES: French, Arabic

MAIN RELIGIONS: Islam, Christianity

CURRENCY: CFA Franc

LITERACY RATE: 26.8%

LIFE EXPECTANCY: 60 years

TIME ZONE: +1

TYPE OF GOVERNMENT: Presidential Republic

HEAD OF STATE: President Mahamat Idriss Déby Itno

HEAD OF GOVT: Prime Minister Allamaye Halina

GDP PER CAPITA: $1,400

POPULATION: 19,093,595

ISD CODE: 235 **INTERNET TLD:** .td

Chad is called the 'Dead Heart of Africa' because of its harsh and inhospitable climate.

CHILE

LOCATION: South America

CAPITAL: Santiago

AREA: 756,102 sq. km

LANGUAGE: Spanish

MAIN RELIGION: Christianity

CURRENCY: Chilean Peso

LITERACY RATE: 97%

LIFE EXPECTANCY: 80.3 years

TIME ZONE: –3

TYPE OF GOVERNMENT: Presidential Republic

HEAD OF STATE AND GOVT: President Gabriel Boric

GDP PER CAPITA: $25,900

POPULATION: 18,664,652

ISD CODE: 56 **INTERNET TLD:** .cl

Chile is the longest and narrowest country in the world. It is 4,300 km long and just 175 km wide (on average).

CHINA

LOCATION: East Asia

CAPITAL: Beijing

AREA: 9,596,960 sq. km

LANGUAGES: Mandarin, Cantonese

MAIN RELIGIONS: Atheism (official), Taoism, Buddhism

CURRENCY: Renminbi

LITERACY RATE: 96.8%

LIFE EXPECTANCY: 78.7 years

TIME ZONE: +8

TYPE OF GOVERNMENT: Communist/Single-party state

HEAD OF STATE: President Xi Jinping

HEAD OF GOVT: Premier Li Qiang

GDP PER CAPITA: $18,200

POPULATION: 1,416,043,270

ISD CODE: 86 **INTERNET TLD:** .cn

The Chinese invented the compass, gunpowder, ice cream and toilet paper. The last invention was used only by emperors.

COLOMBIA

LOCATION: North-west South America

CAPITAL: Bogota

AREA: 1,138,910 sq. km

LANGUAGE: Spanish

MAIN RELIGION: Christianity

CURRENCY: Colombian Peso

LITERACY RATE: 95.6%

LIFE EXPECTANCY: 74.9 years

TIME ZONE: –5

TYPE OF GOVERNMENT: Presidential Republic

HEAD OF STATE AND GOVT: President Gustavo Francisco Petro

GDP PER CAPITA: $15,600

POPULATION: 49,588,357

ISD CODE: 57 **INTERNET TLD:** .co

The river Caño Cristales in La Macarena is known to change colours. It is also called the 'Rainbow River'.

COMOROS

LOCATION: Southern Africa

CAPITAL: Moroni

AREA: 2,235 sq. km

LANGUAGES: Arabic, French, Shikomoro

MAIN RELIGION: Islam

CURRENCY: Comorian Franc

LITERACY RATE: 62%

LIFE EXPECTANCY: 67.5 years

TIME ZONE: +3

TYPE OF GOVERNMENT: Federal Presidential Republic

HEAD OF STATE AND GOVT: President Azali Assoumani

GDP PER CAPITA: $3,200

POPULATION: 900,141

ISD CODE: 269 **INTERNET TLD:** .km

Comoros is called the 'Perfume Isles' because of its fragrant ylang-ylang flower whose oil is a major export traditionally.

(DEMOCRATIC REPUBLIC OF THE) CONGO

LOCATION: Central Africa

CAPITAL: Kinshasa

AREA: 2,344,858 sq. km

LANGUAGE: French

MAIN RELIGION: Christianity

CURRENCY: Congolese Franc

LITERACY RATE: 80%

LIFE EXPECTANCY: 62.6 years

TIME ZONE: +1

TYPE OF GOVERNMENT: Semi-presidential Republic

HEAD OF STATE: President Félix-Antoine Tshisekedi Tshilombo **HEAD OF GOVT:** Prime Minister Judith Suminwa Tuluka

GDP PER CAPITA: $1,100

POPULATION: 115,403,027

ISD CODE: 243

INTERNET TLD: .cd

Congo's current prime minister, Judith Suminwa Tuluka (since 1 April 2024), is the country's first female prime minister.

Background: Comoros

(REPUBLIC OF THE) CONGO

LOCATION: Central Africa

CAPITAL: Brazzaville

AREA: 342,000 sq. km

LANGUAGES: French, Lingala, Monokutuba, other African languages

MAIN RELIGION: Christianity

CURRENCY: CFA Franc

LITERACY RATE: 80.6%

LIFE EXPECTANCY: 72.9 years

TIME ZONE: +2

TYPE OF GOVERNMENT: Presidential Republic

HEAD OF STATE: President Denis Sassou-N'guesso **HEAD OF GOVT:** Prime Minister Anatole Collinet Makosso

GDP PER CAPITA: $3,700

POPULATION: 6,097,665

ISD CODE: 242 **INTERNET TLD:** .cg

For its size, the Republic of Congo has a large number of languages, with up to sixty-two recognized spoken languages, and many more dialects.

COSTA RICA

LOCATION: Central America

CAPITAL: San Jose

AREA: 51,100 sq. km

LANGUAGE: Spanish

MAIN RELIGION: Christianity

CURRENCY: Costa Rican Colon

LITERACY RATE: 98%

LIFE EXPECTANCY: 80.3 years

TIME ZONE: –6

TYPE OF GOVERNMENT: Presidential Republic

HEAD OF STATE AND GOVT: President Rodrigo Chaves Robles

GDP PER CAPITA: $22,100

POPULATION: 5,265,575

ISD CODE: 506

INTERNET TLD: .cr

The 'yigüirro', a clay- coloured thrush, is Costa Rica's national symbol.

COTE D'IVOIRE

LOCATION: Western Africa

CAPITAL: Yamoussoukro

AREA: 322,463 sq. km

LANGUAGES: French, Dioula

MAIN RELIGIONS: Islam, Christianity

CURRENCY: CFA Franc

LITERACY RATE: 89.9%

LIFE EXPECTANCY: 63.2 years

TIME ZONE: 0

TYPE OF GOVERNMENT: Presidential Republic

HEAD OF STATE: President Alassane Ouattara **HEAD OF GOVT:** Prime Minister Robert Beujré Mambé

GDP PER CAPITA: $5,500

POPULATION: 29,981,758

ISD CODE: 225 **INTERNET TLD:** .ci

Elephants are facing extinction in Cote d'Ivoire, once famous for its ivory trade. Its national football team is known as 'Les Elephants', meaning 'The Elephants'.

Background: Costa Rica

CROATIA

LOCATION: South-east Europe

CAPITAL: Zagreb

AREA: 56,594 sq. km

LANGUAGE: Croatian

MAIN RELIGION: Christianity

CURRENCY: Euro

LITERACY RATE: 99.4%

LIFE EXPECTANCY: 77.7 years

TIME ZONE: +1

TYPE OF GOVERNMENT: Parliamentary Republic

HEAD OF STATE: President Zoran Milanović **HEAD OF GOVT:** Prime Minister Andrej Plenković

GDP PER CAPITA: $34,300

POPULATION: 4,150,116

ISD CODE: 385 **INTERNET TLD:** .hr

In 2019, Croatia became the youngest member of the European Parliament.

CUBA

LOCATION: Central America

CAPITAL: Havana

AREA: 110,860 sq. km

LANGUAGE: Spanish

MAIN RELIGION: Christianity

CURRENCY: Cuban Peso

LITERACY RATE: 99.7%

LIFE EXPECTANCY: 80.1 years

TIME ZONE: –5

TYPE OF GOVERNMENT: Communist/ Single-party Republic

HEAD OF STATE: President Miguel Díaz-Canel **HEAD OF GOVT:** Prime Minister Manuel Marrero Cruz

GDP PER CAPITA: $12,300

POPULATION: 10,966,038

ISD CODE: 53 **INTERNET TLD:** .cu

Cubans refer to their island as 'El Cocodrilo' because when viewed from above, it resembles a crocodile.

CYPRUS

LOCATION: Mediterranean

CAPITAL: Nicosia

AREA: 9,251 sq. km

LANGUAGES: Greek, Turkish

MAIN RELIGION: Christianity (Greek Orthodox Church)

CURRENCY: Euro

LITERACY RATE: 99.4%

LIFE EXPECTANCY: 80.2 years

TIME ZONE: +2

TYPE OF GOVERNMENT: Presidential Republic

HEAD OF STATE AND GOVT: President Nikos Christodoulides

GDP PER CAPITA: $45,000

POPULATION: 1,320,525

ISD CODE: 357 **INTERNET TLD:** .cy

The Cyprus mouflon is a kind of wild sheep that was originally found only in Cyprus.

Background: Croatia

CZECHIA

LOCATION: Central Europe

CAPITAL: Prague

AREA: 78,867 sq. km

LANGUAGE: Czech

MAIN RELIGION: Christianity

CURRENCY: Czech Koruna

LITERACY RATE: 99%

LIFE EXPECTANCY: 78.6 years

TIME ZONE: +1

TYPE OF GOVERNMENT: Parliamentary Republic

HEAD OF STATE: President Petr Pavel **HEAD OF GOVT:** Prime Minister Petr Fiala

GDP PER CAPITA: $41,100

POPULATION: 10,837,890

ISD CODE: 420 **INTERNET TLD:** .cz

Prague is also called 'the city of a hundred spires'.

DENMARK

LOCATION: North Europe

CAPITAL: Copenhagen

AREA: 43,094 sq. km

LANGUAGE: Danish

MAIN RELIGION: Christianity (Evangelical Lutheran church)

CURRENCY: Danish Krone

LITERACY RATE: 99%

LIFE EXPECTANCY: 82.1 years

TIME ZONE: +1

TYPE OF GOVERNMENT: Parliamentary Constitutional Monarchy

HEAD OF STATE: King Frederik X

HEAD OF GOVT: Prime Minister Mette Frederiksen

GDP PER CAPITA: $59,900

POPULATION: 5,946,984

ISD CODE: 45 **INTERNET TLD:** .dk

There are 443 named islands in the Danish archipelago and only 76 of these are inhabited.

DJIBOUTI

LOCATION: East Africa

CAPITAL: Djibouti City

AREA: 23,200 sq. km

LANGUAGES: French, Arabic

MAIN RELIGION: Islam

CURRENCY: Djiboutian Franc

LITERACY RATE: 70%

LIFE EXPECTANCY: 65.9 years

TIME ZONE: +3

TYPE OF GOVERNMENT: Presidential Republic

HEAD OF STATE: President Ismaïl Omar Guelleh **HEAD OF GOVT:** Prime Minister Abdoulkader Kamil Mohamed

GDP PER CAPITA: $5,000

POPULATION: 994,974

ISD CODE: 253 **INTERNET TLD:** .dj

Background: Denmark

Lake Assal in Djibouti lies 156 m (512 ft) below sea level, making it the lowest point in Africa.

DOMINICA

LOCATION: Central America

CAPITAL: Roseau

AREA: 751 sq. km

LANGUAGES: English, French

MAIN RELIGION: Christianity

CURRENCY: East Caribbean Dollar

LITERACY RATE: 95.47%

LIFE EXPECTANCY: 78.7 years

TIME ZONE: –4

TYPE OF GOVERNMENT: Parliamentary Republic

HEAD OF STATE: President Sylvanie Burton **HEAD OF GOVT:** Prime Minister Roosevelt Skerrit

GDP PER CAPITA: $11,500

POPULATION: 74,661

ISD CODE: 1-767 **INTERNET TLD:** .dm

Christopher Columbus came to this island in 1493 on a Sunday. That's why he called it 'Dominica', meaning 'Sunday' in Latin.

DOMINICAN REPUBLIC

LOCATION: Central America

CAPITAL: Santo Domingo

AREA: 48,670 sq. km

LANGUAGE: Spanish

MAIN RELIGION: Christianity

CURRENCY: Dominican Peso

LITERACY RATE: 95.5%

LIFE EXPECTANCY: 72.6 years

TIME ZONE: –4

TYPE OF GOVERNMENT: Presidential Republic

HEAD OF STATE AND GOVT: President Luis Abinader

GDP PER CAPITA: $19,300

POPULATION: 10,815,857

ISD CODE: 809 **INTERNET TLD:** .do

The oldest extant cathedral in the Americas is in Santo Domingo – the Cathedral of Santa Maria la Menor. Its construction began in 1512.

ECUADOR

LOCATION: Western South America

CAPITAL: Quito

AREA: 283,561 sq. km

LANGUAGE: Spanish

MAIN RELIGION: Christianity

CURRENCY: US Dollar

LITERACY RATE: 93.9%

LIFE EXPECTANCY: 74.9 years

TIME ZONE: –5

TYPE OF GOVERNMENT: Presidential Republic

HEAD OF STATE AND GOVT: President Daniel Noboa Azin

GDP PER CAPITA: $10,900

POPULATION: 18,309,984

ISD CODE: 593 **INTERNET TLD:** .ec

Ecuador is one of thirteen countries through which the Equator passes.

EGYPT

LOCATION: North Africa

CAPITAL: Cairo

AREA: 1,001,450 sq. km

LANGUAGES: Arabic, English, French

MAIN RELIGION: Islam

CURRENCY: Egyptian Pound

LITERACY RATE: 73.1%

LIFE EXPECTANCY: 75 years

TIME ZONE: +2

TYPE OF GOVERNMENT: Presidential Republic

HEAD OF STATE: President Abdel Fattah Saeed Hussein Khalil El-Sisi

HEAD OF GOVT: Prime Minister Mostafa Madbouly

GDP PER CAPITA: $12,800

POPULATION: 111,247,248

ISD CODE: 20 **INTERNET TLD:** .eg

The Great Pyramid of Giza in Egypt is the only existing ancient wonder of the world.

EL SALVADOR

LOCATION: Central America

CAPITAL: San Salvador

AREA: 21,041 sq. km

LANGUAGE: Spanish

MAIN RELIGION: Christianity

CURRENCY: US Dollar

LITERACY RATE: 89.1%

LIFE EXPECTANCY: 75.9 years

TIME ZONE: –6

TYPE OF GOVERNMENT: Presidential Republic

HEAD OF STATE AND GOVT: President Nayib Bukele

GDP PER CAPITA: $9,400

POPULATION: 6,628,702

ISD CODE: 503 **INTERNET TLD:** .sv

El Salvador, a country with 21 volcanoes, was in an infamous 100-hour war with neighbouring Honduras, over a football game in 1969.

EQUATORIAL GUINEA

LOCATION: Central Africa

CAPITAL: Malabo

AREA: 28,051 sq. km

LANGUAGES: Spanish, French

MAIN RELIGION: Christianity

CURRENCY: CFA Franc

LITERACY RATE: 95.3%

LIFE EXPECTANCY: 63.9 years

TIME ZONE: +1

TYPE OF GOVERNMENT: Presidential Republic

HEAD OF STATE: President Teodoro Obiang Nguema Mbasogo **HEAD OF GOVT:** Prime Minister Manuel Osa Nsue Nsua

GDP PER CAPITA: $14,900

POPULATION: 1,795,834

ISD CODE: 240 **INTERNET TLD:** .gq

Equatorial Guinea is the smallest African country that is a member of the United Nations.

Background: Egypt

ERITREA

LOCATION: East Africa

CAPITAL: Asmara

AREA: 117,600 sq. km

LANGUAGES: Tigrinya, Arabic, English

MAIN RELIGIONS: Islam, Christianity

CURRENCY: Eritrean Nakfa

LITERACY RATE: 76.6%

LIFE EXPECTANCY: 67.5 years

TIME ZONE: +3

TYPE OF GOVERNMENT: Presidential Republic

HEAD OF STATE AND GOVT: President Isaias Afwerki

GDP PER CAPITA: $1,600

POPULATION: 6,343,956

ISD CODE: 291 **INTERNET TLD:** .er

A one-party nation, the country has not held national or presidential elections since independence in 1993.

ESTONIA

LOCATION: East Europe

CAPITAL: Tallinn

AREA: 45,228 sq. km

LANGUAGE: Estonian, Russian

MAIN RELIGION: Christianity

CURRENCY: Euro

LITERACY RATE: 99.9%

LIFE EXPECTANCY: 78.4 years

TIME ZONE: +2

TYPE OF GOVERNMENT: Parliamentary Republic

HEAD OF STATE: President Alar Keris
HEAD OF GOVT: Prime Minister Kristen Michal

GDP PER CAPITA: $37,700

POPULATION: 1,193,791

ISD CODE: 372 **INTERNET TLD:** .ee

Estonia has the highest number of meteorite craters per square kilometre in the world.

ESWATINI

LOCATION: Southern Africa

CAPITAL: Mbabane

AREA: 17,364 sq. km

LANGUAGES: English, Swati

MAIN RELIGIONS: Christianity, Islam

CURRENCY: Lilangeni; South African Rand

LITERACY RATE: 88.4%

LIFE EXPECTANCY: 60.7 years

TIME ZONE: +2

TYPE OF GOVERNMENT: Absolute Monarchy

HEAD OF STATE: King Mswati III
HEAD OF GOVT: Prime Minister Russell Mmiso Dlamini

GDP PER CAPITA: $9,100

POPULATION: 1,138,089

ISD CODE: 268 **INTERNET TLD:** .sz

In 2018, King Mswati III renamed Swaziland as 'Kingdom of Eswatini'. It means 'land of the Swazis'.

 Background: Estonia

ETHIOPIA

LOCATION: East Africa

CAPITAL: Addis Ababa

AREA: 1,104,300 sq. km

LANGUAGES: Amharic, Oromo

MAIN RELIGIONS: Christianity, Islam

CURRENCY: Ethiopian Birr

LITERACY RATE: 51.8%

LIFE EXPECTANCY: 67.7 years

TIME ZONE: +3

TYPE OF GOVERNMENT: Federal Parliamentary Republic

HEAD OF STATE: President Sahle-Work Zewde **HEAD OF GOVT:** Prime Minister Abiy Ahmed

GDP PER CAPITA: $2,400

POPULATION: 118,550,298

ISD CODE: 251 **INTERNET TLD:** .et

Marathoner Abebe Bikila was the first black African to win an Olympic gold at the 1960 Summer Games in Rome, running barefoot. He won another gold at the 1964 Tokyo Olympics.

FIJI

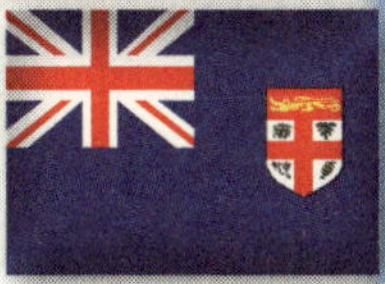

LOCATION: South Pacific Ocean

CAPITAL: Suva

AREA: 18,274 sq. km

LANGUAGES: English, Fijian

MAIN RELIGIONS: Christianity, Hinduism

CURRENCY: Fijian Dollar

LITERACY RATE: 99.1%

LIFE EXPECTANCY: 74.8 years

TIME ZONE: +12

TYPE OF GOVERNMENT: Parliamentary Republic

HEAD OF STATE: President Ratu Wiliame Katonivere **HEAD OF GOVT:** Prime Minister Sitiveni Ligamamada Rabuka

GDP PER CAPITA: $12,400

POPULATION: 951,611

ISD CODE: 679 **INTERNET TLD:** .fj

Off the island of Taveuni, there is a place where one can swim from the current day to the day before as the International Date Line runs through it.

FINLAND

LOCATION: North Europe

CAPITAL: Helsinki

AREA: 338,145 sq. km

LANGUAGE: Finnish

MAIN RELIGION: Christianity (Church of Finland)

CURRENCY: Euro

LITERACY RATE: 100%

LIFE EXPECTANCY: 82.2 years

TIME ZONE: +2

TYPE OF GOVERNMENT: Parliamentary Republic

HEAD OF STATE: President Alexander Stubb **HEAD OF GOVT:** Prime Minister Petteri Orpo

GDP PER CAPITA: $49,400

POPULATION: 5,626,414

ISD CODE: 358 **INTERNET TLD:** .fi

The International Failure Day was initiated in Finland where a National Failure Day has been celebrated on 13 October since 2010.

Background: Fiji

FRANCE

LOCATION: West Europe

CAPITAL: Paris

AREA: 643,801 sq. km

LANGUAGE: French

MAIN RELIGION: Christianity

CURRENCY: Euro

LITERACY RATE: 99%

LIFE EXPECTANCY: 82.6 years

TIME ZONE: +1

TYPE OF GOVERNMENT: Semi-presidential Republic

HEAD OF STATE: President Emmanuel Macron **HEAD OF GOVT:** Prime Minister Gabriel Attal

GDP PER CAPITA: $45,900

POPULATION: 68,374,591

ISD CODE: 33 **INTERNET TLD:** .fr

According to a law passed in 2016, food in French supermarkets cannot be thrown out; it has to be distributed to food banks or other charity organizations.

GABON

LOCATION: West Africa

CAPITAL: Libreville

AREA: 267,667 sq. km

LANGUAGES: French, Fang

MAIN RELIGION: Christianity

CURRENCY: CFA Franc

LITERACY RATE: 85.5%

LIFE EXPECTANCY: 70.4 years

TIME ZONE: +1

TYPE OF GOVERNMENT: Presidential Republic

HEAD OF STATE: Transitional President Gen. Brice Oligui Nguema **HEAD OF GOVT:** Interim Prime Minister Raymond Ndong Sima

GDP PER CAPITA: $13,900

POPULATION: 2,455,105

ISD CODE: 241 **INTERNET TLD:** .ga

The green stripe in Gabon's flag represents its forest, the blue stripe represents the sea and the yellow band which divides the two is meant to be the equator that runs through the country.

(THE) GAMBIA

LOCATION: West Africa

CAPITAL: Banjul

AREA: 11,300 sq. km

LANGUAGES: English, Mandinka

MAIN RELIGION: Islam

CURRENCY: Dalasi

LITERACY RATE: 58.1%

LIFE EXPECTANCY: 68.4 years

TIME ZONE: 0

TYPE OF GOVERNMENT: Presidential Republic

HEAD OF STATE AND GOVT: President Adama Barrow

GDP PER CAPITA: $2,100

POPULATION: 2,523,327

ISD CODE: 220 **INTERNET TLD:** .gm

The country is called 'The' Gambia to prevent confusing it with Zambia.

Background: France

GEORGIA

LOCATION: South-west Asia

CAPITAL: Tbilisi

AREA: 69,700 sq. km

LANGUAGES: Georgian, Russian, Armenian, Azerbaijani

MAIN RELIGION: Christianity

CURRENCY: Lari

LITERACY RATE: 99.6

LIFE EXPECTANCY: 72.8 years

TIME ZONE: +4

TYPE OF GOVERNMENT: Semi-presidential Republic

HEAD OF STATE: President Salome Zourabichvili **HEAD OF GOVT:** Prime Minister Irakli Kobakhidze

GDP PER CAPITA: $17,100

POPULATION: 4,900,961

ISD CODE: 995 **INTERNET TLD:** .ge

Citizens of around ninety-eight countries can enter Georgia without a visa.

GERMANY

LOCATION: West Europe

CAPITAL: Berlin

AREA: 357,022 sq. km

LANGUAGE: German

MAIN RELIGION: Christianity

CURRENCY: Euro

LITERACY RATE: 99%

LIFE EXPECTANCY: 81.9 years

TIME ZONE: +1

TYPE OF GOVERNMENT: Federal Parliamentary Republic

HEAD OF STATE: President Frank-Walter Steinmeier **HEAD OF GOVT:** Chancellor Olaf Scholz

GDP PER CAPITA: $54,000

POPULATION: 84,119,100

ISD CODE: 49 **INTERNET TLD:** .de

German scientists are credited with the discovery of insulin and the invention of the pocket watch, the calculator, the automobile and the jet engine.

GHANA

LOCATION: West Africa

CAPITAL: Accra

AREA: 238,533 sq. km

LANGUAGES: English, indigenous languages

MAIN RELIGION: Christianity

CURRENCY: Cedi

LITERACY RATE: 79%

LIFE EXPECTANCY: 70.1 years

TIME ZONE: 0

TYPE OF GOVERNMENT: Presidential Republic

HEAD OF STATE AND GOVT: President Nana Addo Dankwa Akufo-Addo

GDP PER CAPITA: $5,500

POPULATION: 34,589,092

ISD CODE: 233 **INTERNET TLD:** .gh

Ghana was the first sub-Saharan African country to gain independence from colonial rule.

Background: Germany

GREECE

LOCATION: Southern Europe, bordering the Aegean Sea

CAPITAL: Athens

AREA: 131,957 sq. km

LANGUAGE: Greek

MAIN RELIGION: Christianity (Greek Orthodox Church)

CURRENCY: Euro

LITERACY RATE: 97.9%

LIFE EXPECTANCY: 81.9 years

TIME ZONE: +2

TYPE OF GOVERNMENT: Parliamentary Republic

HEAD OF STATE: President Katerina Sakellaropoulou **HEAD OF GOVT:** Prime Minister Kyriakos Mitsotakis

GDP PER CAPITA: $31,700

POPULATION: 10,461,091

ISD CODE: 30 **INTERNET TLD:** .gr

The ancient Greeks are believed to have invented the yo-yo in 500 BCE.

GRENADA

LOCATION: Central America

CAPITAL: St George's

AREA: 344 sq. km

LANGUAGE: English

MAIN RELIGION: Christianity

CURRENCY: East Caribbean Dollar

LITERACY RATE: 98.6%

LIFE EXPECTANCY: 76.3 years

TIME ZONE: –4

TYPE OF GOVERNMENT: Constitutional Monarchy and Parliamentary Democracy

HEAD OF STATE: King Charles III
HEAD OF GOVT: Prime Minister Dickon Mitchell

GDP PER CAPITA: $14,500

POPULATION: 114,621

ISD CODE: 473 **INTERNET TLD:** .gd

Grenada is home to both black sand and white sand beaches with water so clear that coral formations can be spotted from aircraft above.

GUATEMALA

LOCATION: Central America

CAPITAL: Guatemala City

AREA: 108,889 sq. km

LANGUAGES: Spanish, indigenous languages

MAIN RELIGION: Christianity

CURRENCY: Quetzal

LITERACY RATE: 83.3%

LIFE EXPECTANCY: 73.5 years

TIME ZONE: –6

TYPE OF GOVERNMENT: Presidential Republic

HEAD OF STATE AND GOVT: President Bernardo Arévalo de León

GDP PER CAPITA: $9,200

POPULATION: 18,255,216

ISD CODE: 502 **INTERNET TLD:** .gt

The name Guatemala means 'land of the trees' in the Maya-Toltec language. More than twenty-one Mayan languages are spoken here.

GUINEA

LOCATION: West Africa

CAPITAL: Conakry

AREA: 245,857 sq. km

LANGUAGE: French

MAIN RELIGION: Islam

CURRENCY: Guinean Franc

LITERACY RATE: 45.3%

LIFE EXPECTANCY: 64.6 years

TIME ZONE: 0

TYPE OF GOVERNMENT: Presidential Republic

HEAD OF STATE: President Colonel Mamady Doumbouya **HEAD OF GOVT:** Prime Minister Mamadou Oury Bah

GDP PER CAPITA: $2,700

POPULATION: 13,986,179

ISD CODE: 224 **INTERNET TLD:** .gn

Mount Nimba, located on the border of Guinea and Cote d'Ivoire, is the highest point in both countries.

GUINEA-BISSAU

LOCATION: West Africa

CAPITAL: Bissau

AREA: 36,125 sq. km

LANGUAGE: Portuguese

MAIN RELIGIONS: Islam, Christianity, Animist, indigenous beliefs

CURRENCY: CFA Franc

LITERACY RATE: 52.9%

LIFE EXPECTANCY: 64.5 years

TIME ZONE: 0

TYPE OF GOVERNMENT: Semi-presidential Republic

HEAD OF STATE: President Umaro Sissoco Embaló **HEAD OF GOVT:** Prime Minister Rui Duarte de Barros

GDP PER CAPITA: $1,900

POPULATION: 2,132,325

ISD CODE: 245 **INTERNET TLD:** .gw

The capital's name 'Bissau' was added to the country's name in 1974, to prevent mix-ups with the neighbouring Republic of Guinea.

GUYANA

LOCATION: Central America

CAPITAL: Georgetown

AREA: 214,969 sq. km

LANGUAGES: English, indigenous languages

MAIN RELIGIONS: Christianity, Hinduism

CURRENCY: Guyanese Dollar

LITERACY RATE: 88.8%

LIFE EXPECTANCY: 72.4 years

TIME ZONE: –4

TYPE OF GOVERNMENT: Parliamentary Republic

HEAD OF STATE AND GOVT: President Mohamed Irfaan Ali

GDP PER CAPITA: $35,600

POPULATION: 794,099

ISD CODE: 592 **INTERNET TLD:** .gy

At 250.5 m (822 ft), the Kaieteur Falls is about twice the height of Victoria Falls on the border of Zambia and Zimbabwe.

HAITI

LOCATION: Central America

CAPITAL: Port-au-Prince

AREA: 27,750 sq. km

LANGUAGES: French, Creole

MAIN RELIGIONS: Christianity, Haitian Vodou

CURRENCY: Gourde

LITERACY RATE: 61.7%

LIFE EXPECTANCY: 65.6 years

TIME ZONE: –5

TYPE OF GOVERNMENT: Semi-presidential Republic

HEAD OF STATE AND GOVT: Acting President and Prime Minister Garry Conille

GDP PER CAPITA: $2,800

POPULATION: 11,753,943

ISD CODE: 509 **INTERNET TLD:** .ht

Haiti is the only nation in the world whose independence was gained as part of a successful slave rebellion.

HONDURAS

LOCATION: Central America

CAPITAL: Tegucigalpa

AREA: 112,090 sq. km

LANGUAGE: Spanish

MAIN RELIGION: Christianity

CURRENCY: Lempira

LITERACY RATE: 88.5%

LIFE EXPECTANCY: 73.1 years

TIME ZONE: -6

TYPE OF GOVERNMENT: Presidential Republic

HEAD OF STATE AND GOVT: President Iris Xiomara Castro de Zelaya

GDP PER CAPITA: $5,700

POPULATION: 9,529,188

ISD CODE: 504 **INTERNET TLD:** .hn

The five stars on the flag stand for the five countries of Central America. Honduras is represented by the star in the middle because of its central geographical location.

HUNGARY

LOCATION: Central Europe

CAPITAL: Budapest

AREA: 93,028 sq. km

LANGUAGES: Hungarian, German

MAIN RELIGION: Christianity

CURRENCY: Forint

LITERACY RATE: 99.1%

LIFE EXPECTANCY: 76 years

TIME ZONE: +1

TYPE OF GOVERNMENT: Parliamentary Republic

HEAD OF STATE: President Tamás Sulyok **HEAD OF GOVT:** Prime Minister Viktor Orbán

GDP PER CAPITA: $35,400

POPULATION: 9,855,745

ISD CODE: 36 **INTERNET TLD:** .hu

The country has a pre-approved set of names. If the desired name is not on the list, the parents must apply for it.

Background: Hungary

ICELAND

LOCATION: North Europe

CAPITAL: Reykjavik

AREA: 103,000 sq. km

LANGUAGES: Icelandic, English, German

MAIN RELIGION: Christianity

CURRENCY: Icelandic Krona

LITERACY RATE: 99%

LIFE EXPECTANCY: 84 years

TIME ZONE: 0

TYPE OF GOVERNMENT: Unitary Parliamentary Republic

HEAD OF STATE: President Halla Tómasdóttir

HEAD OF GOVT: Prime Minister Bjarni Benediktsson

GDP PER CAPITA: $55,600

POPULATION: 364,036

ISD CODE: 354 **INTERNET TLD:** .is

Only 1 per cent of the land in Iceland is considered arable.

INDIA

LOCATION: South Asia

CAPITAL: New Delhi

AREA: 3,287,263 sq. km

LANGUAGES: Hindi, English and 21 other official languages

MAIN RELIGIONS: Hinduism, Islam, Sikhism, Christianity, Jainism, Buddhism

CURRENCY: Indian Rupee

LITERACY RATE: 74.4%

LIFE EXPECTANCY: 68.2 years

TIME ZONE: +5.30

TYPE OF GOVERNMENT: Federal Parliamentary Republic

HEAD OF STATE: President Droupadi Murmu **HEAD OF GOVT:** Prime Minister Narendra Modi

GDP PER CAPITA: $7,100

POPULATION: 1,452,998,639

ISD CODE: 91 **INTERNET TLD:** .in

India Post has over 154,000 post offices, making it the largest postal network in the world.

INDONESIA

LOCATION: South-east Asia

CAPITAL: Jakarta

AREA: 1,904,569 sq. km

LANGUAGE: Bahasa

MAIN RELIGION: Islam

CURRENCY: Indonesian Rupiah

LITERACY RATE: 96%

LIFE EXPECTANCY: 73.6 years

TIME ZONE: +7

TYPE OF GOVERNMENT: Presidential Republic

HEAD OF STATE AND GOVT: President Joko Widodo

GDP PER CAPITA: $12,400

POPULATION: 281,562,465

ISD CODE: 62 **INTERNET TLD:** .id

Indonesia comprises more than 17,000 islands, of which around 6,000 are inhabited.

Background: India

IRAN

LOCATION: Middle East

CAPITAL: Tehran

AREA: 1,648,195 sq. km

LANGUAGES: Persian, Azerbaijani, Turkish

MAIN RELIGION: Islam

CURRENCY: Iranian Rial

LITERACY RATE: 88.7%

LIFE EXPECTANCY: 75.6 years

TIME ZONE: +3.30

TYPE OF GOVERNMENT: Theocratic Republic

HEAD OF STATE: Supreme Leader Ali Hosseini-Khamenei **HEAD OF GOVT:** President Dr Masoud Pezeshkian

GDP PER CAPITA: $15,500

POPULATION: 88,386,937

ISD CODE: 98 **INTERNET TLD:** .ir

Iran's proven oil reserves are the fourth largest in the world, after Venezuela, Saudi Arabia and Canada.

IRAQ

LOCATION: Middle East

CAPITAL: Baghdad

AREA: 438,317 sq. km

LANGUAGES: Arabic, Kurdish

MAIN RELIGION: Islam

CURRENCY: New Iraqi Dinar

LITERACY RATE: 85.6%

LIFE EXPECTANCY: 73.7 years

TIME ZONE: +3

TYPE OF GOVERNMENT: Federal Parliamentary Republic

HEAD OF STATE: President Latif Rashid **HEAD OF GOVT:** Prime Minister Mohammed Shia' Al Sudani

GDP PER CAPITA: $9,200

POPULATION: 42,083,436

ISD CODE: 964 **INTERNET TLD:** .iq

Oil exports account for about 95 per cent of Iraq's foreign exchange earnings.

IRELAND

LOCATION: West Europe

CAPITAL: Dublin

AREA: 70,273 sq. km

LANGUAGES: Gaelic, English

MAIN RELIGION: Christianity

CURRENCY: Euro

LITERACY RATE: 99%

LIFE EXPECTANCY: 82 years

TIME ZONE: 0

TYPE OF GOVERNMENT: Parliamentary Republic

HEAD OF STATE: President Michael D. Higgins **HEAD OF GOVT:** Taoiseach (Prime Minister) Simon Harris

GDP PER CAPITA: $112,400

POPULATION: 5,233,461

ISD CODE: 353 **INTERNET TLD:** .ie

Irish surnames are well-known for beginning with Mac/Mc or 'O'. 'Mac' means 'son of' and 'O' means 'grandson of' in Gaelic.

ISRAEL

LOCATION: Middle East

CAPITAL: Jerusalem

AREA: 21,937 sq. km

LANGUAGES: Hebrew, English, Arabic

MAIN RELIGIONS: Judaism, Islam

CURRENCY: Israeli (New) Shekel

LITERACY RATE: 97.8%

LIFE EXPECTANCY: 83.1 years

TIME ZONE: +2

TYPE OF GOVERNMENT: Parliamentary Democracy

HEAD OF STATE: President Isaac Herzog **HEAD OF GOVT:** Prime Minister Benjamin Netanyahu

GDP PER CAPITA: $44,400

POPULATION: 9,402,617

ISD CODE: 972 **INTERNET TLD:** .il

Israeli banknotes have Braille on them to help visually challenged people identify them easily.

ITALY

LOCATION: Southern Europe

CAPITAL: Rome

AREA: 301,340 sq. km

LANGUAGE: Italian

MAIN RELIGION: Christianity

CURRENCY: Euro

LITERACY RATE: 99.2%

LIFE EXPECTANCY: 83 years

TIME ZONE: +1

TYPE OF GOVERNMENT: Parliamentary Republic

HEAD OF STATE: President Sergio Mattarella **HEAD OF GOVT:** Prime Minister Giorgia Meloni

GDP PER CAPITA: $44,300

POPULATION: 60,964,931

ISD CODE: 39 **INTERNET TLD:** .it

Most of the world's top sports cars – Ferrari, Lamborghini, Bugatti, Maserati and Alfa Romeo – are manufactured in Italy.

JAMAICA

LOCATION: Central America

CAPITAL: Kingston

AREA: 10,991 sq. km

LANGUAGE: English

MAIN RELIGION: Christianity

CURRENCY: Jamaican Dollar

LITERACY RATE: 88.7%

LIFE EXPECTANCY: 76.3 years

TIME ZONE: –5

TYPE OF GOVERNMENT: Constitutional Monarchy and Parliamentary Democracy

HEAD OF STATE: King Charles III

HEAD OF GOVT: Prime Minister Andrew Holness

GDP PER CAPITA: $10,100

POPULATION: 2,823,713

ISD CODE: 1-876 **INTERNET TLD:** .jm

Ian Fleming designed and built his home called 'Goldeneye' in Jamaica and wrote ten James Bond novels there.

Background: Italy

JAPAN

LOCATION: East Asia

CAPITAL: Tokyo

AREA: 377,915 sq. km

LANGUAGE: Japanese

MAIN RELIGIONS: Shintoism, Buddhism

CURRENCY: Yen

LITERACY RATE: 99%

LIFE EXPECTANCY: 85.2 years

TIME ZONE: +9

TYPE OF GOVERNMENT: Parliamentary Constitutional Monarchy

HEAD OF STATE: Emperor Naruhito
HEAD OF GOVT: Prime Minister Fumio Kishida

GDP PER CAPITA: $41,600

POPULATION: 123,201,945

ISD CODE: 81 **INTERNET TLD:** .jp

Mt Fuji (3,776.2 m/12,389.2 ft), the tallest mountain in the country, is an active volcano.

JORDAN

LOCATION: Middle East

CAPITAL: Amman

AREA: 89,342 sq. km

LANGUAGES: Arabic, English

MAIN RELIGION: Islam

CURRENCY: Jordanian Dinar

LITERACY RATE: 98.4%

LIFE EXPECTANCY: 76.5 years

TIME ZONE: +2

TYPE OF GOVERNMENT: Parliamentary Constitutional Monarchy

HEAD OF STATE: King Abdullah II
HEAD OF GOVT: Prime Minister Bisher Al-Khasawneh

GDP PER CAPITA: $9,500

POPULATION: 11,174,024

ISD CODE: 962 **INTERNET TLD:** .jo

The world's lowest point on dry land is the Dead Sea shore, shared by Israel and Jordan. It is 418 m/1,371 ft below sea level.

KAZAKHSTAN

LOCATION: Central Asia

CAPITAL: Astana

AREA: 2,724,900

LANGUAGES: Kazakh, Russian

MAIN RELIGIONS: Islam, Christianity

CURRENCY: Tenge

LITERACY RATE: 99.8%

LIFE EXPECTANCY: 73.3 years

TIME ZONE: +6

TYPE OF GOVERNMENT: Presidential Republic

HEAD OF STATE: President Kassym-Jomart Tokayev **HEAD OF GOVT:** Prime Minister Olzhas Bektenov

GDP PER CAPITA: $26,100

POPULATION: 20,260,006

ISD CODE: 7 **INTERNET TLD:** .kz

The Baikonur Cosmodrome is the world's oldest and largest (by area) space launch facility.

Background: Jordan

KENYA

LOCATION: East Africa

CAPITAL: Nairobi

AREA: 580,367 sq. km

LANGUAGES: English, Kiswahili

MAIN RELIGIONS: Christianity, Islam

CURRENCY: Kenyan Shilling

LITERACY RATE: 82.6%

LIFE EXPECTANCY: 70.4 years

TIME ZONE: +3

TYPE OF GOVERNMENT: Presidential Republic

HEAD OF STATE & GOVT: President William Ruto

GDP PER CAPITA: $4,900

POPULATION: 58,246,378

ISD CODE: 254 **INTERNET TLD:** .ke

Wangari Maathai, a social, environmental and political activist, and the first African woman to win a Nobel Peace prize, was Kenyan.

KIRIBATI

LOCATION: Oceania

CAPITAL: Tarawa

AREA: 811 sq. km

LANGUAGES: Kiribati, English

MAIN RELIGION: Christianity

CURRENCY: Australian Dollar

LITERACY RATE: 97.7%

LIFE EXPECTANCY: 68.5 years

TIME ZONE: +12

TYPE OF GOVERNMENT: Presidential Republic

HEAD OF STATE AND GOVT: President Taneti Maamau

GDP PER CAPITA: $2,000

POPULATION: 116,545

ISD CODE: 686 **INTERNET TLD:** .ki

It is the first country to celebrate new year since it is fourteen hours ahead of GMT.

KUWAIT

LOCATION: Middle East

CAPITAL: Kuwait City

AREA: 17,818 sq. km

LANGUAGES: Arabic

MAIN RELIGION: Islam

CURRENCY: Kuwaiti Dinar

LITERACY RATE: 96.5%

LIFE EXPECTANCY: 79.6 years

TIME ZONE: +3

TYPE OF GOVERNMENT: Constitutional Monarchy (Emirate)

HEAD OF STATE: Sheikh Nawaf Al-Ahmad Al-Jaber Al-Sabah **HEAD OF GOVT:** Sheikh Dr Muhammad Sabah Al-Salem Al-Sabah

GDP PER CAPITA: $49,400

POPULATION: 3,138,355

ISD CODE: 965 **INTERNET TLD:** .kw

More than two-thirds of the people who reside in Kuwait do not hold Kuwaiti citizenship and cannot vote in parliamentary elections.

KYRGYZSTAN

LOCATION: Central Asia

CAPITAL: Bishkek

AREA: 199,951 sq. km

LANGUAGES: Kyrgyz, Uzbek, Russian

MAIN RELIGION: Islam

CURRENCY: Som

LITERACY RATE: 99.6%

LIFE EXPECTANCY: 72.9 years

TIME ZONE: +6

TYPE OF GOVERNMENT: Parliamentary Republic

HEAD OF STATE AND GOVT: President Sadyr Japarov

GDP PER CAPITA: $5,100

POPULATION: 6,172,101

ISD CODE: 996 **INTERNET TLD:** .kg

There are more than eighty-eight major mountain ranges in Kyrgyzstan, which make up more than 70 per cent of the country's territory.

LAOS

LOCATION: South-East Asia

CAPITAL: Vientiane

AREA: 236,800 sq. km

LANGUAGES: Lao, French, English

MAIN RELIGION: Buddhism

CURRENCY: Kip

LITERACY RATE: 87.1%

LIFE EXPECTANCY: 69 years

TIME ZONE: +7

TYPE OF GOVERNMENT: Communist state

HEAD OF STATE: President Thongloun Sisoulith **HEAD OF GOVT:** Prime Minister Sonexay Siphandone

GDP PER CAPITA: $7,900

POPULATION: 7,953,556

ISD CODE: 856 **INTERNET TLD:** .la

In Laos, the country is known as Sathalanalat Paxathipatai Paxaxon Lao.

LATVIA

LOCATION: Eastern Europe

CAPITAL: Riga

AREA: 64,589 sq. km

LANGUAGES: Latvian, Russian

MAIN RELIGION: Christianity

CURRENCY: Euro

LITERACY RATE: 99.9%

LIFE EXPECTANCY: 76.4 years

TIME ZONE: +2

TYPE OF GOVERNMENT: Parliamentary Republic

HEAD OF STATE: President Edgars Rinkēvičs **HEAD OF GOVT:** Prime Minister Evika Silina

GDP PER CAPITA: $33,000

POPULATION: 1,801,246

ISD CODE: 371 **INTERNET TLD:** .lv

Tourists can visit the Karosta Prison Hotel in Liepaja, which is a former military jail, for a prison experience, including interrogation and a night stay in a cold cell.

Background: Latvia

LEBANON

LOCATION: Middle East

CAPITAL: Beirut

AREA: 10,400 sq. km

LANGUAGES: Arabic, French, English

MAIN RELIGIONS: Islam, Christianity

CURRENCY: Lebanese Pound

LITERACY RATE: 95.1%

LIFE EXPECTANCY: 79.2 years

TIME ZONE: +2

TYPE OF GOVERNMENT: Parliamentary Republic

HEAD OF STATE: Vacant **HEAD OF GOVT:** Prime Minister Najib Miqati

GDP PER CAPITA: $13,000

POPULATION: 5,364,482

ISD CODE: 961 **INTERNET TLD:** .lb

Lebanon is the only country in the Middle East that does not have even a patch of desert.

LESOTHO

LOCATION: Southern Africa

CAPITAL: Maseru

AREA: 30,355 sq. km

LANGUAGES: Sesotho, English

MAIN RELIGION: Christianity

CURRENCY: Loti

LITERACY RATE: 81%

LIFE EXPECTANCY: 60.2 years

TIME ZONE: +2

TYPE OF GOVERNMENT: Parliamentary Constitutional Monarchy

HEAD OF STATE: King Letsie III
HEAD OF GOVT: Prime Minister Sam Matekane

GDP PER CAPITA: $2,200

POPULATION: 2,227,548

ISD CODE: 266 **INTERNET TLD:** .ls

Lesotho is the only country that lies entirely 1,500 m (4,920 ft) above sea level. Villages can only be reached by riding horses, trekking or by a light aircraft.

LIBERIA

LOCATION: West Africa

CAPITAL: Monrovia

AREA: 111,369 sq. km

LANGUAGES: English, ethnic languages

MAIN RELIGIONS: Indigenous faiths, Christianity, Islam

CURRENCY: Liberian Dollar

LITERACY RATE: 48.3%

LIFE EXPECTANCY: 61.6 years

TIME ZONE: 0

TYPE OF GOVERNMENT: Presidential Republic

HEAD OF STATE AND GOVT: President Joseph Boakai

GDP PER CAPITA: $1,500

POPULATION: 5,437,249

ISD CODE: 231 **INTERNET TLD:** .lr

Liberia was founded by freed people of colour from the USA.

LIBYA

LOCATION: North Africa

CAPITAL: Tripoli

AREA: 1,759,540

LANGUAGES: Arabic, Italian, English

MAIN RELIGION: Islam

CURRENCY: Libyan Dinar

LITERACY RATE: 91%

LIFE EXPECTANCY: 77.7 years

TIME ZONE: +2

TYPE OF GOVERNMENT: Transitional

HEAD OF STATE: Chairman, Presidential Council: Mohammed Al Menfi **HEAD OF GOVT:** Interim Prime Minister Abdul Hamid Dbeibeh

GDP PER CAPITA: $19,800

POPULATION: 7,361,263

ISD CODE: 218 **INTERNET TLD:** .ly

95 per cent of Libya is covered by the Sahara desert. It is very arid, and in some places it rains only once in ten or more years.

LIECHTENSTEIN

LOCATION: Central Europe

CAPITAL: Vaduz

AREA: 160 sq. km

LANGUAGE: German

MAIN RELIGION: Christianity

CURRENCY: Swiss Franc

LITERACY RATE: 99%

LIFE EXPECTANCY: 83 years

TIME ZONE: +1

TYPE OF GOVERNMENT: Constitutional Monarchy

HEAD OF STATE: Prince Hans-Adam II **HEAD OF GOVT:** Prime Minister Daniel Risch

GDP PER CAPITA: $139,100

POPULATION: 40,272

ISD CODE: 423 **INTERNET TLD:** .li

Liechtenstein has no airport. The closest airport is in Zurich in Switzerland.

LITHUANIA

LOCATION: East Europe

CAPITAL: Vilnius

AREA: 65,300 sq. km

LANGUAGES: Lithuanian, Russian

MAIN RELIGION: Christianity

CURRENCY: Euro

LITERACY RATE: 99.8%

LIFE EXPECTANCY: 76.1 years

TIME ZONE: +2

TYPE OF GOVERNMENT: Semi-presidential Republic

HEAD OF STATE: President Gitanas Nausėda **HEAD OF GOVT:** Prime Minister Ingrida Šimonytė

GDP PER CAPITA: $40,000

POPULATION: 2,628,186

ISD CODE: 370 **INTERNET TLD:** .lt

Lithuania was the first Soviet Republic to declare independence from the USSR.

Background: Liechtenstein

LUXEMBOURG

LOCATION: West Europe

CAPITAL: Luxembourg City

AREA: 2,586 sq. km

LANGUAGES: Luxembourgish, French, German, Portuguese

MAIN RELIGION: Christianity

CURRENCY: Euro

LITERACY RATE: 100%

LIFE EXPECTANCY: 83.4 years

TIME ZONE: +1

TYPE OF GOVERNMENT: Constitutional Monarchy

HEAD OF STATE: Grand Duke Henri **HEAD OF GOVT:** Prime Minister Luc Frieden

GDP PER CAPITA: $117,700

POPULATION: 671,254

ISD CODE: 352 **INTERNET TLD:** .lu

Luxembourg is the world's only remaining Grand Duchy, meaning that its head of state is a Grand Duke or Grand Duchess.

MADAGASCAR

LOCATION: Southern African coast

CAPITAL: Antananarivo

AREA: 587,041 sq. km

LANGUAGES: Malagasy, English, French

MAIN RELIGIONS: Indigenous faiths, Christianity, Islam

CURRENCY: Malagasy Ariary

LITERACY RATE: 77.3%

LIFE EXPECTANCY: 68.8 years

TIME ZONE: +3

TYPE OF GOVERNMENT: Semi-presidential Republic

HEAD OF STATE: President Andry Nirina Rajoelina **HEAD OF GOVT:** Prime Minister Christian Ntsay

GDP PER CAPITA: $1,500

POPULATION: 29,452,714

ISD CODE: 261 **INTERNET TLD:** .mg

Madagascar is also known as the Red Island because in many areas the soil has a distinct reddish tint.

MALAWI

LOCATION: Southern Africa

CAPITAL: Lilongwe

AREA: 118,484 sq. km

LANGUAGES: Chichewa, Chinyanja

MAIN RELIGIONS: Christianity, Islam

CURRENCY: Malawian Kwacha

LITERACY RATE: 67.3%

LIFE EXPECTANCY: 73 years

TIME ZONE: +2

TYPE OF GOVERNMENT: Presidential Republic

HEAD OF STATE AND GOVT: President Lazarus Chakwera

GDP PER CAPITA: $1,500

POPULATION: 21,763,309

ISD CODE: 265 **INTERNET TLD:** .mw

Lake Malawi, from which the country gets its name, is also called the 'Calendar Lake' since it is about 365 miles (number of days in a year) (587.4 km) long and 52 miles (number of weeks in a year) (83.7 km) wide.

MALAYSIA

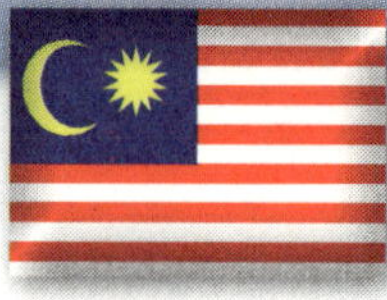

LOCATION: South-East Asia

CAPITAL: Kuala Lumpur

AREA: 329,847 sq. km

LANGUAGES: Bahasa Malaysia (Malay), English, Chinese

MAIN RELIGIONS: Islam, Buddhism

CURRENCY: Ringgit

LITERACY RATE: 95%

LIFE EXPECTANCY: 76.6 years

TIME ZONE: +8

TYPE OF GOVERNMENT: Federal Parliamentary Constitutional Monarchy

HEAD OF STATE: King Sultan Ibrahim ibni al-Marhum Sultan Iskandar **HEAD OF GOVT:** Prime Minister Anwar Ibrahim

GDP PER CAPITA: $28,400

POPULATION: 34,564,810

ISD CODE: 60 **INTERNET TLD:** .my

The world's largest flower, the Rafflesia (1 m/3.3 ft in diameter), is found here.

(THE) MALDIVES

LOCATION: South-East Asia

CAPITAL: Male

AREA: 298 sq. km

LANGUAGES: Dhivehi, English

MAIN RELIGION: Islam

CURRENCY: Rufiyaa

LITERACY RATE: 97.9%

LIFE EXPECTANCY: 77.4 years

TIME ZONE: +5

TYPE OF GOVERNMENT: Presidential Republic

HEAD OF STATE AND GOVT: President Mohamed Muizzu

GDP PER CAPITA: $21,300

POPULATION: 388,858

ISD CODE: 960 **INTERNET TLD:** .mv

In 2009, Maldives became the world's first country to hold an official presidential cabinet meeting underwater.

MALI

LOCATION: West Africa

CAPITAL: Bamako

AREA: 1,240,192 sq. km

LANGUAGES: Bambara, French

MAIN RELIGION: Islam

CURRENCY: CFA Franc

LITERACY RATE: 35.5%

LIFE EXPECTANCY: 63.2 years

TIME ZONE: 0

TYPE OF GOVERNMENT: Semi-presidential Republic

HEAD OF STATE: Transitional President Colonel Assimi Goita **HEAD OF GOVT:** Transitional Prime Minister Choguel Maïga

GDP PER CAPITA: $2,100

POPULATION: 21,990,607

ISD CODE: 223 **INTERNET TLD:** .ml

Mali is home to the world's largest mud-brick building, the Great Mosque of Djenné.

Background: Maldives

MALTA

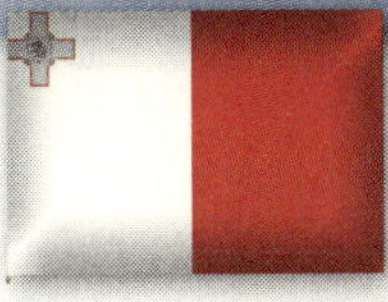

LOCATION: Southern Europe

CAPITAL: Valletta

AREA: 316 sq. km

LANGUAGES: Maltese, English

MAIN RELIGION: Christianity

CURRENCY: Euro

LITERACY RATE: 94.9%

LIFE EXPECTANCY: 83.6 years

TIME ZONE: +1

TYPE OF GOVERNMENT: Parliamentary Republic

HEAD OF STATE: President Myriam Spiteri Debono **HEAD OF GOVT:** Prime Minister Robert Abela

GDP PER CAPITA: $48,600

POPULATION: 469,730

ISD CODE: 356 **INTERNET TLD:** .mt

Malta was known as 'Melita', meaning 'the island of honey', by ancient Greeks and Romans.

MARSHALL ISLANDS

LOCATION: Northern Pacific Ocean

CAPITAL: Majuro

AREA: 181 sq. km

LANGUAGES: Marshallese, English

MAIN RELIGION: Christianity

CURRENCY: US Dollar

LITERACY RATE: 98.3%

LIFE EXPECTANCY: 75.2 years

TIME ZONE: +12

TYPE OF GOVERNMENT: Mixed Presidential Parliamentary Republic

HEAD OF STATE AND GOVT: President Hilda C. Heine

GDP PER CAPITA: $6,000

POPULATION: 82,011

ISD CODE: 692 **INTERNET TLD:** .mh

Almost 2,000,000 sq. km of ocean was declared a shark sanctuary here in 2011. It is the largest shark sanctuary in the world.

MAURITANIA

LOCATION: Western Africa

CAPITAL: Nouakchott

AREA: 1,030,700 sq. km

LANGUAGES: Arabic, Pulaar

MAIN RELIGION: Islam

CURRENCY: Ouguiya

LITERACY RATE: 67%

LIFE EXPECTANCY: 65.9 years

TIME ZONE: 0

TYPE OF GOVERNMENT: Presidential Republic

HEAD OF STATE: President Mohamed Ould Ghazouani **HEAD OF GOVT:** Prime Minister Mokhtar Ould Djay

GDP PER CAPITA: $5,300

POPULATION: 4,328,040

ISD CODE: 222 **INTERNET TLD:** .mr

If you look at Mauritania from space, you can see a clear bull's eye-like geological feature, which is 50 km across, called 'The Eye of Africa.'

MAURITIUS

LOCATION: Indian Ocean

CAPITAL: Port Louis

AREA: 2,040 sq. km

LANGUAGES: Creole, French, Bhojpuri, English

MAIN RELIGIONS: Hinduism, Christianity, Islam

CURRENCY: Mauritian Rupee

LITERACY RATE: 92.2%

LIFE EXPECTANCY: 75.4 years

TIME ZONE: +4

TYPE OF GOVERNMENT: Parliamentary Republic

HEAD OF STATE: President Prithvirajsing Roopun **HEAD OF GOVT:** Prime Minister Pravind Kumar Jugnauth

GDP PER CAPITA: $22,800

POPULATION: 1,310,504

ISD CODE: 230 **INTERNET TLD:** .mu

Inspired by the dodo, an extinct bird once endemic to Mauritius, Lewis Carroll wrote the book *Alice's Adventures in Wonderland* in 1865.

MEXICO

LOCATION: North America

CAPITAL: Mexico City

AREA: 1,964,375 sq. km

LANGUAGE: Spanish

MAIN RELIGION: Christianity

CURRENCY: Mexican Peso

LITERACY RATE: 95.2%

LIFE EXPECTANCY: 74.6 years

TIME ZONE: –6

TYPE OF GOVERNMENT: Federal Presidential Republic

HEAD OF STATE AND GOVT: President Andrés Manuel López Obrador

GDP PER CAPITA: $20,300

POPULATION: 130,739,927

ISD CODE: 52 **INTERNET TLD:** .mx

Mexico City is sinking at the rate of 15–20 cm a year because it is built on an aquifer.

MICRONESIA

LOCATION: Island group in the North Pacific Ocean

CAPITAL: Palikir

AREA: 702 sq. km

LANGUAGE: English

MAIN RELIGION: Christianity

CURRENCY: US Dollar

LITERACY RATE: 98.8%

LIFE EXPECTANCY: 75 years

TIME ZONE: +11

TYPE OF GOVERNMENT: Federal Presidential Republic

HEAD OF STATE AND GOVT: President Wesley W. Simina

GDP PER CAPITA: $3,300

POPULATION: 99,603

ISD CODE: 691 **INTERNET TLD:** .fm

Micronesia houses the ruins of Nan Madol, an artificial group of islands connected by canals built in the eighth or ninth century CE. This gives it the name 'Venice of the Pacific'.

MOLDOVA

LOCATION: East Europe

CAPITAL: Chisinau

AREA: 33,851 sq. km

LANGUAGES: Moldovan, Russian

MAIN RELIGION: Christianity

CURRENCY: Moldovan Leu

LITERACY RATE: 99.6%

LIFE EXPECTANCY: 70.1 years

TIME ZONE: +2

TYPE OF GOVERNMENT: Parliamentary Republic

HEAD OF STATE: President Maia Sandu **HEAD OF GOVT:** Prime Minister Dorin Recean

GDP PER CAPITA: $13,300

POPULATION: 3,599,528

ISD CODE: 372 **INTERNET TLD:** .md

Emil Racovita, a cave in Criva, Moldova, is among the largest caves in the world. There are twenty underground lakes inside the cave.

MONACO

LOCATION: West Europe

CAPITAL: Monaco

AREA: 2 sq. km

LANGUAGES: French, English, Italian

MAIN RELIGION: Christianity

CURRENCY: Euro

LITERACY RATE: 99%

LIFE EXPECTANCY: 89.8 years

TIME ZONE: +1

TYPE OF GOVERNMENT: Constitutional Monarchy

HEAD OF STATE: Prince Albert II **HEAD OF GOVT:** Minister of State Pierre Dartout

GDP PER CAPITA: $115,700

POPULATION: 31,813

ISD CODE: 377 **INTERNET TLD:** .mc

It takes an hour for an average person to walk the width of the entire country.

MONGOLIA

LOCATION: North Asia

CAPITAL: Ulaanbaatar

AREA: 1,564,116 sq. km

LANGUAGE: Mongol

MAIN RELIGIONS: Buddhism, Christianity, Islam

CURRENCY: Togrog/Tugrik

LITERACY RATE: 99.2%

LIFE EXPECTANCY: 71.9 years

TIME ZONE: +8

TYPE OF GOVERNMENT: Semi-presidential Republic

HEAD OF STATE: President Ukhnaagiin Khürelsükh **HEAD OF GOVT:** Prime Minister Luvsannamsrai Oyun-Erdene

GDP PER CAPITA: $12,100

POPULATION: 3,281,676

ISD CODE: 976 **INTERNET TLD:** .mn

Fossilised dinosaur remains and the first dinosaur eggs were found in the Gobi Desert in Mongolia in the 1920s.

Background: Mexico

MONTENEGRO

LOCATION: South-eastern Europe

CAPITAL: Podgorica

AREA: 13,812 sq. km

LANGUAGES: Montenegrin, Serbian

MAIN RELIGIONS: Islam, Christianity

CURRENCY: Euro

LITERACY RATE: 99%

LIFE EXPECTANCY: 78.2 years

TIME ZONE: +1

TYPE OF GOVERNMENT: Parliamentary Republic

HEAD OF STATE: President Jakov Milatović **HEAD OF GOVT:** Prime Minister Milojko Spajić

GDP PER CAPITA: $22,100

POPULATION: 599,849

ISD CODE: 382 **INTERNET TLD:** .me

The name Montenegro, meaning 'Black Mountain', was probably derived from the thick 'black' forests that covered Mount Lovcen, the highest point in Montenegro in medieval times.

MOROCCO

LOCATION: North Africa

CAPITAL: Rabat

AREA: 446,550 sq. km

LANGUAGE: Arabic

MAIN RELIGION: Islam

CURRENCY: Moroccan Dirham

LITERACY RATE: 75.9%

LIFE EXPECTANCY: 74.2 years

TIME ZONE: 0

TYPE OF GOVERNMENT: Parliamentary Constitutional Monarchy

HEAD OF STATE: King Mohammed VI
HEAD OF GOVT: Prime Minister Aziz Akhannouch

GDP PER CAPITA: $8,100

POPULATION: 37,387,585

ISD CODE: 212 **INTERNET TLD:** .ma

Morocco is often called the 'Oasis of the Senses'. From the Sahara Desert to the snow-capped Atlas Mountains, the country's landscape is very diverse.

MOZAMBIQUE

LOCATION: South-eastern Africa

CAPITAL: Maputo

AREA: 799,380 sq. km

LANGUAGES: Makhuwa, Portuguese

MAIN RELIGIONS: Christianity, Islam

CURRENCY: Metical

LITERACY RATE: 63.4%

LIFE EXPECTANCY: 58.3 years

TIME ZONE: +2

TYPE OF GOVERNMENT: Presidential Republic

HEAD OF STATE AND GOVT: President Filipe Nyusi

GDP PER CAPITA: $1,300

POPULATION: 33,350,954

ISD CODE: 258 **INTERNET TLD:** .mz

Mozambique has won two Olympic medals, both won by Maria de Lurdes Mutola (nicknamed 'Maputo Express') in the women's 800 m – a bronze in 1996 and a gold in 2000.

MYANMAR (BURMA)

LOCATION: South-East Asia

CAPITAL: Naypyidaw

AREA: 676,578 sq. km

LANGUAGE: Burmese

MAIN RELIGION: Buddhism

CURRENCY: Kyat

LITERACY RATE: 89.1%

LIFE EXPECTANCY: 70.3 years

TIME ZONE: +6.5

TYPE OF GOVERNMENT: Parliamentary Republic (under dispute)

HEAD OF STATE AND GOVT: Senior General Min Aung Hlaing (Chief of the Myanmar Military Council)

GDP PER CAPITA: $4,200

POPULATION: 57,527,139

ISD CODE: 95 **INTERNET TLD:** .mm

In 2005, the capital of Myanmar was shifted from Yangon to Naypyidaw.

NAMIBIA

LOCATION: Southern Africa

CAPITAL: Windhoek

AREA: 824,292 sq. km

LANGUAGES: English, Afrikaans

MAIN RELIGION: Christianity

CURRENCY: Namibian Dollar

LITERACY RATE: 92.3%

LIFE EXPECTANCY: 65.9 years

TIME ZONE: +1

TYPE OF GOVERNMENT: Presidential Republic

HEAD OF STATE AND GOVT: President Nangolo Mbumba

GDP PER CAPITA: $9,100

POPULATION: 2,803,660

ISD CODE: 264 **INTERNET TLD:** .na

One in four households in Namibia lives in poverty. The wealthiest 10 per cent of people command more than half the country's income.

NAURU

LOCATION: South Pacific Ocean

CAPITAL: No officially designated capital; Yaren is the largest city

AREA: 21 sq. km

LANGUAGES: Nauruan, English

MAIN RELIGION: Christianity

CURRENCY: Australian Dollar

LITERACY RATE: 98%

LIFE EXPECTANCY: 68.6 years

TIME ZONE: +12

TYPE OF GOVERNMENT: Parliamentary Republic

HEAD OF STATE AND GOVT: President Lionel Aingimea

GDP PER CAPITA: $11,000

POPULATION: 9,892

ISD CODE: 674 **INTERNET TLD:** .nr

Nauru is the world's smallest island nation. It is the only republican state in the world without an official capital.

Background: Namibia

NEPAL

LOCATION: South Asia

CAPITAL: Kathmandu

AREA: 147,181 sq. km

LANGUAGE: Nepali

MAIN RELIGION: Hinduism

CURRENCY: Nepalese Rupee

LITERACY RATE: 71.2%

LIFE EXPECTANCY: 73 years

TIME ZONE: +5.45

TYPE OF GOVERNMENT: Federal Parliamentary Republic

HEAD OF STATE: President Ram Chandra Poudel **HEAD OF GOVT:** Prime Minister K.P. Sharma Oli

GDP PER CAPITA: $4,000

POPULATION: 31,122,387

ISD CODE: 977 **INTERNET TLD:** .np

Nepal's flag is the only national flag in the world that is neither a rectangle nor a square.

(THE) NETHERLANDS

LOCATION: North-western Europe

CAPITAL: Amsterdam

AREA: 41,543 sq. km

LANGUAGES: Dutch, Frisian

MAIN RELIGION: Christianity

CURRENCY: Euro

LITERACY RATE: 99%

LIFE EXPECTANCY: 81.9 years

TIME ZONE: +1

TYPE OF GOVERNMENT: Parliamentary Constitutional Monarchy

HEAD OF STATE: King Willem-Alexander **HEAD OF GOVT:** Prime Minister Dick Schoof

GDP PER CAPITA: $59,200

POPULATION: 17,772,378

ISD CODE: 31 **INTERNET TLD:** .nl

The country's landscape is dotted with windmills, a famous hallmark. There are as many as 300 castles open to the general public.

NEW ZEALAND

LOCATION: South-western Pacific Ocean

CAPITAL: Wellington

AREA: 268,838 sq. km

LANGUAGE: English

MAIN RELIGION: Christianity

CURRENCY: New Zealand Dollar

LITEACY RATE: 99%

LIFE EXPECTANCY: 82.9 years

TIME ZONE: +12

TYPE OF GOVERNMENT: Constitutional Monarchy and Parliamentary Democracy

HEAD OF STATE: King Charles III **HEAD OF GOVT:** Prime Minister Christopher Luxon

GDP PER CAPITA: $45,200

POPULATION: 5,161,211

ISD CODE: 64 **INTERNET TLD:** .nz

New Zealand is home to the world's heaviest parrot, the kakapo. The bird can weigh up to 4 kilograms.

NICARAGUA

LOCATION: Central America

CAPITAL: Managua

AREA: 130,370 sq. km

LANGUAGE: Spanish

MAIN RELIGION: Christianity

CURRENCY: Córdoba

LITERACY RATE: 82.6%

LIFE EXPECTANCY: 74.7 years

TIME ZONE: –6

TYPE OF GOVERNMENT: Presidential Republic

HEAD OF STATE AND GOVT: President Jose Daniel Ortega Saavedra

GDP PER CAPITA: $5,800

POPULATION: 6,676,948

ISD CODE: 505 **INTERNET TLD:** .ni

Nicaragua is famous for its dance form known as 'Palo de Mayo'. The country's most popular sport is baseball.

NIGER

LOCATION: West Africa

CAPITAL: Niamey

AREA: 1,267,000 sq. km

LANGUAGES: French, Hausa, Djerma

MAIN RELIGION: Islam

CURRENCY: CFA Franc

LITERACY RATE: 37.3%

LIFE EXPECTANCY: 60.9 years

TIME ZONE: +1

TYPE OF GOVERNMENT: formerly, semi-presidential republic

HEAD OF STATE: President Abdourahame Tchiani **HEAD OF GOVT:** Prime Minister Ali Mahaman Lamine Zeine

GDP PER CAPITA: $1,300

POPULATION: 26,342,784

ISD CODE: 227 **INTERNET TLD:** .ne

The remains of the dinosaur *Nigersaurus*, known for its long neck and hammerhead skull, were discovered in Niger in the 1950s.

NIGERIA

LOCATION: West Africa

CAPITAL: Abuja

AREA: 923,769 sq. km

LANGUAGES: English, Hausa

MAIN RELIGIONS: Islam, Christianity

CURRENCY: Naira

LITERACY RATE: 62%

LIFE EXPECTANCY: 62.2 years

TIME ZONE: +1

TYPE OF GOVERNMENT: Presidential Federal Republic

HEAD OF STATE AND GOVT: President Bola Tinubu

GDP PER CAPITA: $5,000

POPULATION: 236,747,130

ISD CODE: 234 **INTERNET TLD:** .ng

Nigeria is home to Nollywood, the world's second-largest film industry by volume, producing more movies annually than Hollywood and second only to India's Bollywood.

NORTH KOREA

LOCATION: East Asia

CAPITAL: Pyongyang

AREA: 120,538 sq. km

LANGUAGE: Korean

MAIN RELIGIONS: Officially atheist; Buddhism, Chondogyo, Christianity

CURRENCY: Won

LITERACY RATE: 100%

LIFE EXPECTANCY: 73.5 years

TIME ZONE: +9

TYPE OF GOVERNMENT: Communist Dictatorship

HEAD OF STATE: Chairman Kim Jong-un **HEAD OF GOVT:** Supreme People's Assembly President Choe Ryong-hae

GDP PER CAPITA: $1,700

POPULATION: 26,298,666

ISD CODE: 850 **INTERNET TLD:** .kp

The old name for North Korea is Joseon or Choson (Land of Morning Calm).

NORTH MACEDONIA

LOCATION: South-eastern Europe

CAPITAL: Skopje

AREA: 25,713 sq. km

LANGUAGES: Macedonian, Albanian

MAIN RELIGIONS: Christianity (Macedonian Orthodox Church), Islam

CURRENCY: Macedonian Dinar

LITERACY RATE: 98.4%

LIFE EXPECTANCY: 77.3 years

TIME ZONE: +1

TYPE OF GOVERNMENT: Parliamentary Republic

HEAD OF STATE: President Gordana Siljanovska-Davkova **HEAD OF GOVT:** Prime Minister Hristijan Mickoski

GDP PER CAPITA: $17,100

POPULATION: 2,135,622

ISD CODE: 389 **INTERNET TLD:** .mk

Macedonia was formerly a part of Yugoslavia and gained Independence in 1991.

NORWAY

LOCATION: Northern Europe

CAPITAL: Oslo

AREA: 323,802 sq. km

LANGUAGE: Norwegian

MAIN RELIGION: Christianity

CURRENCY: Norwegian Kroner

LITERACY RATE: 100%

LIFE EXPECTANCY: 82.9 years

TIME ZONE: +1

TYPE OF GOVERNMENT: Parliamentary Constitutional Monarchy

HEAD OF STATE: King Harald V

HEAD OF GOVT: Prime Minister Jonas Gahr Støre

GDP PER CAPITA: $67,500

POPULATION: 5,509,733

ISD CODE: 47 **INTERNET TLD:** .no

The Nobel Peace Prize is awarded in Oslo. The Norwegian king is present at the award ceremony.

Background: Norway

OMAN

LOCATION: Middle East

CAPITAL: Muscat

AREA: 309,500 sq. km

LANGUAGES: Arabic, English, Urdu

MAIN RELIGION: Islam

CURRENCY: Omani Rial

LITERACY RATE: 95.7%

LIFE EXPECTANCY: 77.4 years

TIME ZONE: +4

TYPE OF GOVERNMENT: Absolute Monarchy

HEAD OF STATE AND GOVT: Sultan Haitham bin Tariq Al Said

GDP PER CAPITA: $35,300

POPULATION: 3,901,992

ISD CODE: 968 **INTERNET TLD:** .om

The leaves of the *Myrtus communis* or the 'Yas' shrub found in Oman are used for making perfume.

PAKISTAN

LOCATION: South Asia

CAPITAL: Islamabad

AREA: 796,095 sq. km

LANGUAGES: Urdu, Punjabi, Sindhi

MAIN RELIGION: Islam

CURRENCY: Pakistani Rupee

LITERACY RATE: 58%

LIFE EXPECTANCY: 70.3 years

TIME ZONE: +5

TYPE OF GOVERNMENT: Federal Parliamentary Republic

HEAD OF STATE: President Asif Ali Zardari **HEAD OF GOVT:** Prime Minister Shehbaz Sharif

GDP PER CAPITA: $5,400

POPULATION: 252,363,571

ISD CODE: 92 **INTERNET TLD:** .pk

Pakistan is home to the largest earth-filled dam in the world, Tarbela dam.

PALAU

LOCATION: Group of islands in the North Pacific Ocean

CAPITAL: Melekeok

AREA: 459 sq. km

LANGUAGES: Palauan, Filipino, English

MAIN RELIGION: Christianity

CURRENCY: US Dollar

LITERACY RATE: 96.6%

LIFE EXPECTANCY: 75.2 years

TIME ZONE: +9

TYPE OF GOVERNMENT: Presidential Republic

HEAD OF STATE AND GOVT: President Surangel Whipps, Jr

GDP PER CAPITA: $14,100

POPULATION: 21,864

ISD CODE: 680 **INTERNET TLD:** .pw

In 1783, Palau was accidentally discovered by the shipwrecked crew of Captain Henry Wilson when he reached the shores of an island called Ulong.

Background: Oman

PANAMA

LOCATION: Central America

CAPITAL: Panama City

AREA: 75,420 sq. km

LANGUAGE: Spanish

MAIN RELIGION: Christianity

CURRENCY: Balboa, US Dollar

LITERACY RATE: 95.7%

LIFE EXPECTANCY: 79.2 years

TIME ZONE: –5

TYPE OF GOVERNMENT: Presidential Republic

HEAD OF STATE AND GOVT: President José Raúl Mulino

GDP PER CAPITA: $33,300

POPULATION: 4,470,241

ISD CODE: 507 **INTERNET TLD:** .pa

The currency of Panama is named after Vasco Nunez de Balboa, the Spanish explorer who was the first to cross the Isthmus of Panama to the Pacific Ocean in 1513.

PAPUA NEW GUINEA

LOCATION: Between the Coral Sea and the South Pacific Ocean

CAPITAL: Port Moresby

AREA: 462,840 sq. km

LANGUAGES: Tok Pisin, English, Hiri Motu

MAIN RELIGION: Christianity

CURRENCY: Kina

LITERACY RATE: 64.2%

LIFE EXPECTANCY: 70.1 years

TIME ZONE: +11

TYPE OF GOVERNMENT: Constitutional Monarchy and Parliamentary Democracy

HEAD OF STATE: King Charles III
HEAD OF GOVT: Prime Minister James Marape

GDP PER CAPITA: $3,800

POPULATION: 10,046,233

ISD CODE: 675 **INTERNET TLD:** .pg

Seashells were the national currency of Papua New Guinea until 1933.

PARAGUAY

LOCATION: Central South America

CAPITAL: Asuncion

AREA: 406,752 sq. km

LANGUAGES: Spanish, Guarani

MAIN RELIGION: Christianity

CURRENCY: Guarani

LITERACY RATE: 94.5%

LIFE EXPECTANCY: 78.8 years

TIME ZONE: –4

TYPE OF GOVERNMENT: Presidential Republic

HEAD OF STATE AND GOVT: President Santiago Peña Palacios

GDP PER CAPITA: $13,500

POPULATION: 7,522,549

ISD CODE: 595 **INTERNET TLD:** .py

Due to its central location in South America, Paraguay is sometimes referred to as 'Corazon de America', or the Heart of America.

PERU

LOCATION: Western South America

CAPITAL: Lima

AREA: 1,285,216 sq. km

LANGUAGES: Spanish, Quechua

MAIN RELIGION: Christianity

CURRENCY: Nuevo Sol

LITERACY RATE: 94.5%

LIFE EXPECTANCY: 68.9 years

TIME ZONE: –5

TYPE OF GOVERNMENT: Presidential Republic

HEAD OF STATE AND GOVT: President Dina Ercilia Boluarte

GDP PER CAPITA: $12,700

POPULATION: 32,600,249

ISD CODE: 51 **INTERNET TLD:** .pe

There are as many as 3,000–4,000 varieties of potato grown in Peru.

(THE) PHILIPPINES

LOCATION: South-east Asia

CAPITAL: Manila

AREA: 300,000 sq. km

LANGUAGES: Filipino, English

MAIN RELIGION: Christianity

CURRENCY: Philippine Peso

LITERACY RATE: 96.3%

LIFE EXPECTANCY: 70.8 years

TIME ZONE: +8

TYPE OF GOVERNMENT: Presidential Republic

HEAD OF STATE AND GOVT: President Ferdinand 'BongBong' Marcos, Jr

GDP PER CAPITA: $8,600

POPULATION: 118,277,063

ISD CODE: 63 **INTERNET TLD:** .ph

There are more than 200 volcanoes on the islands of the Philippines, though only a few are active.

POLAND

LOCATION: Central Europe

CAPITAL: Warsaw

AREA: 312,685 sq. km

LANGUAGE: Polish

MAIN RELIGION: Christianity

CURRENCY: Zloty

LITERACY RATE: 99.8%

LIFE EXPECTANCY: 76.7 years

TIME ZONE: +1

TYPE OF GOVERNMENT: Parliamentary Republic

HEAD OF STATE: President Andrzej Duda **HEAD OF GOVT:** Prime Minister Donald Tusk

GDP PER CAPITA: $37,700

POPULATION: 38,746,310

ISD CODE: 48 **INTERNET TLD:** .pl

The Poles consider their name-days more important than their birthdays. Name-days are days of the year on which certain Christian saints are honoured. All those who share the name of the saint celebrate the day.

Background: Peru

PORTUGAL

LOCATION: South-western Europe

CAPITAL: Lisbon

AREA: 92,090 sq. km

LANGUAGES: Portuguese

MAIN RELIGION: Christianity

CURRENCY: Euro

LITERACY RATE: 95.9%

LIFE EXPECTANCY: 81.9 years

TIME ZONE: 0

TYPE OF GOVERNMENT: Semi-presidential Republic

HEAD OF STATE: President Marcelo Rebelo de Sousa **HEAD OF GOVT:** Prime Minister Antonio Luís Montenegro

GDP PER CAPITA: $35,800

POPULATION: 10,207,177

ISD CODE: 351 **INTERNET TLD:** .pt

Ferdinand Magellan, a Portuguese explorer, was the first to complete a circumnavigation of the Earth, in 1522.

QATAR

LOCATION: Middle East

CAPITAL: Doha

AREA: 11,586 sq. km

LANGUAGES: Arabic, English

MAIN RELIGION: Islam

CURRENCY: Qatari Riyal

LITERACY RATE: 93.5%

LIFE EXPECTANCY: 80.3 years

TIME ZONE: +3

TYPE OF GOVERNMENT: Absolute Monarchy

HEAD OF STATE: Amir Tamim bin Hamad Al Thani **HEAD OF GOVT:** Prime Minister Sheikh Mohammed bin Abdulrahman Al Thani

GDP PER CAPITA: $96,600

POPULATION: 2,552,088

ISD CODE: 974 **INTERNET TLD:** .qa

Qatar was the first Middle Eastern nation to host the FIFA World Cup, in November–December 2022.

ROMANIA

LOCATION: South-east Europe

CAPITAL: Bucharest

AREA: 238,391 sq. km

LANGUAGES: Romanian, Hungarian

MAIN RELIGION: Christianity

CURRENCY: Romanian Leu

LITERACY RATE: 98.9%

LIFE EXPECTANCY: 76.9 years

TIME ZONE: +2

TYPE OF GOVERNMENT: Semi-presidential Republic

HEAD OF STATE: President Klaus Iohannis **HEAD OF GOVT:** Prime Minister Marcel Ciolacu

GDP PER CAPITA: $32,500

POPULATION: 18,148,155

ISD CODE: 40 **INTERNET TLD:** .ro

The earliest reliably dated European modern human fossils were discovered in 2002 at Pestera cu Oase ('Cave with Bones'). They were 37,800 to 42,000 years old.

RUSSIA

LOCATION: North Asia/east Europe

CAPITAL: Moscow

AREA: 17,098,242 sq. km

LANGUAGE: Russian

MAIN RELIGION: Christianity

CURRENCY: Ruble

LITERACY RATE: 99.7%

LIFE EXPECTANCY: 72.3 years

TIME ZONE: +3 to +12

TYPE OF GOVERNMENT: Semi-presidential Federation

HEAD OF STATE: President Vladimir Putin **HEAD OF GOVT:** Prime Minister Mikhail Mishustin

GDP PER CAPITA: $27,500

POPULATION: 140,820,810

ISD CODE: 7 **INTERNET TLD:** .ru

The game Tetris was invented in Russia. In 1984, Alexey Pajitnov developed the first version of Tetris for the Electronika 60 computer.

RWANDA

LOCATION: Central Africa

CAPITAL: Kigali

AREA: 26,338 sq. km

LANGUAGES: Kinyarwanda, French, English

MAIN RELIGION: Christianity

CURRENCY: Rwandan Franc

LITERACY RATE: 75.9%

LIFE EXPECTANCY: 66.6 years

TIME ZONE: +2

TYPE OF GOVERNMENT: Presidential Republic

HEAD OF STATE: President Paul Kagame **HEAD OF GOVT:** Prime Minister Édouard Ngirente

GDP PER CAPITA: $2,400

POPULATION: 13,623,302

ISD CODE: 250 **INTERNET TLD:** .rw

Sixty per cent of Rwandan parliamentarians are women.

SAINT KITTS AND NEVIS

LOCATION: Islands in the Caribbean Sea

CAPITAL: Basseterre

AREA: 261 sq. km

LANGUAGE: English

MAIN RELIGION: Christianity

CURRENCY: East Caribbean Dollar

LITERACY RATE: 97.8%

LIFE EXPECTANCY: 77.6 years

TIME ZONE: –4

TYPE OF GOVERNMENT: Constitutional Monarchy and Federal Parliamentary Democracy

HEAD OF STATE: King Charles III **HEAD OF GOVT:** Prime Minister Terrance Drew

GDP PER CAPITA: $28,800

POPULATION: 55,133

ISD CODE: 1-869 **INTERNET TLD:** .kn

Christopher Columbus discovered the island and named it after his patron saint, St Christopher. It was later shortened to Saint Kitts.

Background: Russia

SAINT LUCIA

LOCATION: Caribbean

CAPITAL: Castries

AREA: 616 sq. km

LANGUAGE: English

MAIN RELIGION: Christianity

CURRENCY: East Caribbean Dollar

LITERACY RATE: 90.1%

LIFE EXPECTANCY: 79.4 years

TIME ZONE: –4

TYPE OF GOVERNMENT: Constitutional Monarchy and Parliamentary Democracy

HEAD OF STATE: King Charles III
HEAD OF GOVT: Prime Minister Philip J. Pierre

GDP PER CAPITA: $15,100

POPULATION: 168,038

ISD CODE: 1-758 **INTERNET TLD:** .lc

La Soufriere volcano in Malgretoute, Saint Lucia, is the world's only drive-in volcano! You can drive right into its crater.

SAINT VINCENT AND THE GRENADINES

LOCATION: Central America/Caribbean Sea

CAPITAL: Kingstown

AREA: 389 sq. km

LANGUAGE: English

MAIN RELIGION: Christianity

CURRENCY: East Caribbean Dollar

LITERACY RATE: 96%

LIFE EXPECTANCY: 77.2 years

TIME ZONE: –4

TYPE OF GOVERNMENT: Constitutional Monarchy and Parliamentary Democracy

HEAD OF STATE: King Charles III
HEAD OF GOVT: Prime Minister Ralph Gonsalves

GDP PER CAPITA: $14,600

POPULATION: 100,647

ISD CODE: 1-784 **INTERNET TLD:** .vc

The first few scenes of *The Pirates of the Caribbean: The Curse of the Black Pearl* were shot here.

SAMOA

LOCATION: Group of islands in the South Pacific

CAPITAL: Apia

AREA: 2,831 sq. km

LANGUAGES: Samoan, English

MAIN RELIGION: Christianity

CURRENCY: Tala

LITERACY RATE: 99.1%

LIFE EXPECTANCY: 75.7 years

TIME ZONE: +13

TYPE OF GOVERNMENT: Parliamentary Republic

HEAD OF STATE: President Va'aleto'a Sualauvi II **HEAD OF GOVT:** Prime Minister Fiamē Naomi Mata'afa

GDP PER CAPITA: $5,200

POPULATION: 208,853

ISD CODE: 685 **INTERNET TLD:** .ws

Tattooing is a great tradition in Samoa, and both men and women have been getting intricate tattoos for at least 2,000 years.

Background: Saint Lucia

SAN MARINO

LOCATION: Southern Europe

CAPITAL: San Marino

AREA: 61.2 sq. km

LANGUAGE: Italian

MAIN RELIGION: Christianity

CURRENCY: Euro

LITERACY RATE: 99.9%

LIFE EXPECTANCY: 84.2 years

TIME ZONE: +1

TYPE OF GOVERNMENT: Parliamentary Republic

HEAD OF STATE: co-chiefs of state Captains Regent Alessandro Rossi and Milena Gasperoni **HEAD OF GOVT:** Secretary of State for Foreign Affairs Luca Beccari

GDP PER CAPITA: $61,600

POPULATION: 35,095

ISD CODE: 378 **INTERNET TLD:** .sm

The constitution of San Marino, enacted in 1600, is the world's oldest constitution still in effect.

SAUDI ARABIA

LOCATION: Middle East

CAPITAL: Riyadh

AREA: 2,149,690 sq. km

LANGUAGE: Arabic

MAIN RELIGION: Islam

CURRENCY: Saudi Riyal

LITERACY RATE: 97.6%

LIFE EXPECTANCY: 77.2 years

TIME ZONE: +3

TYPE OF GOVERNMENT: Absolute Monarchy

HEAD OF STATE AND GOVT: King Salman bin Abdulaziz Al Saud

GDP PER CAPITA: $50,200

POPULATION: 36,544,431

ISD CODE: 966 **INTERNET TLD:** .sa

Saudi Arabia is the world's largest producer of desalinated water.

SAO TOME AND PRINCIPE

LOCATION: West Central Africa; islands in the Sea of Guinea

CAPITAL: Sao Tome

AREA: 964 sq. km

LANGUAGE: Portuguese

MAIN RELIGION: Christianity

CURRENCY: Dobra

LITERACY RATE: 94.8%

LIFE EXPECTANCY: 67.7 years

TIME ZONE: +0

TYPE OF GOVERNMENT: Semi-presidential Republic

HEAD OF STATE: President Carlos Manuel Vila Nova **HEAD OF GOVT:** Prime Minister Patrice Trovoada

GDP PER CAPITA: $3,400

POPULATION: 223,561

ISD CODE: 239 **INTERNET TLD:** .st

Sao Tome and Principe, comprising two islands, is the smallest nation in Africa. Sao Tome houses 90 per cent of the population.

Background: San Marino

SENEGAL

LOCATION: West Africa

CAPITAL: Dakar

AREA: 196,722 sq. km

LANGUAGES: French, Wolof

MAIN RELIGION: Islam

CURRENCY: CFA Franc

LITERACY RATE: 56.3%

LIFE EXPECTANCY: 70.6 years

TIME ZONE: 0

TYPE OF GOVERNMENT: Presidential Republic

HEAD OF STATE: President Bassirou Diomaye Faye **HEAD OF GOVT:** Prime Minister Ousmane Sonko

GDP PER CAPITA: $3,600

POPULATION: 18,847,519

ISD CODE: 221 **INTERNET TLD:** .sn

Senegal is known for its tradition of storytelling, performed by storytellers called 'griots'. They have kept West African history alive through stories and music.

SERBIA

LOCATION: East Europe

CAPITAL: Belgrade

AREA: 77,474 sq. km

LANGUAGES: Serbian, Hungarian

MAIN RELIGION: Christianity

CURRENCY: Serbian Dinar

LITERACY RATE: 99.5%

LIFE EXPECTANCY: 75.3 years

TIME ZONE: +1

TYPE OF GOVERNMENT: Parliamentary Republic

HEAD OF STATE: President Aleksandar Vučić **HEAD OF GOVT:** Prime Minister Miloš Vučević

GDP PER CAPITA: $20,900

POPULATION: 6,652,212

ISD CODE: 381 **INTERNET TLD:** .rs

Serbia is one of the biggest producers and exporters of raspberries in the world. In the harvest season, more than 200,000 people are employed in this industry.

SEYCHELLES

LOCATION: Indian Ocean

CAPITAL: Victoria

AREA: 455 sq. km

LANGUAGES: Creole, English, French

MAIN RELIGION: Christianity

CURRENCY: Seychelles Rupee

LITERACY RATE: 95.9%

LIFE EXPECTANCY: 76.6 years

TIME ZONE: +4

TYPE OF GOVERNMENT: Presidential Republic

HEAD OF STATE AND GOVT: President Wavel Ramkalawan

GDP PER CAPITA: $25,200

POPULATION: 98,187

ISD CODE: 248 **INTERNET TLD:** .sc

Medusagyne oppositifolia or the jellyfish tree (named so after the shape of its fruit), which is endemic to Seychelles, was thought extinct until a few plants were discovered in the 1970s.

Background: Senegal

SIERRA LEONE

LOCATION: West Africa

CAPITAL: Freetown

AREA: 71,740 sq. km

LANGUAGES: English, Krio, Temne

MAIN RELIGIONS: Islam, Christianity

CURRENCY: Leone

LITERACY RATE: 48.6%

LIFE EXPECTANCY: 59.4 years

TIME ZONE: +0

TYPE OF GOVERNMENT: Presidential Republic

HEAD OF STATE AND GOVT: President Julius Maada Bio

GDP PER CAPITA: $1,600

POPULATION: 9,121,049

ISD CODE: 232 **INTERNET TLD:** .sl

Sierra Leone gets its name from Portuguese 'Serra Leao', meaning 'lion mountain range'.

SINGAPORE

LOCATION: South-East Asia

CAPITAL: Singapore City

AREA: 719 sq. km

LANGUAGES: English, Mandarin, Malay

MAIN RELIGION: Buddhism, Islam

CURRENCY: Singapore Dollar

LITERACY RATE: 97.5%

LIFE EXPECTANCY: 86.7 years

TIME ZONE: +8

TYPE OF GOVERNMENT: Parliamentary Republic

HEAD OF STATE: President Tharman Shanmugaratnam **HEAD OF GOVT:** Prime Minister Lawrence Wong

GDP PER CAPITA: $108,000

POPULATION: 6,028,459

ISD CODE: 65 **INTERNET TLD:** .sg

A city, a capital and a state all at once, Singapore is one of only three city states in the world. The other two are Monaco and Vatican City.

SLOVAKIA

LOCATION: Central Europe

CAPITAL: Bratislava

AREA: 49,035 sq. km

LANGUAGES: Slovak, Hungarian

MAIN RELIGION: Christianity

CURRENCY: Euro

LITERACY RATE: 99.6%

LIFE EXPECTANCY: 77.2 years

TIME ZONE: +1

TYPE OF GOVERNMENT: Parliamentary Republic

HEAD OF STATE: President Peter Pellegrini **HEAD OF GOVT:** Prime Minister Robert Fico

GDP PER CAPITA: $33,200

POPULATION: 5,563,649

ISD CODE: 421 **INTERNET TLD:** .sk

Stefan Banic, a Slovak, invented the first actively used parachute, patenting it in 1913.

Background: Singapore

SLOVENIA

LOCATION: Central Europe

CAPITAL: Ljubljana

AREA: 20,273 sq. km

LANGUAGE: Slovene

MAIN RELIGIONS: Christianity, Islam

CURRENCY: Euro

LITERACY RATE: 99.7%

LIFE EXPECTANCY: 82.2 years

TIME ZONE: +1

TYPE OF GOVERNMENT: Parliamentary Republic

HEAD OF STATE: President Nataša Pirc Musar **HEAD OF GOVT:** Prime Minister Robert Golob

GDP PER CAPITA: $41,000

POPULATION: 2,097,893

ISD CODE: 386 **INTERNET TLD:** .si

A grapevine that grows in the city of Maribor here is believed to be the world's oldest extant vine. It's over 450 years old.

SOLOMON ISLANDS

LOCATION: South Pacific Ocean

CAPITAL: Honiara

AREA: 28,896 sq. km

LANGUAGES: Pijin (Solomonese Pidgin), English

MAIN RELIGION: Christianity

CURRENCY: Solomon Island Dollar

LITERACY RATE: 84.1%

LIFE EXPECTANCY: 77.2 years

TIME ZONE: +11

TYPE OF GOVERNMENT: Constitutional Monarchy and Parliamentary Democracy

HEAD OF STATE: King Charles III **HEAD OF GOVT:** Prime Minister Jeremiah Manele

GDP PER CAPITA: $2,200

POPULATION: 726,799

ISD CODE: 677 **INTERNET TLD:** .sb

Marovo Lagoon, the largest saltwater lagoon in the world, is located in New Georgia in the Solomon Islands.

SOMALIA

LOCATION: East Africa

CAPITAL: Mogadishu

AREA: 637,657 sq. km

LANGUAGES: Somali, Arabic

MAIN RELIGION: Islam

CURRENCY: Somali Shilling

LITERACY RATE: 37.8%

LIFE EXPECTANCY: 56.5 years

TIME ZONE: +3

TYPE OF GOVERNMENT: Federal Parliamentary Republic

HEAD OF STATE: President Hassan Sheikh Mohamud **HEAD OF GOVT:** Prime Minister Hamza Abdi Barre

GDP PER CAPITA: $1,400

POPULATION: 13,017,273

ISD CODE: 252 **INTERNET TLD:** .so

Somalia is located on a peninsula in East Africa, which juts out into the Arabian Sea. It is called the 'Horn of Africa' for its horn-like shape.

Background: South Africa

SOUTH AFRICA

LOCATION: Southern Africa

CAPITAL: Pretoria (executive), Cape Town (judicial), Bloemfontein (legislative)

AREA: 1,219,090 sq. km

LANGUAGES: IsiZulu, IsiXhosa, Afrikaans, and seven other official languages

MAIN RELIGIONS: Christianity, Islam, Hinduism, traditional African religions

CURRENCY: South African Rand

LITERACY RATE: 95%

LIFE EXPECTANCY: 71.9 years

TIME ZONE: +2

TYPE OF GOVERNMENT: Parliamentary Republic

HEAD OF STATE AND GOVT: President Cyril Ramaphosa

GDP PER CAPITA: $13,500

POPULATION: 60,442,647

ISD CODE: 27 **INTERNET TLD:** .za

The Vredefort Dome is the world's largest meteor scar (originally 300-km wide!).

SOUTH KOREA

LOCATION: East Asia

CAPITAL: Seoul

AREA: 99,720 sq. km

LANGUAGE: Korean

MAIN RELIGIONS: Christianity, Buddhism

CURRENCY: South Korean Won

LITERACY RATE: 97.97%

LIFE EXPECTANCY: 83.4 years

TIME ZONE: +9

TYPE OF GOVERNMENT: Presidential Republic

HEAD OF STATE: President Yoon Suk Yeol **HEAD OF GOVT:** Prime Minister Han Duck-soo

GDP PER CAPITA: $45,600

POPULATION: 52,081,799

ISD CODE: 82 **INTERNET TLD:** .kr

South Korean men above eighteen years have to serve in the army for two years.

SOUTH SUDAN

LOCATION: East-central Africa

CAPITAL: Juba

AREA: 619,745 sq. km

LANGUAGES: English, indigenous languages, including Dinka, Nuer, Bari and Zande

MAIN RELIGIONS: Animist, Christianity, Islam

CURRENCY: South Sudanese Pound

LITERACY RATE: 34.5%

LIFE EXPECTANCY: 60.3 years

TIME ZONE: +3

TYPE OF GOVERNMENT: Presidential Republic

HEAD OF STATE AND GOVT: President Salva Kiir Mayardit

GDP PER CAPITA: $1,600

POPULATION: 12,703,714

ISD CODE: 211 **INTERNET TLD:** .ss

South Sudan is the world's youngest country, having gained independence from Sudan in 2011 after a two-decade-long civil war.

SPAIN

LOCATION: South-western Europe

CAPITAL: Madrid

AREA: 505,370 sq. km

LANGUAGE: Spanish

MAIN RELIGION: Christianity

CURRENCY: Euro

LITERACY RATE: 98.6%

LIFE EXPECTANCY: 83 years

TIME ZONE: +1

TYPE OF GOVERNMENT: Parliamentary Constitutional Monarchy

HEAD OF STATE: King Felipe VI

HEAD OF GOVT: President and Prime Minister Pedro Sánchez

GDP PER CAPITA: $40,200

POPULATION: 47,280,433

ISD CODE: 34 **INTERNET TLD:** .es

'La Tomatina' festival held in Buñol is a popular festival where participants engage in a massive tomato fight.

SRI LANKA

LOCATION: South Asia

CAPITAL: Sri Jayawardenepura Kotte; Colombo (commercial capital)

AREA: 65,610 sq. km

LANGUAGES: Sinhala, Tamil

MAIN RELIGIONS: Buddhism, Hinduism

CURRENCY: Sri Lankan Rupee

LITERACY RATE: 92.3%

LIFE EXPECTANCY: 76.8 years

TIME ZONE: +5.30

TYPE OF GOVERNMENT: Presidential Republic

HEAD OF STATE AND GOVT: President Ranil Wickremesinghe

GDP PER CAPITA: $12,200

POPULATION: 21,982,608

ISD CODE: 94 **INTERNET TLD:** .lk

Sri Lanka was known as Ceylon before 1972. In 1960, Sirimavo Bandaranaike of Sri Lanka (then Ceylon) became the first woman prime minister in history.

SUDAN

LOCATION: North-eastern Africa

CAPITAL: Khartoum

AREA: 1,861,484 sq. km

LANGUAGES: Arabic, English

MAIN RELIGIONS: Islam, Christianity

CURRENCY: Sudanese Pound

LITERACY RATE: 60.7%

LIFE EXPECTANCY: 67.8 years

TIME ZONE: +2

TYPE OF GOVERNMENT: Federal Presidential Democratic Republic

HEAD OF STATE AND GOVT: Sovereign Council Chairman and Commander-in-Chief of Sudanese Armed Forces General Abd-al-Fattah al-BURHAN Abd-al-Rahman

GDP PER CAPITA: $3,600

POPULATION: 50,467,278

ISD CODE: 249 **INTERNET TLD:** .sd

Sudan is home to more pyramids than Egypt.

SURINAME

LOCATION: North-eastern South America

CAPITAL: Paramaribo

AREA: 163,820 sq. km

LANGUAGES: Dutch, English

MAIN RELIGIONS: Christianity, Hinduism

CURRENCY: Surinamese Dollar

LITERACY RATE: 95%

LIFE EXPECTANCY: 72.7 years

TIME ZONE: –3

TYPE OF GOVERNMENT: Presidential Republic

HEAD OF STATE AND GOVT: President Chan Santokhi

GDP PER CAPITA: $15,000

POPULATION: 646,758

ISD CODE: 597 **INTERNET TLD:** .sr

Tropical rainforests cover about 80 per cent of the land area in Suriname.

SWEDEN

LOCATION: Northern Europe

CAPITAL: Stockholm

AREA: 450,295 sq. km

LANGUAGE: Swedish

MAIN RELIGION: Christianity

CURRENCY: Swedish Krona

LITERACY RATE: 99%

LIFE EXPECTANCY: 82.9 years

TIME ZONE: +1

TYPE OF GOVERNMENT: Parliamentary Constitutional Monarchy

HEAD OF STATE: King Carl XVI Gustaf

HEAD OF GOVT: Prime Minister Ulf Kristersson

GDP PER CAPITA: $55,300

POPULATION: 10,589,835

ISD CODE: 46 **INTERNET TLD:** .se

A popular Swedish souvenir is the road sign for 'moose crossing'. Every year, many of these signs are stolen from the roads.

SWITZERLAND

LOCATION: Central Europe

CAPITAL: Bern (de facto); no official capital

AREA: 41,277 sq. km

LANGUAGES: German, French, Italian

MAIN RELIGION: Christianity

CURRENCY: Swiss Franc

LITERACY RATE: 99%

LIFE EXPECTANCY: 83.9 years

TIME ZONE: +1

TYPE OF GOVERNMENT: Federal Republic

HEAD OF STATE AND GOVT: President of the Swiss Confederation Viola Amherd

GDP PER CAPITA: $72,300

POPULATION: 8,860,574

ISD CODE: 41 **INTERNET TLD:** .ch

Seventy per cent of the country is covered with mountains and it has over 1,500 lakes.

Background: Sweden

SYRIA

LOCATION: Middle East

CAPITAL: Damascus

AREA: 187,437 sq. km

LANGUAGE: Arabic

MAIN RELIGION: Islam

CURRENCY: Syrian Pound

LITERACY RATE: 86.4%

LIFE EXPECTANCY: 74.8 years

TIME ZONE: +2

TYPE OF GOVERNMENT: Presidential Republic

HEAD OF STATE: President Bashar al-Assad **HEAD OF GOVT:** Prime Minister Hussein Arnous

GDP PER CAPITA: $2,900

POPULATION: 23,865,423

ISD CODE: 963 **INTERNET TLD:** .sy

Damascus has been inhabited for more than 4,000 years, making it one of the oldest continuously inhabited settlements in the world.

TAJIKISTAN

LOCATION: Central Asia

CAPITAL: Dushanbe

AREA: 144,100 sq. km

LANGUAGES: Tajik, Russian

MAIN RELIGION: Islam

CURRENCY: Somoni

LITERACY RATE: 99.8%

LIFE EXPECTANCY: 71.9 years

TIME ZONE: +5

TYPE OF GOVERNMENT: Presidential Republic

HEAD OF STATE: President Emomali Rahmon **HEAD OF GOVT:** Prime Minister Kokhir Rasulzoda

GDP PER CAPITA: $4,100

POPULATION: 10,394,063

ISD CODE: 992 **INTERNET TLD:** .tj

The Iskanderkul Lake of Tajikistan has been named after Alexander the Great. The country was an integral part of the ancient Silk Route.

TANZANIA

LOCATION: East Africa

CAPITAL: Dodoma

AREA: 947,300 sq. km

LANGUAGES: Swahili, English

MAIN RELIGIONS: Islam, Christianity, indigenous faiths

CURRENCY: Tanzanian Shilling

LITERACY RATE: 81.8%

LIFE EXPECTANCY: 70.8 years

TIME ZONE: +3

TYPE OF GOVERNMENT: Presidential Republic

HEAD OF STATE AND GOVT: President Samia Suluhu Hassan **HEAD OF GOVT:** Prime Minister Kassim Majalivi

GDP PER CAPITA: $2,600

POPULATION: 67,462,121

ISD CODE: 255 **INTERNET TLD:** .tz

At 264 sq. km, the Ngorongoro Crater, in the Crater Highlands area of Tanzania, is the largest inactive, intact and unfilled crater in the world. It is home to many wild animals.

Background: Thailand

THAILAND

LOCATION: South-east Asia

CAPITAL: Bangkok

AREA: 513,120 sq. km

LANGUAGE: Thai

MAIN RELIGION: Buddhism

CURRENCY: Baht

LITERACY RATE: 94.1%

LIFE EXPECTANCY: 78.2 years

TIME ZONE: +7

TYPE OF GOVERNMENT: Constitutional Monarchy

HEAD OF STATE: King Vajiralongkorn **HEAD OF GOVT:** Prime Minister Paetongtarn Shinawatra

GDP PER CAPITA: $17,500

POPULATION: 69,920,998

ISD CODE: 66 **INTERNET TLD:** .th

Thailand is the only South-East Asian country to have never been dominated by a Western power and hence retains most of its original culture.

TIMOR-LESTE

LOCATION: South-east Asia

CAPITAL: Dili

AREA: 14,874 sq. km

LANGUAGES: Tetum, Portuguese

MAIN RELIGION: Christianity

CURRENCY: US Dollar

LITERACY RATE: 68.1%

LIFE EXPECTANCY: 70.5 years

TIME ZONE: +9

TYPE OF GOVERNMENT: Semi-presidential Republic

HEAD OF STATE: President José Ramos-Horta **HEAD OF GOVT:** Prime Minister Xanana Gusmão

GDP PER CAPITA: $3,900

POPULATION: 1,506,909

ISD CODE: 670 **INTERNET TLD:** .tl

Nine days after East Timor gained independence from Portugal in 1975, it was occupied by Indonesia. It became independent of Indonesian rule in 2002.

TOGO

LOCATION: West Africa

CAPITAL: Lome

AREA: 56,785 sq. km

LANGUAGES: French, Ewe, Mina, Kabye, Dagomba, other indigenous languages

MAIN RELIGIONS: Indigenous beliefs, Christianity, Islam

CURRENCY: CFA Franc

LITERACY RATE: 66.5%

LIFE EXPECTANCY: 72.1 years

TIME ZONE: +0

TYPE OF GOVERNMENT: Presidential Republic

HEAD OF STATE: President Faure Gnassingbé **HEAD OF GOVT:** Prime Minister Victoire Tomegah Dogbé

GDP PER CAPITA: $2,200

POPULATION: 8,917,994

ISD CODE: 228 **INTERNET TLD:** .tg

Togo is the world's fourth largest producer of phosphate, a mineral used for fertilisers.

TONGA

LOCATION: South Pacific Ocean

CAPITAL: Nuku'alofa

AREA: 747 sq. km

LANGUAGES: Tongan, English

MAIN RELIGION: Christianity

CURRENCY: Pa'anga

LITERACY RATE: 99.4%

LIFE EXPECTANCY: 78 years

TIME ZONE: +13

TYPE OF GOVERNMENT: Constitutional Monarchy

HEAD OF STATE: King Tupou VI **HEAD OF GOVT:** Prime Minister Hu'akavameiliku

GDP PER CAPITA: $6,100

POPULATION: 104,889

ISD CODE: 676 **INTERNET TLD:** .to

Captain James Cook, the famous British navigator, named Tonga the 'Friendly Islands'.

TRINIDAD AND TOBAGO

LOCATION: Caribbean Sea

CAPITAL: Port of Spain

AREA: 5,128 sq. km

LANGUAGE: English

MAIN RELIGIONS: Christianity, Hinduism

CURRENCY: Trinidad and Tobago Dollar

LITERACY RATE: 99%

LIFE EXPECTANCY: 76.5 years

TIME ZONE: –4

TYPE OF GOVERNMENT: Parliamentary Republic

HEAD OF STATE: President Christine Kangaloo **HEAD OF GOVT:** Prime Minister Keith Rowley

GDP PER CAPITA: $23,300

POPULATION: 1,408,966

ISD CODE: 1-868 **INTERNET TLD:** .tt

It is believed that Daniel Defoe and Robert Louis Stevenson based their respective novels, *Robinson Crusoe* and *Treasure Island*, on the islands of Trinidad and Tobago.

TUNISIA

LOCATION: Northern Africa

CAPITAL: Tunis

AREA: 163,610 sq. km

LANGUAGES: Arabic, French

MAIN RELIGION: Islam

CURRENCY: Tunisian Dinar

LITERACY RATE: 82.7%

LIFE EXPECTANCY: 77.3 years

TIME ZONE: +1

TYPE OF GOVERNMENT: Parliamentary Republic

HEAD OF STATE: President Kais Saied **HEAD OF GOVT:** Prime Minister Kamel Madouri

GDP PER CAPITA: $10,600

POPULATION: 12,048,847

ISD CODE: 216 **INTERNET TLD:** .tn

The city of Kairouan in Tunisia is considered one of the most important cities for Islam after Mecca, Medina and Jerusalem.

Background: Turkey

TURKEY (TURKIYE)

LOCATION: West Asia/East Europe

CAPITAL: Ankara

AREA: 783,562 sq. km

LANGUAGE: Turkish

MAIN RELIGION: Islam

CURRENCY: Turkish Lira

LITERACY RATE: 96.7%

LIFE EXPECTANCY: 76.7 years

TIME ZONE: +3

TYPE OF GOVERNMENT: Presidential Republic

HEAD OF STATE AND GOVT: President Recep Tayyip Erdoğan

GDP PER CAPITA: $33,100

POPULATION: 84,119,531

ISD CODE: 90 **INTERNET TLD:** .tr

Istanbul, the largest city in Turkey by population, is the only city in the world built on two continents (Asia and Europe).

TURKMENISTAN

LOCATION: Central Asia

CAPITAL: Ashgabat

AREA: 488,100 sq. km

LANGUAGES: Turkmen, Russian

MAIN RELIGION: Islam

CURRENCY: Turkmenistani Manat

LITERACY RATE: 99.7%

LIFE EXPECTANCY: 72.4 years

TIME ZONE: +5

TYPE OF GOVERNMENT: Presidential Republic; authoritarian

HEAD OF STATE AND GOVT: President Serdar Berdimuhamedow

GDP PER CAPITA: $14,700

POPULATION: 5,744,151

ISD CODE: 993 **INTERNET TLD:** .tm

In Turkmenistan's Karakum Desert, the Darvaza Gas Crater ('The Burning Gates') gives off a glow that can be seen from kilometres away.

TUVALU

LOCATION: South Pacific Ocean

CAPITAL: Funafuti

AREA: 26 sq. km

LANGUAGES: Tuvaluan, English

MAIN RELIGION: Christianity (Church of Tuvalu)

CURRENCY: Tuvaluan Dollar, Australian Dollar

LITERACY RATE: Not available

LIFE EXPECTANCY: 69 years

TIME ZONE: +12

TYPE OF GOVERNMENT: Constitutional Monarchy and Parliamentary Democracy

HEAD OF STATE: King Charles III

HEAD OF GOVT: Prime Minister Feleti Penitala Teo

GDP PER CAPITA: $4,600

POPULATION: 11,733

ISD CODE: 688; **INTERNET TLD:** .tv

Eight of the nine islands of Tuvalu are inhabited; the name 'Tuvalu' means 'eight standing together'.

UGANDA

LOCATION: East-central Africa

CAPITAL: Kampala

AREA: 241,038 sq. km

LANGUAGES: English, Swahili

MAIN RELIGIONS: Christianity, Islam

CURRENCY: Ugandan Shilling

LITERACY RATE: 79%

LIFE EXPECTANCY: 69.7 years

TIME ZONE: +3

TYPE OF GOVERNMENT: Presidential Republic

HEAD OF STATE AND GOVT: President Yoweri Museveni

GDP PER CAPITA: $2,300

POPULATION: 49,283,041

ISD CODE: 256 **INTERNET TLD:** .ug

There are large reserves of crude oil and natural gas in Uganda that are still largely untapped. The largest export is coffee.

UKRAINE

LOCATION: Eastern Europe

CAPITAL: Kiev

AREA: 603,550 sq. km

LANGUAGES: Ukrainian, Russian

MAIN RELIGION: Christianity (Ukrainian Orthodox Church)

CURRENCY: Hryvnia

LITERACY RATE: 100%

LIFE EXPECTANCY: 70.5 years

TIME ZONE: +2

TYPE OF GOVERNMENT: Semi-presidential Republic

HEAD OF STATE: President Volodymyr Zelenskyy **HEAD OF GOVT:** Prime Minister Denys Shmyhal

GDP PER CAPITA: $10,700

POPULATION: 35,661,826

ISD CODE: 380 **INTERNET TLD:** .ua

The town called Rakhiv and the village of Dilove near Rakhiv are two of the contenders for the geographical centre of Europe.

UNITED ARAB EMIRATES

LOCATION: Middle East

CAPITAL: Abu Dhabi

AREA: 83,600 sq. km

LANGUAGE: Arabic

MAIN RELIGION: Islam

CURRENCY: UAE Dirham

LITERACY RATE: 98.1%

LIFE EXPECTANCY: 79.9 years

TIME ZONE: +4

TYPE OF GOVERNMENT: Federation of Monarchies

HEAD OF STATE: President Mohammed bin Zayed Al Nahyan **HEAD OF GOVT:** Prime Minister Mohammed bin Rashid Al Maktoum

GDP PER CAPITA: $74,900

POPULATION: 10,032,213

ISD CODE: 971 **INTERNET TLD:** .ae

If you've ever dreamed of walking up to an ATM and withdrawing a gold bar, then head to Dubai, UAE, where you can find such a machine.

COUNTRIES

UNITED KINGDOM

LOCATION: West Europe

CAPITAL: London

AREA: 243,610 sq. km

LANGUAGE: English

MAIN RELIGION: Christianity

CURRENCY: Pound Sterling

LITERACY RATE: 99%

LIFE EXPECTANCY: 82.2 years

TIME ZONE: +0

TYPE OF GOVERNMENT: Parliamentary Constitutional Monarchy

HEAD OF STATE: King Charles III **HEAD OF GOVT:** Prime Minister Keir Starmer

GDP PER CAPITA: $47,600

POPULATION: 68,459,055

ISD CODE: 44 **INTERNET TLD:** .uk

The United Kingdom was the first country in the world to use postage stamps.

UNITED STATES OF AMERICA

LOCATION: North America

CAPITAL: Washington DC

AREA: 9,833,517 sq. km

LANGUAGES: English, Spanish

MAIN RELIGION: Christianity

CURRENCY: US Dollar

LITERACY RATE: 99%

LIFE EXPECTANCY: 80.9 years

TIME ZONE: –3 to –10

TYPE OF GOVERNMENT: Constitutional Federal Republic

HEAD OF STATE AND GOVT: President Joseph R. Biden, Jr

GDP PER CAPITA: $64,600

POPULATION: 341,963,408

ISD CODE: 1 **INTERNET TLD:** .us

The USA is the only country to have ever used nuclear weapons.

URUGUAY

LOCATION: Southern South America

CAPITAL: Montevideo

AREA: 176,215 sq. km

LANGUAGES: Spanish, Portunol

MAIN RELIGION: Christianity

CURRENCY: Uruguayan Peso

LITERACY RATE: 98.8%

LIFE EXPECTANCY: 78.9 years

TIME ZONE: –3

TYPE OF GOVERNMENT: Presidential Republic

HEAD OF STATE AND GOVT: President Luis Lacalle Pou

GDP PER CAPITA: $24,400

POPULATION: 3,425,330

ISD CODE: 598 **INTERNET TLD:** .uy

Uruguay has the world's longest national anthem (six minutes). Greece actually has the longest one, but generally uses a shorter version.

Background: United Kingdom

UZBEKISTAN

LOCATION: Central Asia

CAPITAL: Tashkent

AREA: 447,400 sq. km

LANGUAGES: Uzbek, Russian

MAIN RELIGION: Islam

CURRENCY: Uzbekistani Som

LITERACY RATE: 100%

LIFE EXPECTANCY: 76.2 years

TIME ZONE: +5

TYPE OF GOVERNMENT: Presidential Republic

HEAD OF STATE: President Shavkat Miromonovich Mirziyoyev **HEAD OF GOVT:** Prime Minister Aripov Abdulla Nigmatovich

GDP PER CAPITA: $8,100

POPULATION: 36,520,593

ISD CODE: 998 **INTERNET TLD:** .uz

Uzbekistan has the fourth largest gold deposits in the world. The country mines 80 tonnes of gold every year.

VANUATU

LOCATION: South Pacific Ocean

CAPITAL: Port Vila

AREA: 12,189 sq. km

LANGUAGES: Bislama, English

MAIN RELIGION: Christianity

CURRENCY: Vanuatu Vatu

LITERACY RATE: 89.1%

LIFE EXPECTANCY: 75.7 years

TIME ZONE: +11

TYPE OF GOVERNMENT: Parliamentary Republic

HEAD OF STATE: President Nikenike Vurobaravu **HEAD OF GOVT:** Prime Minister Charlot Salwai

GDP PER CAPITA: $2,800

POPULATION: 318,007

ISD CODE: 678 **INTERNET TLD:** .vu

Vanuatu is an archipelago consisting of approximately eighty-two islands of volcanic origin.

VATICAN CITY

LOCATION: Southern Europe (a city state in Rome, Italy)

CAPITAL: Vatican City

AREA: 0.44 sq. km

LANGUAGES: Italian, Latin, French

MAIN RELIGION: Christianity

CURRENCY: Euro

LITERACY RATE: 100%

LIFE EXPECTANCY: Not available

TIME ZONE: +1

TYPE OF GOVERNMENT: Ecclesiastical Elective Monarchy

HEAD OF STATE: Pope Francis **HEAD OF GOVT:** President of the Pontifical Commission for Vatican City State Fernando Vérgez Alzaga

GDP PER CAPITA: Not applicable

POPULATION: 1,000

ISD CODE: 379 **INTERNET TLD:** .va

Vatican City is the smallest country in the world by both area and population. St Peter's Basilica in Vatican City is the largest church in the world.

Background: Vatican City

VENEZUELA

LOCATION: Northern South America

CAPITAL: Caracas

AREA: 912,050 sq. km

LANGUAGE: Spanish

MAIN RELIGION: Christianity

CURRENCY: Bolivar Soberano

LITERACY RATE: 97.5%

LIFE EXPECTANCY: 74.5 years

TIME ZONE: –4

TYPE OF GOVERNMENT: Federal Presidential Republic

HEAD OF STATE AND GOVT: President Nicolás Maduro Moros

GDP PER CAPITA: $7,704

POPULATION: 31,250,306

ISD CODE: 58 **INTERNET TLD:** .ve

The world's highest uninterrupted waterfall, Angel Falls, is in Venezuela. Its height is 979 m (3,212 ft).

VIETNAM

LOCATION: South-east Asia

CAPITAL: Hanoi

AREA: 331,210 sq. km

LANGUAGES: Vietnamese, English

MAIN RELIGIONS: Buddhism, Christianity

CURRENCY: Vietnamese Dong

LITERACY RATE: 95.8%

LIFE EXPECTANCY: 76.1 years

TIME ZONE: +7

TYPE OF GOVERNMENT: Communist state

HEAD OF STATE: President To Lam
HEAD OF GOVT: Prime Minister Pham Minh Chinh

GDP PER CAPITA: $11,400

POPULATION: 105,758,975

ISD CODE: 84
INTERNET TLD: .vn

Vietnam is the world's largest producer of cashew nuts and black pepper.

YEMEN

LOCATION: South-west Asia

CAPITAL: Ataq city (interim capital)

AREA: 527,968 sq. km

LANGUAGE: Arabic

MAIN RELIGION: Islam

CURRENCY: Yemeni Rial

LITERACY RATE: 70.1%

LIFE EXPECTANCY: 68.2 years

TIME ZONE: +3

TYPE OF GOVERNMENT: Transitional

HEAD OF STATE: Chairman of the Presidential Leadership Council Rashad al-Alimi **HEAD OF GOVT:** Prime Minister Ahmed Awad bin Mubarak

GDP PER CAPITA: $2,500

POPULATION: 32,140,443

ISD CODE: 967 **INTERNET TLD:** .ye

The *Dracaena cinnabari* or the dragon blood tree, a uniquely umbrella-shaped tree, grows in the Yemeni island of Socotra. It gets its name from its dark red resin.

Background: Zambia

COUNTRIES

ZAMBIA

LOCATION: Southern Africa

CAPITAL: Lusaka

AREA: 752,618 sq. km

LANGUAGES: English, Bemba, Nyanja

MAIN RELIGIONS: Christianity, Islam

CURRENCY: Zambian Kwacha

LITERACY RATE: 86.7%

LIFE EXPECTANCY: 66.9 years

TIME ZONE: +2

TYPE OF GOVERNMENT: Presidential Republic

HEAD OF STATE AND GOVT: President Hakainde Hichilema

GDP PER CAPITA: $3,400

POPULATION: 20,799,116

ISD CODE: 260

INTERNET TLD: .zm

***Termitomyces titanicus*, the largest edible mushroom in the world, is found in Zambia. Its cap is about 1 m (3.3 ft) in diameter.**

ZIMBABWE

LOCATION: Southern Africa

CAPITAL: Harare

AREA: 390,757 sq. km

LANGUAGES: English, Shona, Ndebele

MAIN RELIGIONS: Christianity, indigenous faiths

CURRENCY: Zimbabwe Dollar

LITERACY RATE: 89.7%

LIFE EXPECTANCY: 67.2 years

TIME ZONE: +2

TYPE OF GOVERNMENT: Presidential Republic

HEAD OF STATE AND GOVT: President Emmerson Mnangagwa

GDP PER CAPITA: $2,200

POPULATION: 17,150,352

ISD CODE: 263 **INTERNET TLD:** .zw

Background: Zimbabwe

Lake Kariba in Zimbabwe, constructed on the River Zambezi, is one of the largest man-made lakes in the world.

CHANGING Shapes of Nations

THE country that was called Yugoslavia was divided into seven countries in the 1990s.

1. Bosnia and Herzegovina
2. Croatia
3. Kosovo*
4. Macedonia
5. Montenegro
6. Serbia
7. Slovenia

When the Soviet Union broke up in 1991, these were the independent countries it was divided into:

1. Armenia 2. Azerbaijan 3. Belarus 4. Estonia 5. Georgia 6. Kazakhstan 7. Kyrgyzstan 8. Latvia 9. Lithuania 10. Moldova 11. Russia 12. Tajikistan 13. Turkmenistan 14. Ukraine 15. Uzbekistan

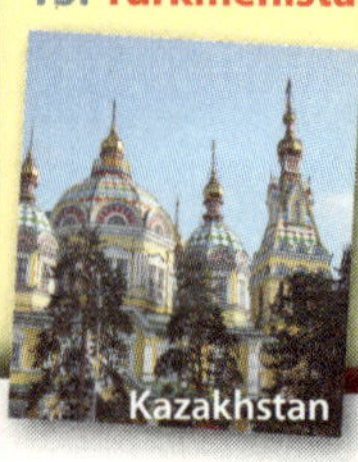

Kazakhstan

Lithuania

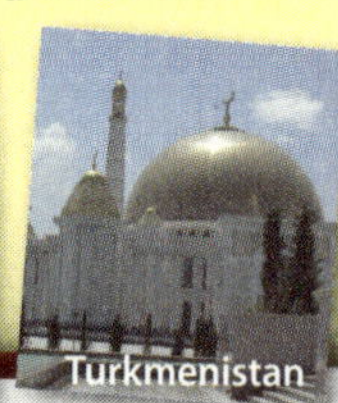

Turkmenistan

*The Republic of Kosovo declared its independence in 2008, and is partially recognised. Serbia still claims it as part of its territory. It is administered by the UN.

SUPERLATIVES

Fastest Animal (land) Cheetah (speed: 80–120 km/h)

Largest Animal (land) African elephant (length: 2.5–4 m/ 8.2–13 ft; weight: 2.5–7 tonnes)

Largest Animal (sea) Blue whale (length: 25–32 m/ 82–105 ft; weight: 170 tonnes)

Slowest Animal Sloth (speed: 1.8–2.4 m/6–8 ft per minute)

Largest Archipelago Malay Archipelago > 25,000 islands (Indonesia and Malaysia)

Tallest Animal (land) Giraffe (height: 4.2–5.7 m/ 14–19 ft; weight 794–1,900 kg)

Largest Bay Hudson Bay, Canada (shoreline: 12,268 km)

Fastest Bird (dive) Peregrine Falcon (length: 36–49 cm/ 14.2–19.3 in; speed: 300 km/h)

Largest Bird Ostrich (length: 2.1–2.7 m/7–9 ft; weight: 90–130 kg)

Smallest Bird Hummingbird (length: 7.5–13 cm/3–5 in)

Longest Bridge Danyang–Kunshan Grand Bridge, China (length: 165 km/541,338 ft)

Tallest Building (office) Burj Khalifa, Dubai, UAE (height: 829.8 m/ 2,722 ft)

Busiest Canal (ship) Kiel Canal (linking North Sea at Brunsbuttel to Baltic Sea at Kiel–Holtenau) (length: 98.26 km)

Highest Capital City La Paz, Bolivia (altitude: 3,640 m/ 11,942 ft)

Longest Canal (ship) Suez Canal (linking Red Sea and the Mediterranean) (length: 193.3 km)

Largest Cinema Kinepolis-Madrid Ciudad de la Imagen megaplex, Spain (seating capacity: 9,200; screens: 25)

Smallest Country Vatican City (0.44 sq. km)

Highest City La Rinconada, Peru; (altitude: 5,100 m/16,728 ft)

Most Populated City Tokyo, Japan (est. population: 37,115,035)

* Twenty-foot Equivalent Unit

Largest Continent

Asia (area: 44.58 million sq. km)

Smallest Continent

Australia (area: 7.741 million sq. km)

Largest Country

Russia (area: 17,098,242 sq. km)

Largest Coral Formation

The Great Barrier Reef, Australia (stretching over 2,300 km)

Longest Corridor

Ramanathaswamy Temple, Rameswaram, Tamil Nadu, India (length: 1,220 m/4,002 ft)

Most Populated Country

India (est. population, 2024: 1,452,787,348)

Largest Dam

Three Gorges Dam, China (over River Yangtze; length: 2,309 m/7,575.46 ft; height: 185 m/606.96 ft)

Largest Desert

Antarctic Polar Desert, Antarctica (area: 14,244,935 sq. km)

Biggest Dome

Singapore National Stadium, Singapore (diameter: 312 m/1023 ft)

Largest Delta

Ganga–Brahmaputra Delta, Bay of Bengal (area: 105,641 sq. km)

Longest Epic

The Mahabharata (over 200,000 verse lines)

Largest Flower

Rafflesia arnoldii (diameter: 1 m/3.3 ft)

Tallest Geyser (active)

Steamboat Geyser, Yellowstone National Park, USA (height: 2,316 m/7,598 ft)

Largest Gorge

Grand Canyon, USA (average depth: 1,584 m/5,200 ft)

Largest Gulf

Gulf of Mexico (shoreline: 5,000 km)

Deepest Lake

Lake Baikal, Siberia, Russia (max. depth: 1,642 m/5,387 ft)

Largest Island

Greenland, Kingdom of Denmark (area: 2,166,086 sq. km)

Smallest Ocean

Arctic Ocean (surface area: 14 million sq. km)

Largest Lake (inland waterbody)

Caspian Sea (surface area: 371,000 sq. km)

Largest Lake (freshwater)
Lake Superior, USA and Canada (surface area: 82,000 sq. km)

Biggest Library
The British Library, UK (catalogued items: 170–200 million)

Most Venomous Animal
Box Jellyfish (its sting can cause death in humans in minutes)

Highest Melting Point
Tungsten (3,422°C)

Tallest Minaret (freestanding)
Qutub Minar, Delhi, India (height: 72.5 m/238 ft)

Tallest Minaret
Djamaa el Djazair, Algeria (height: 265 m/870 ft)

Longest Mountain Range (above water)
Andes, South America (length: 7,242 km)

Highest Mountain Peak
Mt Everest, Himalayan mountain range (height: 8,848 m/29,029 ft)

Biggest Museum
The Louvre, Paris, France (area: 72,735 sq. m/782,910 sq. ft)

Deepest Ocean Point
Challenger Deep (Mariana Trench, Pacific Ocean) (depth: 11,033.76 m/36,200 ft)

Largest Ocean
The Pacific (surface area: 361,132,000 sq. km)

Largest Palace
Forbidden City, Beijing, China (area: 720,000 sq. m/7,750,015 sq. ft)

Largest Peninsula
Arabian Peninsula (3,250,000 sq. km)

Driest Place*
Arica, Chile (average annual rainfall: 0.76 mm/0.03 in.)

Coldest Place (region)
Antarctica (lowest recorded temperature: –89.2°C; average annual temperature: –50°C.)

Highest Plateau
Tibetan Plateau (altitude: 4,500 m/ 14,800 ft)

Longest Mountain Range (underwater)
Mid-Atlantic Ridge (length: around 16,000 km) in the Atlantic Ocean

Railway Station with Most Platforms
Grand Central Terminal, New York, USA; (platforms: 44; area: 190,000 sq. m/2,045,143 sq. ft)

Longest Platform (railway)
Gorakhpur Station, Uttar Pradesh, India (length:1,366.33 m/4,482.7 ft)

** Outside of polar regions*

WORLD

Longest Railway Route
Trans-Siberian Railway (length: 9,289 km)

Longest River
Nile, Egypt (length: 6,650 km)

Largest River (volume)
The Amazon, South America (average discharge: 219,000 cubic m/sec)

Longest Earthen Dam
Hirakud Dam, Odisha, India (length: 25.79 km)

Largest River Basin
Amazon Basin, South America (area: 7,000,000 sq. km)

Largest Seabird
Wandering albatross (wingspan: 3.3–3.6 m/ 10.83–11.81 ft)

Rainiest Spot
Mawsynram, Meghalaya, India (average annual rainfall: 11,873 mm/467 in.)

Largest Stadium
Narendra Modi Stadium, India (seating capacity: 132,000)

Tallest Statue
Statue of Unity, Gujarat, India (height: 182 m/597 ft)

Tallest Dam
Jinping–I Dam, Sichuan, China (height: 305 m/1,000 ft)

Broadest Strait
Davis Strait, Greenland and Canada (length: 950 km)

Longest Strait
Strait of Malacca (Andaman Sea–South China Sea) (length: 800 km)

Longest Tunnel (canal)
Delaware Aqueduct, New York, USA (length: 137 km)

Longest Tunnel (railway)
Gotthard Base Tunnel, Switzerland (length: 57 km)

Longest Tunnel (road)
Laerdal Tunnel, Norway (length: 24.5 km)

Highest Volcano
Nevados Ojos del Salado, Andes, Argentina–Chile (height: 6,893 m/22,615 ft)

Largest Volcano
Pūhāhonu, Hawaii, USA (volume: 150,000 cubic km)

Highest Waterfall
Angel Falls, Venezuela (height: 979 m/3,212 ft)

Longest Wall
Great Wall of China, Beijing, China (length: 21,196 km)

Largest LED Screen (sphere)
The MSG Sphere, Las Vegas, USA (total screen area of approximately 180,000 sq. ft)

5 EARTH

Earth is 4.54 billion years old. From outer space, it looks like a huge blue marble ball with white swirls and areas of brown, yellow, green and white. It is the only planet with liquid water on the surface.

EARTH NUMBERS

Diameter from North to South Pole
12,714 km (7,900 miles)

Diameter from equator
12,756 km (7,926 miles)

Earth's rotation per hour
15 degrees

Equatorial circumference
40,030.2 km

Surface Area
510,064,472 km^2

Density
5.513g/cm^3

Volume
1,083,206,916,846 km^3

DAYS ON EARTH ARE BECOMING LONGER: Around 4.5 billion years ago, when Earth was formed, the average day is speculated to be approximately six hours long. By 260 million years ago, this had increased to 21.9 hours. Today, as we know, a day is 24 hours long. However, it is constantly increasing by 1.7 milliseconds per day.

EARTH IS RECYCLABLE: The tectonic forces present within the Earth moves the land upward and downward, altering the layers of crust, pushing it further to the magma-filled layer of the Earth. Eventually, the crust melts due to the heat and emerges back as crust through the volcanic eruptions of lava.

EARTH'S ROTATION IS SLOWING DOWN: Earth's spin is known to be slowing down by 17 milliseconds per hundred hours. Due to this, our days will lengthen eventually. However, since the rate of rotation is so slow, it is said that our days would increase to 25 hours only in around 140 million years.

LAND: Earth comprises 32.1 per cent iron, 30.1 per cent oxygen, 15.1 per cent silicon and 13.9 per cent magnesium. Iron is the dominant element in the Earth's core. A sample from there would have 88 per cent of iron. Additionally, Earth's crust is made of 47 per cent oxygen.

AIR: Earth's atmosphere is made of 78 per cent nitrogen, 21 per cent oxygen and 1 per cent other elements, making it conducive to sustaining life.

WATER: The larger part of Earth is covered by water. It exists in three forms: solid, liquid and gas. As a solid, it is found on mountaintops in the form of snow or glaciers. It is present in rivers, oceans, streams as a liquid and as water vapour (or a gaseous form) in the atmosphere.

KNOW YOUR PLANET

Unlike gas planets like Jupiter, Earth is one of the four solar terrestrial planets (planets with a rocky body, as opposed to gas).

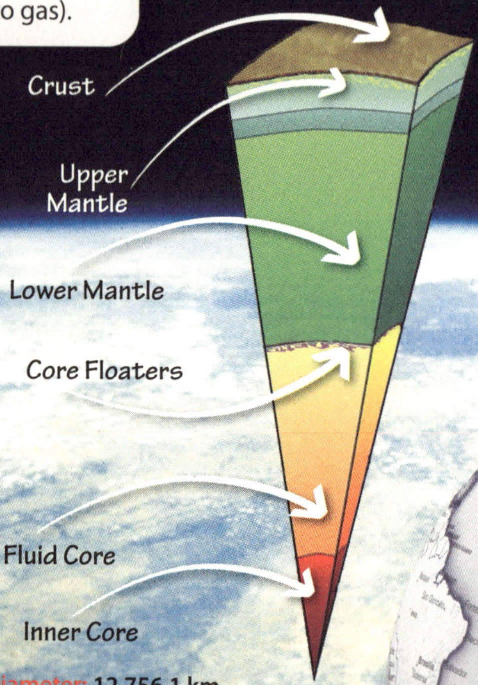

CHEMICAL COMPOSITION

The mass of Earth is approximately 5.9722×10^{24} kg. Earth is made up of nearly a hundred elements, of which oxygen, silicon, aluminium, iron, calcium, sodium, potassium and nickel are the main ones.

Diameter: 12,756.1 km
Distance from the Sun: 152 million km (at aphelion); average: 149.6 million km
Temperature: Maximum: 57.7°C; Minimum: –89.1°C

SHAPE

If you take an orange and squish it at the top and bottom, it will bulge out towards the centre. In a similar way, Earth is a sphere slightly squished at the poles and bulging at the equator. So, if you were to draw a line across the equator and a line through the poles, the line across the equator would actually be 43 km longer than the one through the poles. Therefore, Earth is not a perfect sphere, and is instead what is termed an 'oblate spheroid'. This shape is caused by the rotation of Earth.

INTERNAL STRUCTURE

PLATE TECTONICS

The outer layer of Earth, called the **lithosphere**, is separated into vast pieces known as the tectonic plates, from 80 km to 400 km thick, which drift atop the soft, underlying mantle. They move both sideways, and up and down, at an estimated speed of 1 cm to 10 cm per year. Most of Earth's seismic activity (volcanoes and earthquakes) occurs at the boundaries where the plates interact.

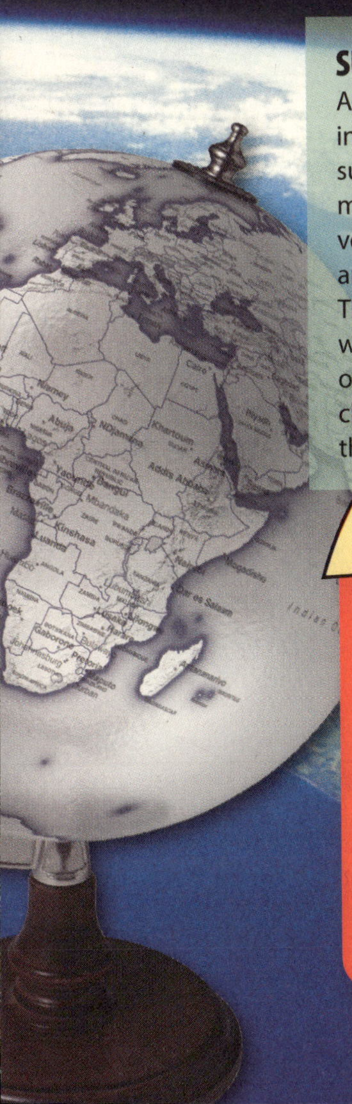

SURFACE

About 70.8 per cent of Earth's surface is covered in water. There are many physical features submerged under it, such as the longest mountain ranges (the Mid-Atlantic Ridge), volcanoes, trenches, canyons, oceanic plateaus and plains. This is known as the **hydrosphere**. The remaining 29.2 per cent of Earth is covered with mountains, deserts, plains, plateaus and other features. This surface undergoes constant changes due to the effects of the movement of the tectonic plates and erosion.

> **"Seventy-five per cent of Earth's atmosphere is found within the first 11 km above the planet's surface. The outermost layer (the exosphere) is the largest, extending from the top of the thermosphere (about 700 km above sea level) to about 10,000 km. It merges with outer space, where there is no atmosphere."**

GEOLOGIC TIMELINE

PHANEROZOIC EON

540 mya–today

'Visible Life': organisms with skeletons or hard shells

MESOZOIC ERA

'The Age of Reptiles'

248–65 mya

Cretaceous Period
146–65 mya

Lower
First flowering plants, primates, crocodilians

Upper
Extinction of dinosaurs

CENOZOIC ERA

'The Age of Mammals'

65 mya–now

Quaternary Period
'The Age of Man'
(1.8 mya–now)

Holocene Epoch
(11,000 years ago –now): Human civilization

Pleistocene Epoch
(1.8–0.011 mya): (Last Ice Age) First human (*Homo sapiens*); mammoths, mastodons, giant ground sloths; mass extinction

Tertiary Period
65–1.8 mya

Neogene Period
24-1.8 mya

Pliocene Epoch
(5–1.8 mya): First hominids (Australopithecines); megalodons; modern whales

Miocene Epoch
(24–5 mya): More mammals (horses, dogs, bears); modern birds; apes and monkeys

Palaeogene Period
(65–24 mya)

Oligocene Epoch
(38–24 mya): Small extinction; new mammals (pigs, deer, cats, rhinos, tapirs); grasses common

Eocene Epoch
(54–38 mya): Mammals abound; rodents, primitive whales appear

Palaeocene Epoch
(65–54 mya): First large mammals; primitive primates

Jurassic Period
(208–146 mya): Dinosaurs diversify; first birds, ferns, gingkos, conifers

Triassic Period
(248–208 mya): First dinosaurs, first mammals; many molluscs, reptiles; small-scale extinction

Permian Period
(280–248 mya): Reptiles and amphibians dominate; first bugs and beetles; major extinctions

Pennsylvanian Period
(325–280 mya): First reptiles; many ferns; cockroaches and mayflies

Carboniferous Period
(360–280 mya): Coal swamps, corals, seed ferns, other plants; amphibians common

Mississippian Period
(360–325 mya): Seed ferns; first winged insects

Devonian Period
(408–360 mya): First amphibians; many coral reefs

Silurian Period
438–408 mya: First vascular land plants; jawed fishes

PALAEOZOIC ERA
540–248 mya

Ordovician Period
(505–438 mya): Primitive plants; first corals, fishes, seaweed, fungi, bivalves

EARTH IS FORMED 4.54 BILLION YEARS AGO

Cambrian Period
(540–500 mya): First fishes, marine invertebrates, like shellfish

PROTEROZOIC EON

2.5 bya–540 mya: First multicelled animals, including sponges

Vendian/ Ediacaran Period
(600–540 mya)

ARCHEOZOIC EON

3.9–2.5 bya: First life forms: one-celled organisms; algae; bacteria appear in sea

HADEAN EON

4.6–3.9 mya: The solidifying of Earth's continental and oceanic crusts

Note: mya: million years ago; bya: billion years ago

THE BIG SEVEN

Earth's land surface is divided broadly into continents and there are many theories defining them. The most accepted definition for a 'continent' would be 'a large, continuous, discrete mass of land, separated from others by expanses of water'. Conventionally, there are seven continents: Asia, Africa, Europe, North America, South America, Australia/Oceania (Australia, New Zealand and islands of South-east Asia) and Antarctica.

NORTH AMERICA

Area: 21,330,000 sq. km; **Percentage of Earth's landmass:** 16.5%; **Population:** 613,149,877; **Percentage of world population*:** 7.51%; **Density of population per sq. km:** 29

SOUTH AMERICA

Area: 17,461,112 sq. km; **Percentage of Earth's landmass:** 12%; **Population:** 435,611,301; **Percentage of world population:** 5.34%; **Density of population per sq. km:** 25

ANTARCTICA

Area: 13,720,000 sq. km; **Percentage of Earth's landmass:** 9.2%; **Population:** Summer 2024 (December to February): 4,713, Winter 2024, (June to August): 1,056; **Percentage of world population:** 0.00002%; **Density of population per sq. km:** 0.00003

EUROPE

Area: 22,134,710 sq. km; **Percentage of Earth's landmass:** 6.8%; **Population:** 743,230,911; **Percentage of world population:** 9.11%; **Density of population per sq. km:** 34

ASIA

Area: 44,614,000 sq. km; **Percentage of Earth's landmass:** 29.5%; **Population:** 4,950,360,147; **Percentage of world population:** 61.84%; **Density of population per sq. km:** 155

AUSTRALIA/ OCEANIA

Area: 8,486,460 sq. km; **Percentage of Earth's landmass:** 5.9%; **Population:** 46,502,478; **Percentage of world population:** 0.57%; **Density of population per sq. km:** 5

AFRICA

Area: 29,648,481 sq. km; **Percentage of Earth's landmass:** 20.4%; **Population:** 1,515,135,613; **Percentage of world population: 18.93%; Density of population per sq. km:** 51

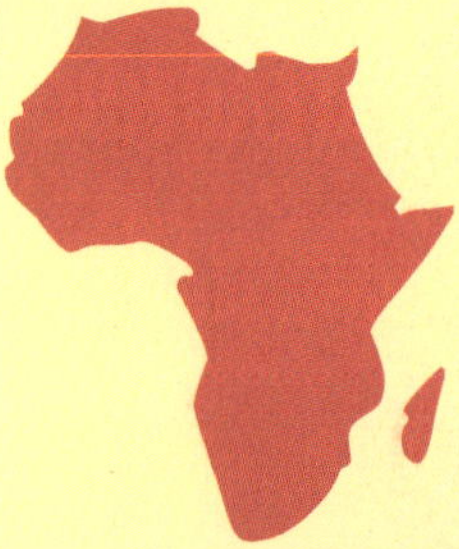

*Note: *Population figures are from 2020; percentages may not add up to 100 due to rounding off of numbers.*

Warmest year on record

NASA's investigation shows that the average surface temperature of Earth in 2023 was the warmest on record. The world is much warmer now than 100 years ago, as humans keep releasing record amounts of greenhouse gases like carbon dioxide into the atmosphere. But at the beginning of 2023, no one expected the year to be the hottest year on record because of the complicated way in which the Earth's climate behaves. During the first few months of the year, only a small number of days broke air temperature records. But the world then went on a remarkable, almost unbroken streak of daily records in the second half of 2023. Last year was about 1.48°C warmer than the long-term average before humans started burning large amounts of fossil fuels.

Heatwaves all over the world

Heatwaves (prolonged period of abnormally hot weather) have affected certain parts of the world this summer, including India, which has been affected the worst. Temperatures in New Delhi exceeded 53°C in late May of 2024 – the capital's highest temperature on record. It is also considered the country's hottest summer in 120 years. The other regions affected include Mexico, southern United States, Central America, Greece, Mecca and South-east Asia. These heatwaves have serious impacts on health, and a substantial amount of people have died from heat strokes.

Dholavira

Discovery of the crater that possibly wiped out the Harappan civilization

A new study finds that a crater in Gujarat may have been caused by the largest meteorite to strike the planet in the last 50,000 years. At the time of impact, this meteorite could have caused a massive fireball, shockwaves and wildfires that would have spread through the area where people from the Indus Valley Civilization lived thousands of years ago.

Scientists have long suspected that the Luna structure (named after the small settlement of Luna nearby) could be a meteorite crater. A new study of the soil near the crater has reinforced the theory of the meteorite origin of the structure, revealing large amounts of iron. At the time, Indus Valley was a powerful civilization on par with Egyptian and Mesopotamian, with its own writing, art and science. Today, at least 1,000 Harappan settlements are known to exist. One of the largest settlements, Dholavira, is located just outside the Luna structure. In 1900 BC, the Harappan civilization began a rapid decline. By 1700 BC, almost all cities had been abandoned. Therefore, the influence of a powerful meteorite impact on these events cannot be ruled out.

Dinosaur that had huge horns has been named after Norse god Loki

Scientists revealed in June that the *Lokiceratops rangiformis* is an entirely new species of dinosaur previously undiscovered by palaeontologists. It was a huge plant-eating dinosaur with an enormous set of horns. That's how it gets its name 'Loki' from the Norse trickster god who used weapons that were similar to the dinosaur's curved horns; '*rangiformis*' comes from the dinosaur's asymmetric (non-identical) horns. It is thought to have been around 6.7 metres long and to have weighed 5 tonnes. Scientists think that the *Lokiceratops* lived around 78 million years ago, in a swampy area of land in what is today the northern part of the United States, near Canada. Its fossil had been discovered in Montana in the US, in 2019, and is currently on display at the Museum of Evolution in Denmark.

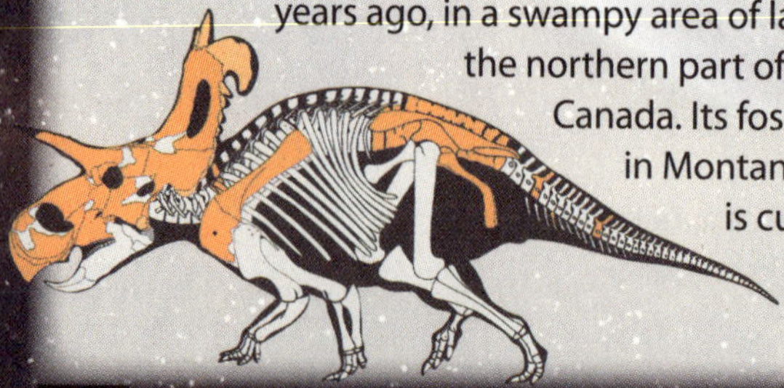

Hydrothermal vents discovered in the dark heart of the Pacific Ocean

A research mission carried out – with the help of undersea robot and a human-occupied submersible – deep in the floor of the eastern Pacific Ocean uncovered new hydrothermal vents. Five new deep-sea hydrothermal vent sites were located on the seafloor at a depth of 2,550 metres (8,366 feet). The East Pacific Rise tectonic plates are continually splitting apart. That is why the vents, which spit fluids hotter than 300°C, have appeared.

Scientists have learned that this location is responsible for 75 per cent of the volcanic activity in the world. The abundance of minerals found in hydrothermal vents supplies the energy needed by animal life to support thriving ecosystems. The finding fundamentally alters our knowledge of the conditions necessary for life to exist on Earth possibly elsewhere in our solar system.

Coral bleaching and its effect on ocean circulation

Many of the world's largest coral reefs are experiencing widespread bleaching and deaths, and they could possibly disappear in the near future. Increased warming of both hot and cold ocean currents shows that horizontal mixing of tropical heat to the poles is accelerating, and that vertical mixing with cold deep water is slowing down, which will cause sea surface temperature to increase even more rapidly.

Corals that have thin tissue layers, branching growth forms and quick growth rates seem to be the most vulnerable to bleaching; if they are severely bleached, they typically perish. Massive, slow-growing corals with thick tissue seem less sensitive and usually bounce back from all but the most extreme situations. As a result, bleaching causes some species to be removed from reefs on a selective basis and can significantly alter the geographic distribution of coral species and the structures of reef communities. Changes in ocean temperature and freshwater discharge have raised concerns that ocean thermohaline circulation (THC) may eventually stop. The ocean's circulation and upwelling patterns would be significantly altered by a slowdown of THC, which might have an impact on coral reef environments.

Prithvi weather-climate AI foundation model: A NASA and IBM collaboration

NASA and IBM have collaborated on a research project that supports a variety of weather and climate applications. This research project has led to the development of a new AI foundation model called the Prithvi weather-climate model. This model supports applications that include the identification and forecasting of extreme weather patterns and natural disasters, the development of targeted predictions based on localized observations, the enhancement of global climate simulations' spatial resolution down to the regional level and the advancement of the representation of the physical processes included in weather and climate models. Because of the model's architectural flexibility, the Prithvi weather-climate model can depict the intricate dynamics of atmospheric physics even in the absence of missing data. Without compromising on resolution, this fundamental model of weather and climate can be scaled to both global and regional locations.

New record holder for smallest dispersers of ingested seeds: Woodlice

Many plants offer fruit to animals so that they eat the seeds and leave them at a distant place after they have passed through the animal's digestive tract. For this to work, the seeds need to be small enough to actually pass through. Considering that seeds of some plants can be as small as dust particles, even bugs can disperse seeds they eat. The woodlice has set a new record for the smallest animal recorded to do so.

Woodlice sometimes destroy some of the seeds they eat, but with these findings, we know that it does not necessarily make them harmful to the ecosystem. Through the discovery, scientists are reevaluating the strategies for preserving diverse habitats that support a wide range of species, including those that were previously considered 'ecologically insignificant'. They also want to investigate if similar dispersal mechanisms exist for other plant species, because this possibility has been overlooked so far.

Amazon rainforest is experiencing a drought

One trigger for the drought is El Niño – a phenomenon where sea surface temperatures increase in the East Pacific Ocean, which affects global rainfall patterns, particularly in South America. But the main cause is climate change. And so one of our planet's most vital defences against global warming is itself being destroyed by climate change. The Amazon rainforest is described as the 'lungs of the planet' because it plays an important role in removing carbon dioxide from the atmosphere. It now faces the worst drought in at least half a century, which has disrupted ecosystems and has impacted millions of people who rely on rivers for transport, food and income. More frequent and intense droughts would test the Amazon's resilience which is already being challenged by deforestation, because around one-fifth of the rainforest has been lost over the last fifty years.

Noto earthquake in Japan

On 1 January 2024, around 4.10 p.m. local time in Japan, a 7.6 magnitude earthquake struck Suzu, located on the Noto Peninsula of Ishikawa Prefecture. It caused large waves, so officials urged people in coastal areas to move to higher ground; it also caused buildings to collapse, trapping several people under the rubble.
There were 230 confirmed deaths. Thousands of people spent the night in evacuation centres as the Japanese military handed out food, water and blankets to those forced to leave their homes. Due to blocked roads, humanitarian aid was sent to the peninsula using ships, while other isolated areas were accessed through helicopters. The Japanese government estimated the total cost of damage at US $17.6 billion.

Rare wild horses are back on Kazakhstan's Golden Steppe

The Przewalski's Horse is the last wild horse species on the planet. By the time they were discovered by Russian geographer Nikolai Przewalski in 1879, their habitat had been reduced to a small area of western Mongolia. Competition from livestock, human activity and changes to their environment had nearly wiped them out.

The species originated millennia ago from the steppes of Central Asia and was taken by researchers to Europe and North America in the nineteenth and twentieth centuries, where populations were established in zoos. Some of them ended up in zoos in Munich and Prague, and it is their descendants that have now been reintroduced in Kazakhstan. In early June, a Czech Army CASA aircraft landed in central Kazakhstan with four of these endangered animals on board. Tessa, Wespe, Umbra and Sary took an eighteen-hour flight from Berlin and a seven-hour truck ride to reach their new home. Two large paddocks of eighty hectares in size have been set up in Altyn Dala – the Kazakh name for the Golden Steppe. Before being released into the wild, they need to demonstrate that they are resistant to frost and parasites and can find food under the heavy snow that falls on the Golden Steppe in winter.

Zombie virus found

The melting Arctic 'permafrost' may start a new disease outbreak due to the release of ancient viruses that have been trapped in the ice for thousands of years. One virus sample was found to be 48,500 years old. The isolated viruses posed no threat to humans but pointed out the presence of genomic traces of poxviruses (associated with diseases like smallpox, which has been eradicated, and human monkeypox, which is a severe generalized infection involving organs such as the lungs) and herpesviruses (associated with herpes, which causes sores or blisters in or around the mouth or genitals, alongside other symptoms).

Escalating temperatures caused by global warming have led to the thawing of previously frozen ice, thus releasing these 'zombie viruses'.

Did you know?

The permafrost, covering a fifth of the Northern Hemisphere, has acted as a time capsule, preserving extinct creatures' remains, along with ancient viruses.

6 SPACE

Space has always been called the final frontier, but its exploration by humans has revealed many of its secrets. Here are just a few, while several more are still clouded in mystery!

The highest mountain known to us so far is on an asteroid called Vesta. Measuring a tremendous **22 km** in height, it is three times taller than Mount Everest!

99 per cent of the mass of the solar system is the Sun.

Consider yourself lucky that you have ground beneath your feet on Earth! You wouldn't be able to walk on Jupiter, Saturn, Uranus or Neptune because these planets have no solid surface!

Humans have sent spacecraft to all of the planets in our solar system – Mercury, Venus, Earth, Mars, Jupiter, Saturn, Uranus and Neptune – as well as two dwarf planets, Pluto and Ceres.

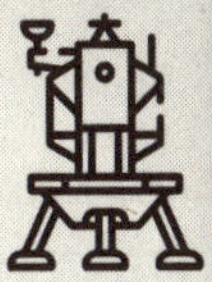

The huge canyon system on Mars, known as Valles Marineris, is **4,000** km long, more than **10 times** longer than the Grand Canyon on Earth. Early spacecrafts to Mars did not spot it because they flew over other parts of the planet. It was finally noticed by the global mapping mission Mariner 9 in 1971.

Currently, the biggest star known to us is called UY Scuti. This red supergiant star is located **9,500** light years away in the Scutum constellation. It is more than **1,708** times the size of the Sun. The star with the highest mass is RMC 136a1, whose mass equals **315** Suns.

It has been estimated that the Milky Way will collide with the Andromeda galaxy, our closest neighbour in the galaxy, in around 4.5 billion years. This is likely to result in a vast elliptical galaxy.

The planet Neptune was discovered in 1846, but since then it has not yet completed one full orbit around the Sun. It takes **165** years to complete one such orbit!

LIFE WITH SPACE TOURISM: TO INFINITY AND BEYOND

The night sky has always been a thing of fascination for people, a glimpse into the endless mystery that is space. Some of its mysteries began to be answered in October 1957, when the USSR launched its first artificial satellite named Sputnik 1 to orbit Earth, unlocking a world of space exploration. With the passing years, technological advances made it possible for existing research to broaden its horizons and learn more about the endless universe. Hence, we saw more and more space travel, with satellites and humans crossing limits as far and wide as the Moon or interstellar space. Additionally, these advancements have let a more commercial side of space exploration to emerge and persist. It's no longer just a plot we read in science fiction books or the story we see unfold in movies or shows; rather, it's now part of our reality, as evident from the eight-day expedition Dennis Tito went on aboard the Soyuz TM-32/ISS EP-1 mission in 2001, as a space tourist.

Space tourism is space travel that people can go on for leisure. After Tito's 2001 journey to the International Space Station (ISS), seven space tourists contracted Space Adventures, the American company that Tito contacted, to let them accompany the crew from 2001 to 2009. After this, the market for space tourism grew as more private agencies ventured into this industry. There are two types of space tourism journeys that are available or will, most likely, be available in the near future:

- **Suborbital flights:** In space tourism, suborbital flights offer an experience of space travel without achieving a full orbit around Earth. These experiences typically involve a short, parabolic ascent towards the edge of space, allowing passengers to experience a few minutes of weightlessness as the vehicle reaches its highest point. Passengers then experience a descent back to Earth under the influence of gravity.

- **Orbital flights:** These flights reach Earth's orbit, allowing passengers to experience weightlessness for a longer duration and see the planet for an extended period when compared to suborbital flights.

Orbital missions also provide extended views of our planet, showcasing the marvellous curvature of Earth against the vast expanse of space.

Inspired in part by the case of Tito, as of 2024, there are four aerospace companies, headquartered in the US, who cater to tourists wanting to visit space and enjoy its majestic beauty with their own eyes:

VIRGIN GALACTIC: Founded by Richard Branson in 2004, Virgin Galactic is a British-American spaceflight company based in California with its operations running from New Mexico. It develops suborbital space shuttles and provides tourists the opportunity to visit space. Its suborbital space flights are known to take tourists approximately ninety km from Earth on board its VSS *Unity* spaceships. Each seat on board a Virgin Galactic spaceflight costs around US$450,000.

SPACEX: Founded by former Tesla chairman Elon Musk in 2002, SpaceX has opened the possibility of space tourism, working towards their goal of maintaining sustainable space travel and making life multiplanetary. The company's headquarters is based in California with its operations and launches located in Texas. It develops and manufactures its spaceflights and software in-house, while also providing services to take interested travellers for a multiple-day trip to space. There are four kinds of destinations available on their website: a three - to six-day low-Earth orbit, a ten-day journey to the ISS, a seven-day trip to the Moon and a journey to Mars.

BLUE ORIGIN: Founded by Amazon founder Jeff Bezos, Blue Origin is a private aerospace company focused on developing reusable suborbital launch vehicles for space tourism and space research. The company is based in Washington, while operating the launches from their Texas site called Launch Site One (LS1). It takes tourists on suborbital missions crossing the Kármán line, letting the people on board experience weightlessness while floating around the spacecraft. The mission functions for ten minutes from launch to landing. Aside from space tourism, Blue Origin is also currently contracted by NASA to develop the former's Blue Moon landing system for the latter's Artemis V mission for US$3.4 billion.

Did you know?
Thirty-year-old Gopi Thotakura became the first Indian space tourist on 19 May 2024 as he experienced space and weightlessness on board Blue Origin's seventh suborbital human spaceflight.

SPACE ADVENTURES: Founded by Eric Anderson in 1998, Space Adventures

HOW TO GET TICKETS

1. CHOOSE YOUR SPACE PROVIDER COMPANY: Research space tourism providers like Virgin Galactic, Blue Origin or SpaceX. Consider factors like the type of experience (suborbital vs. orbital flight), duration, cost and amenities offered.

2. RESERVE YOUR SEAT: Visit the chosen company's website or contact them directly for booking information. Be prepared for potential waitlists and upfront deposits.

3. TRAIN AND PREPARE FOR YOUR FLIGHT: Space tourism companies will provide specific training requirements and health checks. This may involve physical and mental fitness tests, familiarization with safety procedures and briefings on what to expect during the flight.

4. TAKE OFF TO THE COSMOS: Buckle up and prepare for an unforgettable launch experience. Depending on your chosen provider, you might experience weightlessness, witness the curvature of Earth or orbit the planet.

is a private company that offers its services in zero-gravity atmospheric flights, orbital flights with optional spacewalking for interested participants and other spaceflight-related events.

Aside from the economic benefit of space tourism, the programme is not without its challenges. Here are some of the challenges one may encounter:

Affordability: Space tourism is currently **very expensive**. Early flights have cost hundreds of thousands or even millions of dollars. Virgin Galactic has ticket prices ranging from US$50,000 to US$450,000 per seat. Blue Origin's ticket price is tailored to individual passengers based on a variety of factors. Hence, the space tourism industry only caters to a section of individuals.

Environmental impact: There are also **environmental concerns** about the pollution caused by space flights. Black carbon emissions, commonly known as soot produced from rocket fuel combustion, prove to be a major contributor towards climate change.

First in space

Squadron Leader **Rakesh Sharma** (b. 13 January 1949) flew aboard spacecraft Soyuz T-11 that was launched on 2 April 1984, as part of the Intercosmos programme and spent over seven days orbiting Earth. He was the first Indian to travel to space.

Dr Kalpana Chawla (1962–2003) from Karnal, Haryana, was an American cosmonaut who became the first woman of Indian origin in space onboard space shuttle Columbia that took off on 19 November 1997 on a sixteen-day scientific mission, along with five fellow astronauts. She returned to Cape Canaveral on 5 December 1997. In 2003, Chawla died in space along with six other crew members when the shuttle Columbia tragically disintegrated while re-entering Earth's atmosphere.

RAKESH SHARMA

DR KALPANA CHAWLA

First to land a Rover near the Lunar South Pole

With the thundering success of Chandrayaan-3, India became the first country in the world to land a rover on the south pole of the Moon. Chandrayaan-3 was launched on LVM3-M4 rocket on 14 July 2023 from the Satish Dhawan Space Centre in Sriharikota, Andhra Pradesh. The lander entered the lunar orbit on 5 August 2023 and in a thrilling countdown, it touched down on the lunar surface on 23 August 2023. This also made India the fourth country in the world after the erstwhile USSR, US and China to land on the Moon.

First 10 living organisms in space

Decades before humans successfully travelled into space, there were various other organisms that were sent to space.

	Organism	Rocket	Date
1.	Fruit Flies	V2	20 February 1947
2.	Moss	V2	1947
3.	Rhesus Monkey (Albert II)	V2	14 June 1949
4.	Mouse	V2	31 August 1950
5.	Dog (Laika)	SPUTNIK 2	3 November 1957
6.	Squirrel Monkey (Gordo)	JUPITER IRBM AM-13	13 December 1958
7.	Rabbit (Marfusha)	R2	2 July 1959
8.	Chimpanzee (Ham)	MERCURY-REDSTONE 2	31 January 1961
9.	Guinea Pigs, Frogs, Mice	VOSTOK-3A	March 1961
10.	Tortoise	Zond 5	18 September 1968

NASA's first Artemis flight with crew, Artemis III

NASA is ready to achieve a significant milestone with its Artemis lunar exploration programme by landing the first woman and first person of colour on the moon.

The Artemis II, scheduled to launch in 2025, will be NASA's first mission with a crew under Artemis; and with Artemis III, NASA hopes to land the first woman and next man on the Moon, to explore the region near the lunar South Pole. Mike Sarafin, Artemis's mission manager, said, 'This mission will prove (the spacecraft) Orion's critical life support systems are ready to sustain our astronauts on longer duration missions ahead and allow the crew to practise operations essential to the success of Artemis III.' The Artemis II crew will travel approximately 7,403 kilometres miles beyond the far side of the Moon. From this vantage point, they will be able to see Earth and the Moon from Orion's windows, with the Moon close in the foreground and the Earth nearly a quarter-million miles in the background. The SLS core stage was successfully transported from NASA's Michoud Assembly Facility in New Orleans to NASA's Kennedy Space Center in Florida in July 2024.

55 years marked to first Moon landing

20 July 2024 marked fifty-five years since the first time man set foot on moon. In 1969, in the month of June, the crew of Apollo 11–Neil A. Armstrong, Michael Collins and Edwin E. 'Buzz' Aldrin–were very busy. To train for the different phases of their mission, the had astronauts conducted many sessions in the Command Module and Lunar Module simulators at the Manned Spacecraft Centre, now NASA's Johnson Space Centre in Houston. Armstrong and Aldrin practised setting up a television camera that would relay their activities back to Earth during

the two-and-a-half-hour excursion, during which they would have to conduct three scientific experiments and collect rock and moon samples for return to Earth. Between 14 and 16 June, Armstrong flew the Lunar Landing Training Vehicle (LLTV) eight times and completed the simulation twelve times in the LLTV and its predecessor, the Lunar Landing Research Vehicle (LLRV). Boy, did the hard work pay off!

Space start-up Agnikul Cosmos flies world's first 3D-printed rocket engine

Indian space start-up Agnikul Cosmos on 30 May 2024 successfully launched its first sub-orbital test vehicle powered by the world's first single-piece 3D-printed rocket engine. Getting it right in their fifth attempt, the company is the first to use a private launchpad that is set up at the country's only operational spaceport in Srihari kota. 'It signals the ability to rapidly assemble rockets that is unparalleled,' Satyanarayanan Chakravarthy of Agnikul Cosmos, who is also a professor of aerospace engineering at the Indian Institute of Technology (IIT) in Madras, said. The Indian Space Research Organisation (ISRO) also congratulated Agnikul in a post on social media, saying it is 'a major milestone, as the first-ever controlled flight of a semi-cryogenic liquid engine realised through additive manufacturing'.

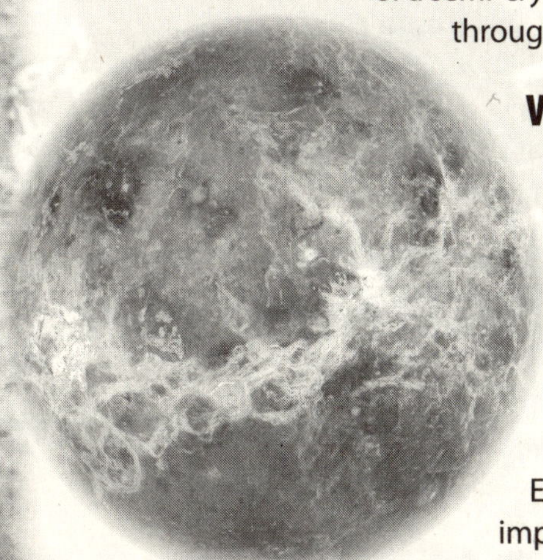

Venus's tectonic history

A recent study at Brown University suggests that Venus, affectionately known as Earth's planetary sister, might have undergone tectonic activity from 4.5 to 3.5 billion years ago. The study suggests that plate tectonics, like those on Earth, may have had a significant impact on the formation of

Venus's atmosphere, which is abundant in carbon dioxide and nitrogen. Understanding the atmospheric composition of Venus is vital as it consists of around 96.5 per cent carbon dioxide and less than 3.5 per cent nitrogen. Furthermore, it is plausible that Venus harboured microbial life billions of years ago because of geological processes.

Verification of the existence of an ancient lake on Mars

The Mars Perseverance rover from NASA, containing ground-penetrating radar, has verified that the Lezero Crater, created by a meteor collision, included a large lake and river delta in its area which is situated somewhat above the equator of Mars. Over a long period of time, the process of sediment deposition and erosion has sculpted the geological features of Mars that are seen on the surface at present. The identification of lake deposits increases the prospect of finding traces of life on Mars.

NASA's next-generation Solar Sail Boom technology launched in April

The Advanced Composite Solar Sail System (ACS3) is a next-generation solar sail technology that was launched in April onboard Rocket Lab's Electron rocket from Launch Complex 1 in Māhia, New Zealand. It harnesses solar force that, according to NASA, is equivalent to merely the weight of a paperclip in your palm. The data obtained from ACS3 will help NASA design future larger scale composite solar sail systems that could be used for space weather early warning satellites, near-Earth asteroid reconnaissance missions or communications relays for crewed exploration missions.

When the spacecraft reached its Sun-synchronous orbit, around 1,000 km above Earth, it started unfolding its composite booms, and

unfurling its solar sail which measures approximately 30 feet per side, or about the size of a small apartment. If all goes well with ACS3, it could lead to scaling up the design enough to travel across the solar system.

Gaganyaan: India's first manned space mission

The Indian Space Research is set to launch Gaganyaan, India's first manned mission to space in 2025. The mission aims to launch a three-member crew to an orbit of 400 km for a three-day mission and bring them safely back to Earth.

Features of the programme:

- The spacecraft weighs 5.3 metric tonnes and will use launch vehicle, Human Rated LVM3 (HLVM3).
- The Crew Escape System (CES) in the rocket will ensure the safe escape of the members in case of any difficulty.
- The Orbital Module, which will be orbiting Earth, is composed of two parts: Crew Module (CM) and Service Module (SM). The CM is the habitable Earth-like space where the crew is stationed. The SM is an unpressurized structure that contains the thermal system, propulsion system and power systems, among others, and is used to provide necessary support to the CM.

Vyommitra, the female humanoid robot developed by ISRO who is equipped with the capability to monitor Module Parameters, issue alerts, execute life support operations and even communicate in two languages, will be heading to space as a part of the Gaganyaan

SPACE NEWS

mission in 2024. Vyommitra's name is derived from the Sanskrit words 'vyoma', meaning space, and 'mitra', meaning friend.

The four Air Force officers that have been selected for the mission are Group Captain Prashanth Balakrishnan Nair, Group Captain Ajit Krishnan, Group Captain Angad Pratap and Wing Commander Shubhanshu Shukla. They trained in Russia and later at the Astronaut Training Facility, Bengaluru. Wing Commander Shukla and Group Captain Nair have also been selected as prime and backup pilots for the upcoming Axiom-4 mission to the ISS, where they will gain necessary experience for the Indian human spaceflight programme. In tradition with renaming the term 'astronauts' according to each country, those part of this mission will be called 'Vyomanauts'. If this mission is successful, India will join USA, Russia and China as the only countries to have sent humans to space.

Did you know?
Future ISRO missions includes a Low Earth Orbit (LEO) obsevatory, jointly developed with NASA; a mission to Venus to study its atmospheric structure and composition; as well as the development of the Bharatiya Antariksha Station, India's first space station.

7 HISTORY

History is the study of what happened in the past, based on what has been written down or documented. Events before written records are generally considered prehistory. History is about our efforts to make sense of the past, by using information gained from what people remember, by discovering things and by interpreting all that we know about these events. Here are a few useful words related to history:

Annals: Historical accounts of facts and events ranged in chronological order, year by year.

Antiquarianism: Historical study focusing on the empirical evidence of the past, including manuscripts and archives, and archaeological and historic sites and artefacts. Now the term is used as a criticism to describe a narrow approach that excludes a historical context.

Antiquities: Objects or artefacts from ancient history, especially from the classical civilizations, the cultures of the Mediterranean region and the ancient Near East (modern Middle East).

Archaeology: The study of human history and prehistory through the excavation of sites and the analysis of physical remains.

Archive: A collection of historical documents and records.

Artefact: Any material object associated with a culture, such as a tool, clothing or food item.

Chronicle: A historical account of facts and events arranged in chronological order.

Chronology: The study of the sequence of past events.

Epigraphy: The study of ancient inscriptions.

Illuminated manuscript: A manuscript in which the text is supplemented by the addition of decoration.

Macrohistory: The study of long-term trends in world history to uncover patterns across diverse cultures.

Microhistory: The detailed investigation of a small unit (an event, a community or an individual) to cast light on broader historical issues.

Numismatics: The study of coins.

Phaleristics: The study of military orders, decorations and medals.

Presentism: Application of present-day ideas to interpretations of the past.

Primary source: Material from or directly related to the past. Documents and records of the period under study, such as diaries, letters, legal documents, accounts, photographs, news reports and artefacts.

WORLD: A BRIEF TIMELINE

5000 BCE

- Rise of the Sumerian Civilization in Mesopotamia in what is roughly present-day Iraq.
- First recorded settlements in the fertile valley of the River Nile in Egypt.

3500 BCE The wheel, the first written language and the use of bronze are located in this period. In the Indus Valley the first use of pottery is recorded.

2600 BCE The emergence of Mayan Civilization in the Yucatán Peninsula in South America. In 2620 BCE, Imhotep builds the first pyramid – the 'step pyramid' at Saqqara – as a tomb for the pharaoh Djoser, and Egypt begins its first era of remarkable monuments.

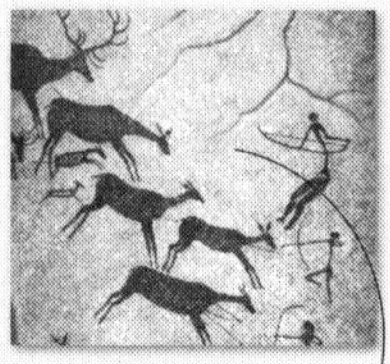

2300 BCE Civilization recorded in China. Astronomy appears as a science. This time also marks the Neolithic Age in Europe.

2200 BCE First records of a civilization in the Malay Peninsula.

1500 BCE Rise of the Vedic culture in north India. The Rig Veda is compiled around this time.

1480 BCE Moses leads Israelites out of Egypt.

5000 BCE | 3500 BCE | 2500 BCE | 2000 BCE | 1500 BCE

2700–2600 BCE The Pyramids are built in Egypt.

2500 BCE Building of the city of Mohenjo-Daro in the Indus Valley, the third oldest civilization after Mesopotamia and Egypt.

2500–2000 BCE First records of the Andean Civilization, the first of its kind in the Americas.

2250–1122 BCE Rise of the Chinese Civilization along the banks of the River Huang He.

2000–1200 BCE The Iron Age civilizations discover the use of iron and start using it for various activities, both for practical purposes and craft.

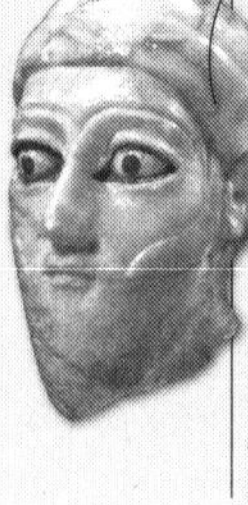

2000 BCE

- The rise of Babylon in the Mesopotamian Civilization.
- King Hammurabi raises the first trained army in the world.
- The Bronze Age reaches Europe.
- Britain is invaded by the Scandinavian tribes for the first time.
- A civilization rises in Japan, soon after which Chinese and Korean groups invade it.

1027 BCE The Chou Dynasty is established in China.

1000 BCE The decline of Egypt begins.

347 BCE Death of Greek philosopher Plato, disciple of Socrates and founder of the Academy, a school of philosophy in Athens, Greece.

660 BCE Birth of Zoroaster, the founder of Zoroastrianism in Media, Iran.

753 BCE The city of Rome is founded by Romulus.

586 BCE Fall of Jerusalem to the Babylonians.

336 BCE Accession of Alexander at the age of 22 to the throne of Macedon in south-east Europe. He will become one of the most successful conquerors of all time.

215 BCE Work begins on the Great Wall of China.

4 BCE–7 CE The birth of Jesus Christ (variously recorded).

44 BCE Julius Caesar is killed by Brutus and other conspirators.

1000 BCE — 500 BCE — 250 BCE — 0 BCE

850 BCE *The Iliad* and *The Odyssey* are composed by Homer.

776 BCE The first Olympic Games are held in Olympia, Greece.

509 BCE Founding of the Roman Republic. The great architecture of Rome can be traced to this period.

560 BCE Gautama Buddha, founder of Buddhism, is born in Lumbini in present-day Nepal.

399 BCE Socrates, the Greek philosopher, is sentenced to death.

264 BCE Ashoka is crowned, marking the start of the Golden Age in India.

73 BCE For the first time in history, slaves revolt against the Roman Republic in the Spartacist Uprising.

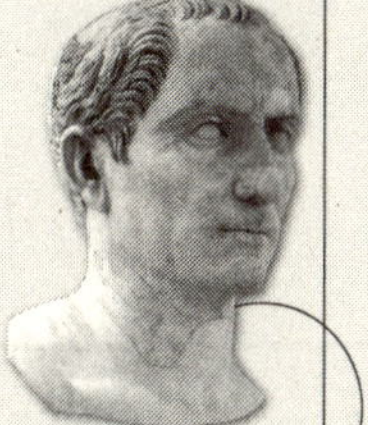

55 BCE Julius Caesar conquers Britain, having already captured Gaul in present-day France.

0 CE | 1000 CE | 1500 CE | 1750 CE

29 CE Jesus Christ is crucified.

64 CE A fire, which lasts for six days, destroys Rome.

570 CE Birth of Prophet Muhammad, the founder of Islam, in Mecca.

1163 The University of Oxford is founded in England.

1215 The Magna Carta, the historic charter of rights and laws in England, is signed.

1337 Beginning of the Hundred Years' War between England and France; ends only in 1453.

1431 Joan of Arc is burnt at the stake in France for allegedly practising witchcraft.

1455 CE The War of Roses, a civil war in England, begins; ends in 1485.

1492 Christopher Columbus discovers the Americas.

1504 The *Mona Lisa* is painted by Leonardo da Vinci.

1564 Birth of poet and playwright William Shakespeare in England.

1642 Civil war in England. King Charles I is in a feud with the Parliament, as they demand democratic powers. Eventually, he is executed in 1653.

1666 London is engulfed by the 'Great Fire'.

1689 Constitutional monarchy is established in England.

1756 Britain, Prussia and Hanover combine to battle Austria, France, Russia, Saxony, Sweden and Spain in the Seven Years' War.

1770 Captain James Cook discovers Australia.

1776 Declaration of American Independence.

1789 On 14 July, the French Revolution begins with the storming of the Bastille prison to free prisoners and end monarchy.

1854 Admiral Perry of the USA visits Japan and forces trade with the West.
- The Crimean War takes place between 1853 and 1856. Lord Cardigan leads the British cavalry against the Russians in what becomes known as 'The Charge of the Light Brigade'.

1860 Herman Hollerith invents an electronic tabulator for the US census. He starts a company that eventually becomes International Business Machines (IBM) Corporation.

1795 The Metric system of measurement is introduced in France.

1861–65 American Civil War; President Lincoln bans slavery; some states attempt to break the Union.

1812 On 24 June, Napoleon takes Moscow, but it is a hollow victory. The city is burned to the ground, yet the Tsar does not surrender. Napoleon and the French army retreat.

1848 Karl Marx and Friedrich Engels publish *The Communist Manifesto*.

1847 US troops, led by General Winfield Scott, enter Mexico City in September. A treaty ending the Mexican–American War is signed in February 1848.

1800 CE | 1825 CE | 1850 CE | 1875 CE

1815 On 18 June, Napoleon is finally defeated at Waterloo, Belgium, by the Duke of Wellington.

1859 Charles Darwin publishes *On the Origin of Species*.

1856 Louis Pasteur shows that diseases spread from tiny organisms. Modern-day germ theory is born.

1814 The Battle of Trafalgar: The British fleet under the command of Horatio Nelson defeats a combined French and Spanish fleet.

1845–48 The Great Hunger (aka Potato Famine) in Ireland. More than 1.5 million die of starvation and disease.

1866 Prussia invades Austria.
- The United States and Europe are connected by a 4,000 km long telegraph cable.

1833 England outlaws slavery and frees more than 780,000 slaves.

1804 Napoleon Bonaparte is crowned emperor of France.

1838 On 24 January, Samuel Morse demonstrates the telegraph machine.

1901 Guglielmo Marconi sends the first transatlantic wireless radio signal.

1904 Russo–Japanese War: The Russians underestimate the modern Japanese fleet, which destroys most of the already depleted Russian Navy a year later. The Japanese use the new Marconi radios to keep track of the Russian Navy.

1898 The Spanish–American War starts. Reports of atrocities by the Spaniards against Cubans compel the USA to intervene.

1905 While working as a patent clerk, Albert Einstein publishes his theory of relativity and also states energy equals matter ($E = mc^2$). He publishes four papers in one year. Three of them are Nobel Prize-winning material.

1939 Hitler invades Poland on 1 September. The British Commonwealth and France declare war on Germany, starting the Second World War.

1876 Alexander Graham Bell patents the telephone.

1930 The first FIFA World Cup starts: Lucien Laurent scores the first goal for France, against Mexico.

1928 Scottish bacteriologist Alexander Fleming notices penicillin mould killing a staphylococcus culture. The 'antibiotics revolution' begins.

1875 CE | 1900 CE | 1915 CE | 1940 CE

1899–1902 Boer War: The descendants of the Dutch in present-day South Africa fight for independence from Britain.

1938 Adolf Hitler, Chancellor of Germany since 1933, launches *Kristallnacht*, the 'night of broken glass'. Hundreds of Jews are killed by Nazis.

1903 Orville and Wilbur Wright fly the first aircraft.

1912 The 'unsinkable' *Titanic* sinks with more than 1,500 passengers.

1918 On 11 November, the First World War ends.

1914 On 3 August, Germany declares war on France, starting the 'Great War' (First World War).

1941 On 22 June, Operation Barbarossa, the invasion of Russia by Germany, is launched 129 years (to the day) after Napoleon invaded Russia.
- On 8 December, the Japanese attack Pearl Harbor, effectively bringing the USA into the Second World War.

1883 The island volcano of Krakatoa in Indonesia erupts on 23 August. More than 36,000 people are killed. Its impact is seen as far away as London and New York. The sound of the explosion is heard 5,000 km away.

1917 The USA enters the First World War against Germany. Ten million people will die in the war.

1942 At the University of Chicago, USA, Enrico Fermi conducts the first nuclear reaction.

1944 The largest offshore landing in history, the invasion of Normandy, referred to as D-Day, starts on 6 June. This spells the end for Hitler's Third Reich.

1945 On 6 August, the USA drops an atomic bomb, 'Little Boy', on Hiroshima, Japan, killing an estimated 66,000 civilians. On 9 August, another bomb, 'Fat Man', is dropped on Nagasaki. Japan announces its surrender to the Allied powers on 15 August; it signs the Instrument of Surrender on 2 September.

1957 Russian-made Sputnik I becomes the first man-made satellite.

1961 On 11 April, Yuri A. Gagarin becomes the first human in space.

1969 On 20 July, Neil Armstrong lands on the surface of the Moon.

1990 Apartheid ends in South Africa.
- The First Gulf War begins when the USA attacks Iraq in response to Iraq's invasion of Kuwait.

1991 The Soviet Union dissolves, and with it, the Cold War with the USA.

1994 Rwanda is engulfed in a bloody civil war.

2001 On 11 September, terrorists in planes crash into the World Trade Center twin towers in New York, and the Pentagon in Washington DC.

2003 US and British forces invade Iraq. Saddam Hussein is caught, and executed in 2006.

2004 On 26 December, a huge tsunami kills thousands in Indonesia, Thailand, Sri Lanka, India, Maldives and Somalia.

2009 On 20 January, Barack Obama is sworn in as the first African-American president of the USA.

1950 CE | 1975 CE | 2010 CE | 2022 CE

1989 In Tiananmen Square, the Chinese army crushes a demonstration, killing hundreds of students.
- In November, the Berlin Wall that divided West Berlin from East Berlin is torn down. Germany is united for the first time since the Second World War.

2011 On 1 May, Osama bin Laden, head of terrorist organization al-Qaeda, is killed in Pakistan by US Special Forces.

2014 In March, Russia annexes Crimea.

2017 The USA pulls out of the landmark Paris Climate Accord.

2018 Former cricketer Imran Khan of the Tehreek-e-Insaaf party becomes Pakistan's prime minister.

2019 Boris Johnson becomes UK prime minister after Theresa May resigns.

2020 COVID-19, a global pandemic, fans out from Wuhan, China, in December 2019, and is declared a Public Health Emergency of International Concern by WHO on 30 January 2020.
- The UK withdraws from the European Union (EU) on 31 January, a move popularly known as 'Brexit'.

2021 Democrat nominee Joe Biden begins his tenure as US president.
- In August, the USA withdraws troops from Afghanistan, resulting in the Taliban taking over Kabul and more than two-thirds of the country.

2022 Russia invades Ukraine on 21 February.
- Pakistan's prime minister Imran Khan is removed from office after losing a no-confidence vote on 4 April and replaced by Shehbaz Sharif, president of the Pakistani Muslim League.
- Boris Johnson resigns as British prime minister on 8 July.

2024 Bangladesh prime minister Sheikh Hasina forced to resign, and flees the country amid student protests.
- Protests demanding ceasefire erupt globally as conflict and violence between Israel and Palestine continues to cause humanitarian crises.

ANCIENT INDIA TIMELINE

3000 BCE	The beginning of the Harappan (Indus Valley) Civilization.
2500 BCE	The establishment of the cities of Harappa and Mohenjo-Daro in the **Valley of the River Indus**.
2000 BCE	The decline of the Harappan Civilization.
1500 BCE	The people later referred to as the 'Vedic' people set up a recognizable Vedic culture in the Gangetic plains.
1100 BCE	With the discovery of iron, the Vedic people start using iron tools.
1800–1100 BCE	One of the earliest sacred scriptures of the Hindus, the **Rig Veda** (variously dated) is composed.
750 BCE	The Upanishads, a set of sacred texts of Hinduism, are composed.
600 BCE	Sixteen Mahajanapadas (Great States) are formed on the subcontinent.
543 BCE	King Bimbisara conquers the Magadha region in the east and becomes emperor of the Magadha Empire.
527 BCE	**Prince Siddhartha Gautama** attains Enlightenment, becomes the Buddha, and establishes Buddhism.
500 BCE	Prince Mahavira establishes Jainism in north India.
493 BCE	Bimbisara dies and is succeeded by Ajatashatru.
461 BCE	Ajatashatru expands the Magadha territory and dies shortly afterwards.
327 BCE	**Alexander of Macedonia** invades the Indus Valley on the Indian subcontinent, fights a famous battle with Puru (Porus).
304 BCE	Magadha king Chandragupta Maurya establishes the Mauryan dynasty with Pataliputra as the capital.
500–300 BCE	The Ramayana, the famous Hindu epic, is composed. There are various dates (between 500 and 300 BCE) put down for Valmiki's Ramayana.
300 BCE	The Chola dynasty establishes the first kingdom in southern India with its capital at Thanjavur.
290 BCE	Chandragupta's son Bindusara extends the Mauryan Empire to the Deccan region.
259 BCE	Mauryan emperor **Ashoka** converts to Buddhism.
220 BCE	The Mauryan dynasty expands to nearly all of India.
200 BCE	The famous epic, the **Mahabharata**, is composed. (Some sources put it down between 500 BCE and 200 BCE and others between 200 BCE and 200 CE).
184 BCE	The Mauryan dynasty ends and makes way for the beginning of the Sunga dynasty.

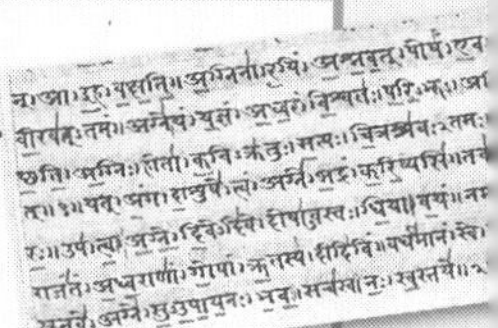

78 BCE	The Sunga dynasty declines.
50 CE	The first Buddhist stupa is built at Sanchi (now in Madhya Pradesh).
300 CE	The Pallava dynasty is established in Kanchipuram (now in Tamil Nadu).
350 CE	The Sangam is compiled in Tamil in the kingdom of Madurai. The Puranas are composed.
390 CE	**Chandragupta II** extends the Gupta kingdom to Gujarat.
450 CE	Kumaragupta, who succeeds Chandragupta II, builds the monastic university of Nalanda (in present-day Bihar).
499 CE	Mathematician Aryabhata writes the *Aryabhatiya,* a compendium of mathematics and astronomy.
500 CE	The beginning of the Bhakti cult in Tamil Nadu.
528 CE	The Gupta Empire sees a downfall due to continuous invasions.
550 CE	The **Chalukya kingdom** is established in central India with its capital at Badami.
606 CE	Harshavardhana rules the kingdom of Thanesar in north India and Nepal with its capital at Kannauj (in present-day Uttar Pradesh).

MEDIEVAL INDIA

761 CE	Muhammad bin Qasim battles Raja Dahir in Sind.
1000 CE	Invasion of Mahmud of Ghazni.
1017–30 CE	**Al-Biruni**, the scholar from Persia, travels in India.
1191 CE	The First Battle of Tarain is fought between Muhammad Ghori (from present-day Afghanistan) and Prithviraj Chauhan. Ghori is defeated by Prithviraj.
1192 CE	The Second Battle of Tarain is fought between Ghori and **Prithviraj Chauhan**.
1194 CE	Muhammad Ghori and Jaichandra, the Gahadavala king of Kannauj, fight the Battle of Chandawar.
1221 CE	**Genghis Khan** invades Punjab.
1310 CE	Alauddin Khilji's army occupies Devagiri, destroying the Seuna Yadava kingdom.
1336 CE	The **Vijayanagara Empire** is established by Harihara I and his brother Bukka Raya I in the Deccan.
1347 CE	Governor Hasan Gangu revolts against Muhammad bin Tughlaq, founding the Bahmani Sultanate.

1370 CE	Bukka, the Vijayanagara ruler, and his son Kumara Kampana capture the entire Tamil-speaking region.
1407 CE	Zafar Khan, governor of Gujarat, declares himself Sultan Muzaffar Shah, founding the Gujarat Sultanate/Muzaffarid dynasty.
1451 CE	Bahlul Khan Lodi ascends the throne of the Delhi Sultanate, starting the Lodi dynasty.
1469 CE	**Guru Nanak**, the founder of Sikhism, is born.
1486 CE	**Sher Shah Suri**, founder of the Suri Empire, is born in Sasaram.
1490 CE	Ahmadnagar declares independence, followed by Bijapur and Berar in the same year, thus breaking up the Bahmani Sultanate.
1497–99 CE	**Vasco da Gama** makes his first voyage from Europe to India and back.
1503 CE	The kingdom of Kochi is taken over by the Portuguese; this is the first European settlement in India.
1509 CE	The Battle of Diu marks the beginning of the dominance of the Europeans in the Asian naval theatre.
1522 CE	The Portuguese land on the Coromandel Coast.

MUGHAL ERA

1526 CE	Sultan Ibrahim Lodi of the Delhi Sultanate angers local nobles, who respond by inviting Babur, the ruler of Kabul, to invade Delhi and Agra.
1527 CE	**Babur** annexes Mewar.
1530 CE	Babur completes his *Baburnama*. He dies, and is succeeded by his son Humayun.
1539 CE	The Battle of Chausa is fought between Humayun and Sher Shah Suri. Humayun is defeated.
1540 CE	The Battle of Kannauj: Humayun is defeated by the Afghans (Suri Dynasty), and spends 12 years in exile.
1552 CE	**Humayun** regains the throne of Delhi.
1556 CE	Humayun dies, and is succeeded by his son Akbar.
1556 CE	The Second Battle of Panipat is fought between Hemu (Hem Chandra Vikramaditya) and Akbar.
1565 CE	The Battle of Talikota results in the conquest of the Vijayanagara Empire by the Deccan sultanates.
1572 CE	**Akbar** annexes Gujarat.
1574 CE	Akbar annexes Bengal.
1586 CE	Akbar annexes Kashmir.
1600 CE	The East India Company is formed in England. It gets exclusive trading rights in India.

1605 CE	Akbar dies, and is succeeded by his son Jahangir.
1628 CE	Jahangir dies, and is succeeded by his son Shah Jahan.
1630 CE	Birth of **Chhatrapati Shivaji Maharaj**.
1658 CE	After completing the Taj Mahal, the Jama Masjid and the Red Fort, Shah Jahan dies. He is succeeded by his son Aurangzeb.
1674 CE	Forces led by Chhatrapati Shivaji Maharaj defeat Aurangzeb's troops, and establish the Maratha Empire.
1675 CE	Guru Tegh Bahadur, the ninth Guru of the Sikhs, is executed in Delhi on the orders of Mughal emperor Aurangzeb.
1680 CE	Chhatrapati Shivaji Maharaj dies at Raigad.
1681 CE	Aurangzeb invades the Deccan.
1699 CE	**Guru Gobind Singh**, the tenth Guru of the Sikhs, creates Dal Khalsa, a military force.
1707 CE	Aurangzeb dies, and is succeeded by his son Bahadur Shah I.
1708 CE	Guru Gobind Singh survives an assassination attempt in Maharashtra.
1719 CE	**Bajirao I** is appointed the Peshwa by Maratha emperor Shahu.
1735 CE	The annexation of Rajputana by Peshwa Bajirao I.
1737 CE	Bajirao I conquers Delhi; the Mughal emperor is spared and kept as a symbolic head.
1740 CE	Bajirao I dies, with the distinction of winning every battle he fought. He is succeeded by Balaji Bajirao.
1757 CE	The British East India Company's private army under **Robert Clive** annexes Bengal in the Battle of Plassey.
1760 CE	The Marathas comprehensively defeat the Nizam of Hyderabad; the Maratha Empire reaches its zenith.
1761 CE	The Afghans dominate in the Third Battle of Panipat, blocking Maratha expansion.
1766 CE	The Sikhs defeat Ahmad Shah Abdali; establish Sikh rule in Punjab. The First Anglo-Mysore War between Mysore's (now Mysuru) Hyder Ali and the East India Company.
1779 CE	Maratha Mahadji Shinde routs the British at the Battle of Wadgaon.
1782 CE	The First Anglo-Maratha War ends with the Treaty of Salbai.
1790 CE	The Marathas defeat the Rajputs of Jaipur and their Mughal allies at the Battle of Patan.
1799 CE	The Fourth Anglo-Mysore War ends with the death of **Tipu Sultan** and the restoration of the Wodeyar dynasty that had ruled Mysore earlier.

1801	**Maharaja Ranjit Singh** establishes Khalsa rule over Punjab, ruling from present-day Lahore.
1807	The East India Company signs the Treaty of Amritsar with Maharaja Ranjit Singh.
1818	The Third Anglo-Maratha War ends with the defeat of Bajirao II and the end of the Maratha Empire, leaving the British in control of most of India.

BRITISH RAJ

1853	First passenger train runs from Bori Bunder in Bombay to Thane in present-day Maharashtra.
1857	**Widespread uprising** in north India against British rule (the First War of Independence). It is crushed and the queen of England declares India a colony.
1858	The British Crown officially takes over Indian governance.
1877	The queen of England is proclaimed empress of India.
1885	The first meeting of the Indian National Congress.
1899	**Lord Curzon** becomes Governor General and viceroy of India.
1905	The first partition of Bengal takes place.
1906	The All-India Muslim League is formed.
1912	The capital of British India is shifted to Delhi from Calcutta.
1919	The **Jallianwala Bagh** massacre takes place in the wake of protests against the Rowlatt Act, which allows political cases to be tried without juries and suspects to be imprisoned without trial.
1920	Mahatma Gandhi launches the Non-cooperation movement.
1922	The violent Chauri Chaura incident takes place during the Civil Disobedience movement; Mahatma Gandhi calls off the protest.
1928	Simon Commission comes to India and is boycotted by all parties.
1930	**Salt Satyagraha**, which begins with the Dandi March, is launched as an agitation against the salt tax.
	The First Round Table Conference takes place in London.
1931	The Second Round Table Conference takes place and the Gandhi–Irwin Pact is signed.
1934	The Civil Disobedience movement is called off.
1942	Gandhi meets the Cripps Mission; the Quit India movement is launched.
1943	Netaji Subhas Chandra Bose takes charge of the Indian National Army.
1947	**Lord Mountbatten** draws up plans for Partition of India.
	Partition of India and independence from British rule, at midnight of 14/15 August.

MODERN HISTORY (POST-INDEPENDENCE)

1947–48	Thousands die in widespread communal riots during and after the Partition of India into two nations: India and Pakistan.
1948	On 30 January, Mahatma Gandhi, on his way to his daily prayer meeting, is assassinated by Nathuram Godse. The first conflict with Pakistan breaks out over the territory of Kashmir.
1951–52	The first general elections are held and the Congress party wins. **Jawaharlal Nehru** is elected prime minister (PM).
1962	India loses brief war with China.
1964	Prime Minister Jawaharlal Nehru dies. Lal Bahadur Shastri becomes India's second prime minister.
1965	The second war with Pakistan over Kashmir is fought.
1966	**Indira Gandhi**, Nehru's daughter, is elected prime minister.
1971	Third war with Pakistan over creation of Bangladesh. The Soviet Union and India sign a 20-year treaty of friendship.
1974	India's first underground nuclear test is carried out.
1975	Indira Gandhi declares Emergency in the country.
1975–77	Nearly 1,000 political opponents are imprisoned during the Emergency.
1977	Indira Gandhi loses the general elections.
1980	Indira Gandhi returns to power, heading a Congress party splinter group – Congress (Indira) – and winning by a huge margin.
1983	The Indian cricket team wins the (Prudential) World Cup for the first time, under the captaincy of Kapil Dev.
1984	Troops storm the Golden Temple in Amritsar, Punjab, the hideout of Sikh militants demanding self-rule. Prime Minister Indira Gandhi is assassinated by bodyguards, sparking off anti-Sikh riots in Delhi and across India. **Rajiv Gandhi**, her son, becomes prime minister. Toxic gas leaks at the Union Carbide pesticides plant in Bhopal. Thousands are killed and many more affected.
1987	India sends troops for peacekeeping operations in Sri Lanka's civil conflict with the Liberation Tigers of Tamil Eelam (LTTE).
1989	Congress is routed in the elections. V.P. Singh (Janata Dal) is PM.
1990	Indian troops are withdrawn from Sri Lanka.
1991	Rajiv Gandhi is assassinated by a suicide bomber.
1992	The Babri mosque in Ayodhya is demolished, triggering widespread communal violence.

1996	The Congress party suffers electoral defeat and the Bharatiya Janata Party (BJP) emerges as the largest single party.
1998	The BJP forms a coalition government under Prime Minister **Atal Bihari Vajpayee**. This will be the first non-Congress government to complete a full term. India conducts five nuclear tests, closely followed by Pakistan.
1999	Vajpayee takes the new bus service to Pakistan to meet its prime minister, Nawaz Sharif, and signs the Lahore Peace Declaration.
2000	The billionth Indian citizen is born.
2001	Vajpayee meets President Pervez Musharraf of Pakistan in the first summit of the neighbours in more than two years. On 13 December, the Parliament is attacked by five terrorists from the Lashkar-e-Taiba and Jaish-e-Mohammed, leading to nine deaths and a stand-off between India and Pakistan. The attackers are killed.
2002	Scientist **A.P.J. Abdul Kalam** is elected president of India.
2003	India and Pakistan resume flights between the two countries, which were banned after the December 2001 terrorist attack on the Indian Parliament.
2004	The United Progressive Alliance (UPA), with the Congress as the largest member party, forms the government after the general elections. Dr Manmohan Singh becomes prime minister.
2006	President George W. Bush of the USA signs an agreement with Prime Minister Manmohan Singh to share nuclear technology.
2007	Pratibha Patil becomes India's first woman president.
2008	Terrorists from Pakistan terrorists **attack landmark spots** in Mumbai.
2009	India's unmanned lunar probe Chandrayaan-1 discovers water molecules on the Moon's surface.
2010	The Indian rupee gets a symbol: ₹ The Indian government initiates the Right of Children to Free and Compulsory Education Act to provide free and compulsory education to all children between six and fourteen years of age. The 19th Commonwealth Games are held in Delhi, from 3 to 14 October 2010.
2011	Mamata Banerjee's Trinamool Congress ends the thirty-four-year rule of the Left coalition led by the Communist Party of India (Marxist) [CPI(M)] in West Bengal.
2012	Pranab Mukherjee is elected as India's thirteenth president. Hamid Ansari is re-elected as vice-president of India. Terrorist Ajmal Kasab is hanged for his role in the 2008 Mumbai attacks.
2013	The Criminal Law (Amendment) Act 2013 is passed after the 16 December 2012 'Nirbhaya' case.

2014	The National Democratic Alliance (NDA), led by the BJP, wins the general elections. Narendra Modi becomes the fifteenth Indian PM.
2016	The Goods and Services Tax (GST), the biggest tax reform since Independence, is launched on the midnight of 30 June. Ram Nath Kovind becomes the second Dalit president of India after K.R. Narayanan (1997–2002).
2018	The BJP wins the legislative assembly elections in Tripura, a Left stronghold for twenty-five years.
2019	The BJP wins the general elections with a thumping majority and **Narendra Modi** becomes prime minister for a second term. The government abrogates Article 370 of the Constitution, which gave special status to Jammu and Kashmir, and bifurcates the state into two Union Territories: Jammu and Kashmir, and Ladakh.
2020	Prime Minister Narendra Modi announces a twenty-one-day lockdown throughout India, the largest in world history, to prevent the spread of COVID-19. National Education Policy 2020 (NEP 2020), a new policy on education, is approved by the Union cabinet. Prime Minister Modi performs *bhoomipujan* and lays the foundation stone of the Ram Temple in Ayodhya, Uttar Pradesh. Three Indian agriculture acts of 2020, referred to as the Farm Bills, are initiated by the Parliament of India in September 2020.
2021	For the first time in history, the Union budget is presented on an India-made tablet as a paperless budget. The contentious Farm Bills are repealed on 19 November. The Supreme Court permits women to take the National Defence Academy examination.
2022	Droupadi Murmu, a member of the BJP, becomes the fifteenth president of India on 25 July 2022, the first person belonging to the tribal community and the second woman after Pratibha Patil to hold the office.
2023	Chandrayaan-3, the third and most recent lunar Indian space research exploration mission, is launched from Sriharikota.
2024	The BJP forms the ruling government for the third consecutive term, as a part of the National Democratic Alliance (NDA) alliance. **Narendra Modi** is sworn in as the prime minister, continuing his service as the head of government since 2014.

HISTORY

Perfectly preserved Pompeian paintings uncovered

Pompeii is an ancient Roman city which was buried after the eruption of Mount Vesuvius in 79 AD. Fortunately, it was entirely preserved under the volcanic debris. Archaeologists have uncovered new frescoes, a type of painting style from the Renaissance period, at the Black Room, assumed to be a banquet hall back then, depicting scenes from Greek mythology. The two paintings include the key figures of the Trojan war. The first being of Paris, prince of Troy, meeting Helen. The second fresco depicts the event of Cassandra, the Trojan priestess, refusing the advances of Apollo, the god of the sun, music and prophecies, which led to her being cursed by him.

New Crete airport gives way to an a-mazing discovery

Remains of a 4,000-year-old labyrinth have been discovered at the summit of Papoura Hill, near Kastelli. Interestingly, the discovery was made during the preparations of a new airport. The labyrinth of Crete is the home of the Minotaur, one of the most famous stories of Greek mythology.

It is 48 metres in diameter, with eight concentric stone walls, and spans a total area of 1,800 sq. m.

Potential Harappan trading town's remains discovered

Villagers from Lodrani village, Kutch district, Gujarat, unearthed remains of a possibly fortified settlement. Experts from the Oxford School of Archaeology confirmed after an investigation that the artefacts found had many similarities with those recovered at Dholavira. The new site has been named 'Morodharo', and can be dated back to 4,500 years. The Harappan pottery found at the site included perforated jar sherds, terracotta cakes and reserved slipware, hinting at the possibility of trade between the two towns.

8 INDIA: STATES AND UNION TERRITORIES

TOP STATES/UNION TERRITORY STATISTICS

Largest by area: Rajasthan

Smallest by area: Goa

State with the longest coastline: Gujarat, with a mainland coastline of 1,600 km (approx.)

State with longest international border: West Bengal; 2,216.7-km-long border with Bangladesh

State sharing borders with most states/UTs: Uttar Pradesh; shares borders with nine Indian states/UTs – Bihar, Chhattisgarh, Delhi, Haryana, Himachal Pradesh, Jharkhand, Madhya Pradesh, Rajasthan and Uttarakhand

Most populated: Uttar Pradesh

Least populated: Lakshadweep

Highest population density: Delhi

Lowest population density: Arunachal Pradesh

Highest literacy rate: Kerala

Longest railway network: Uttar Pradesh

Longest road network: Maharashtra

State with most rivers flowing through it: Uttar Pradesh (48 rivers)

City with most lakes: Udaipur, Rajasthan (seven)

Rainiest area: Mawsynram district, Meghalaya (12 m of annual rainfall)

State with the most UNESCO World Heritage elements (intangible, cultural, historical or other sites): Rajasthan (Hill forts, Jaipur city, Jantar Mantar, Keoladeo Ghana National Park, Kalbelia songs and folk dances) and Maharashtra (Ajanta, Ellora and Elephanta caves, Chhatrapati Shivaji Maharaj Terminus, Kumbh Mela [shared] at Nashik, and Victorian Gothic and art deco ensembles of Mumbai and [shared] Western Ghats)

UT with the most UNESCO World Heritage Sites: Delhi, with the Red Fort complex, Qutub Minar complex and Humayun's Tomb

Cities with UNESCO Heritage City status: Ahmedabad and Dholavira (Gujarat), Jaipur (Rajasthan)

First UNESCO City of Literature: Kozhikode, Kerala

Cleanest City Award 2023: Indore (seven-time winner) and Surat

States/UTs with most wildlife sanctuaries and national parks: Madhya Pradesh and the Andaman and Nicobar Islands: nine national parks each; Andaman and Nicobar Islands: 96 wildlife sanctuaries

* All information has been updated up to 1 August 2024

ANDHRA PRADESH

Capital: Amaravati
Location: South-eastern coast
Area: 160,205 sq. km
Population: 49,634,314
History: Formed in 1956; reorganized in 2014
Language: Telugu, Urdu
Literacy Rate: 67.02%
Governor: S. Abdul Nazeer
Chief Minister: Chandrababu Naidu
Major Rivers: Godavari, Krishna
Industries: Textiles, shipbuilding, aquaculture, auto parts, cement, coal mining
Agriculture: Rice, cotton, maize
State Animal: Blackbuck
State Bird: Rose-ringed parakeet

ARUNACHAL PRADESH

Capital: Itanagar
Location: North-east
Area: 83,743 sq. km
Population: 1,383,727
History: Formed in 1987
Languages: Nisi, Dafla and others
Literacy Rate: 65.38%
Governor: Lt Gen Kaiwalya Trivikram Parnaik
Chief Minister: Pema Khandu
Major Rivers: Siang
Industries: Forest products, handloom, clay
Agriculture: Rice, potato, tea, apple, pineapple
State Animal: Gayal (Mithun)
State Bird: Great hornbill

ASSAM

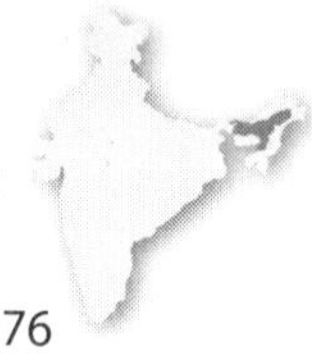

Capital: Dispur
Location: North-east
Area: 78,438 sq. km
Population: 31,205,576
History: Formed in 1947
Languages: Assamese, Bengali, Bodo, Karbi, Dimasa
Literacy Rate: 72.19%
Governor: Lakshman Acharya
Chief Minister: Himanta Biswa Sarma
Major Rivers: Brahmaputra, Barak
Industries: Tea, cement, textiles, sericulture, oil refining, coal mining
Agriculture: Rice, jute, tea, cotton
State Animal: Indian rhinoceros
State Bird: White-winged wood duck

BIHAR

Capital: Patna
Location: East
Area: 94,163 sq. km
Population: 104,099,452
History: Formed in 1936; reorganized in 2000
Languages: Hindi, Bhojpuri
Literacy Rate: 61.8%
Governor: Rajendra Vishwanath Arlekar
Chief Minister: Nitish Kumar
Major Rivers: Ganga, Gandak, Son
Industries: Food and beverages, plastic and rubber, tobacco, textiles, leather, dairy
Agriculture: Rice, wheat, maize, pulses, sugar cane, jute
State Animal: Gaur
State Bird: House sparrow

Background: Andhra Pradesh

CHHATTISGARH

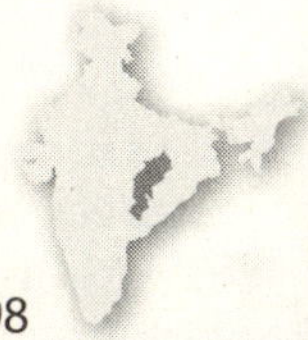

Capital: Raipur
Location: East-central
Area: 135,194 sq. km
Population: 25,545,198
History: Formed in 2000
Languages: Chhattisgarhi, Hindi
Literacy Rate: 70.28%
Governor: Ramen Deka
Chief Minister: Vishnu Deo Sai
Major Rivers: Mahanadi, Indravati
Industries: Cement, mining, steel, aluminium, electricity
Agriculture: Rice, maize, wheat, niger seed, pulses
State Animal: Wild buffalo
State Bird: Hill mynah

GOA

Capital: Panaji
Location: West
Area: 3,702 sq. km
Population: 1,458,545
History: Formed in 1987
Languages: Konkani, Marathi
Literacy Rate: 88.7%
Governor: P.S. Sreedharan Pillai
Chief Minister: Dr Pramod Sawant
Major Rivers: Mandovi, Zuari
Industries: Mining, textiles, tourism and hospitality, fisheries
Agriculture: Rice, millets, maize, cashew, coconut, bananas, sugar cane, pineapples, areca nuts
State Animal: Gaur
State Bird: Ruby-throated yellow bulbul

GUJARAT

Capital: Gandhinagar
Location: West
Area: 196,024 sq. km
Population: 60,383,628
History: Formed in 1960
Language: Gujarati
Literacy Rate: 78.03%
Governor: Acharya Devvrat
Chief Minister: Bhupendrabhai Patel
Major Rivers: Narmada, Tapti, Sabarmati, Mahi
Industries: Fertilizers, textiles, petroleum, engineering, diamonds
Agriculture: Groundnuts, cotton, rice, wheat
State Animal: Asiatic lion
State Bird: Greater flamingo

HARYANA

Capital: Chandigarh
Location: North
Area: 44,212 sq. km
Population: 25,351,462
History: Formed in 1966
Languages: Hindi, Haryanvi
Literacy Rate: 75.55%
Governor: Bandaru Dattatreya
Chief Minister: Nayab Singh Saini
Major Rivers: Yamuna, Ghaggar
Industries: Handloom, electrical appliances, automobiles, IT
Agriculture: Sugar cane, oilseeds, rice, groundnuts, maize, wheat, pulses, mustard
State Animal: Blackbuck
State Bird: Black francolin

Background: Chhattisgarh

HIMACHAL PRADESH

Capital: Shimla; Dharamshala (winter)
Location: North
Area: 55,673 sq. km
Population: 6,864,602
History: Formed in 1971
Languages: Hindi, Pahari
Literacy Rate: 82.8%
Governor: Shiv Pratap Shukla
Chief Minister: Sukhvinder Singh Sukhu
Major Rivers: Beas, Ravi, Chenab, Sutlej, Yamuna
Industries: Food and beverages, electronics, pharmaceuticals, hydroelectricity
Agriculture: Wheat, rice, maize, barley, fruits, olives, sugar cane
State Animal: Snow leopard
State Bird: Western tragopan

JHARKHAND

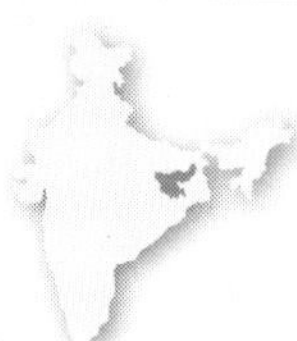

Capital: Ranchi
Location: East
Area: 79,714 sq. km
Population: 32,988,134
History: Formed in 2000
Languages: Hindi, Santhali
Literacy Rate: 66.41%
Governor: Santosh Gangwar
Chief Minister: Hemant Soren
Major Rivers: Damodar, Subarnarekha
Industries: Steel, locomotives, mining, sericulture
Agriculture: Rice, wheat, maize, pulses, mustard
State Animal: Indian elephant
State Bird: Koel

KARNATAKA

Capital: Bengaluru
Location: South-west
Area: 191,791 sq. km
Population: 61,095,297
History: Formed in 1956 as Mysore State; named Karnataka in 1973
Language: Kannada
Literacy Rate: 75.36%
Governor: Thawar Chand Gehlot
Chief Minister: Siddaramaiah
Major Rivers: Krishna, Kaveri
Industries: IT, telecom, electronics, floriculture, silk
Agriculture: Rice, ragi, sorghum, pulses, pearl millet, coffee
Animal: Indian elephant
State Bird: Indian roller

KERALA

Capital: Thiruvananthapuram
Location: South-west
Area: 38,863 sq. km
Population: 33,406,061
History: Formed in 1956
Language: Malayalam
Literacy Rate: 94%
Governor: Arif Muhammad Khan
Chief Minister: Pinarayi Vijayan
Major Rivers: Periyar, Bharatapuza, Pamba, Chaliyar, Chalakudy
Industries: Handlooms and textiles, coir, marine products, agro-industries, electronics, tourism and hospitality, handicrafts
Agriculture: Coconut, rubber, tea, coffee, cashew, spices, rice, tapioca
State Animal: Indian elephant
State Bird: Great hornbill

 Background: Himachal Pradesh

MADHYA PRADESH

Capital: Bhopal
Location: Central
Area: 308,000 sq. km
Population: 72,626,809
History: Formed in 1956; reorganized in 2000
Language: Hindi
Literacy Rate: 69.32%
Governor: Mangubhai Chhaganbhai Patel
Chief Minister: Mohan Yadav
Major Rivers: Narmada, Chambal, Betwa, Tapti
Industries: Automotive, electronics, cement, tourism, telecom, IT, forestry, textiles
Agriculture: Rice, wheat, millets, pulses, cotton, soyabean
State Animal: Barasingha
State Bird: Indian paradise flycatcher

MAHARASHTRA

Capital: Mumbai
Location: West
Area: 307,713 sq. km
Population: 112,374,333
History: Formed in 1960
Language: Marathi
Literacy Rate: 82.34%
Governor: C.P. Radhakrishnan
Chief Minister: Eknath Shinde
Major Rivers: Godavari, Wainganga, Penganga, Wardha, Bhima, Tapti
Industries: Textiles, engineering, pharmaceuticals, sugar, automotive, cinema, food products, breweries, printing and publishing
Agriculture: Rice, millets, sugar cane, pulses, oranges, mango
State Animal: Indian giant squirrel
State Bird: Yellow-footed green pigeon

MANIPUR

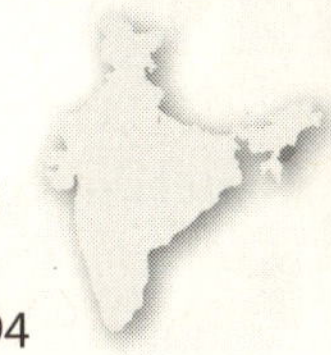

Capital: Imphal
Location: North-east
Area: 22,327 sq. km
Population: 2,855,794
History: Formed in 1972
Language: Manipuri
Literacy Rate: 76.94%
Governor: Lakshman Prasad Acharya
Chief Minister: N. Biren Singh
Major Rivers: Barak, Imphal
Industries: Handloom, bamboo
Agriculture: Rice, wheat, maize, pulses, apricot, oranges
State Animal: Sangai
State Bird: Nongyeen

MEGHALAYA

Capital: Shillong
Location: North-east
Area: 22,429 sq. km
Population: 2,966,889
History: Formed in 1972
Languages: Garo, Khasi, Bengali, Assamese
Literacy Rate: 74.43%
Governor: C.H. Vijayashankar
Chief Minister: Conrad Kongkal Sangma
Major Rivers: Simsang, Umiam, Umtrew
Industries: Plywood, horticulture, agro-industries, cement, tourism handicrafts, sericulture
Agriculture: Rice, maize, oilseeds, tea, coffee, mushrooms, potato, fruits, including pineapple, betel nut
State Animal: Clouded leopard
State Bird: Hill mynah

Background: Manipur

MIZORAM

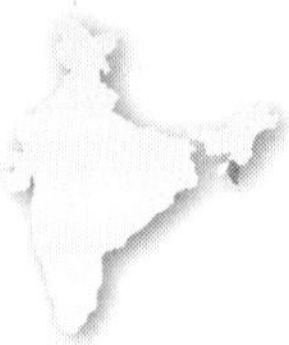

Capital: Aizawl
Location: North-east
Area: 21,087 sq. km
Population: 1,091,014
History: Formed in 1987
Language: Mizo
Literacy Rate: 91.33%
Governor: Dr Hari Babu Kambhampati
Chief Minister: Pu Lalduhawma
Major Rivers: Tlawng, Tiau, Chhimtuipui, Tuirial, Tut, Tuivai
Industries: Handloom, bamboo, food processing, tea, sericulture
Agriculture: Maize, rice, sugar cane, tapioca, ginger, cotton
State Animal: Serow
State Bird: Mrs Hume's pheasant/ Bar-tailed pheasant

NAGALAND

Capital: Kohima
Location: North-east
Area: 16,579 sq. km
Population: 1,978,502
History: Formed in 1963
Languages: Angami, Ao, Chang, Konyak, Lotha, Sangtam, Sema and Chakhesang
Literacy Rate: 79.55%
Governor: La Ganesan
Chief Minister: Neiphiu Rio
Major Rivers: Dhansiri, Doyang
Industries: Handloom, handicrafts, bamboo, food processing, forestry products
Agriculture: Rice, maize, millets, tea, bananas, pineapples, ginger
State Animal: Mithun
State Bird: Blyth's tragopan

ODISHA

Capital: Bhubaneswar
Location: East
Area: 155,707 sq. km
Population: 31,512,070
History: Formed in 1936
Language: Odia
Literacy Rate: 72.87%
Governor: Raghubar Das
Chief Minister: Mohan Charan Majhi
Major Rivers: Mahanadi, Brahmani, Baitarani, Subarnarekha, Salandi
Industries: Steel, aluminium, thermal power, cement, IT, petrochemicals, food processing
Agriculture: Rice, wheat, millets, oilseeds, coconut, cotton
State Animal: Sambar deer
State Bird: Indian roller

PUNJAB

Capital: Chandigarh
Location: North
Area: 50,362 sq. km
Population: 27,743,338
History: Formed in 1966
Language: Punjabi
Literacy Rate: 75.84%
Governor: Gulab Chand Kataria
Chief Minister: Bhagwant Singh Mann
Major Rivers: Beas, Jhelum, Ravi, Sutlej, Chenab
Industries: Sugar, dairy, machine tools, textiles, sports goods
Agriculture: Wheat, rice, oilseeds, maize, sugar cane, cotton, pulses
State Animal: Blackbuck
State Bird: Northern goshawk

Background: Odisha

RAJASTHAN

Capital: Jaipur
Location: North-west
Area: 342,239 sq. km
Population: 68,548,437
History: Formed in 1949
Languages: Rajasthani dialects such as Marwari, Mewari and others; Hindi
Literacy Rate: 66.11%
Governor: Haribhau Bagde
Chief Minister: Bhajanlal Sharma
Major Rivers: Banas, Luni, Sabarmati, Chambal, Mahi, Gambhir
Industries: Zinc and copper, cement, sugar, glass, semi-precious stones
Agriculture: Millets, pulses, maize, oilseeds, barley, cotton, chillies, rice
State Animal: Camel, Chinkara
State Bird: Great Indian bustard

TAMIL NADU

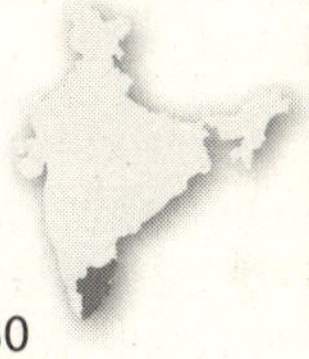

Capital: Chennai
Location: South
Area: 130,058 sq. km
Population: 72,147,030
History: Formed in 1956
Language: Tamil
Literacy Rate: 80.09%
Governor: Ravindra Narayan Ravi
Chief Minister: M.K. Stalin
Industries: Textiles, commercial vehicles, sugar, paper, electronic hardware, cement
Agriculture: Rice, sugar cane, cotton, coconut, cashew, tea, rubber, coffee
State Animal: Nilgiri tahr
State Bird: Emerald dove

SIKKIM

Capital: Gangtok
Location: North-east
Area: 7,096 sq. km
Population: 610,577
History: Formed in 1975
Languages: Nepali, Bhutia, Lepcha
Literacy Rate: 81.42%
Governor: Om Prakash Mathur
Chief Minister: Prem Singh Tamang
Major Rivers: Teesta, Rangeet, Takcham Chu, Ramphu Chu
Industries: Bamboo, handicrafts, handloom, carpet-weaving, floriculture, jewellery, tea, electronics
Agriculture: Oranges, cardamom, ginger, turmeric, cherry, pepper, baby corn
State Animal: Red panda
State Bird: Blood pheasant

TELANGANA

Capital: Hyderabad
Location: South-east
Area: 112,077 sq. km
Population: 35,004,674
History: Formed in 2014
Languages: Telugu, Urdu
Literacy Rate: 66.54%
Governor: Jishnu Dev Varma
Chief Minister: A. Revanth Reddy
Major Rivers: Godavari, Krishna, Musi
Industries: Sugar, textiles, IT, pharmaceuticals, cement
Agriculture: Rice, maize, millets, tobacco, sugar cane
State Animal: Jinka (spotted deer)
State Bird: Palapitta

Background: Rajasthan

TRIPURA

Capital: Agartala
Location: North-east
Area: 10,491 sq. km
Population: 3,673,917
History: Formed in 1972
Languages: Kokborok, Bengali
Literacy Rate: 87.22%
Governor: Indrasena Reddy Nallu
Chief Minister: Dr Manik Saha
Major Rivers: Gomti, Khowai, Longai
Industries: Natural gas, food processing, rubber, tea, bamboo, handloom, handicrafts, sericulture
Agriculture: Fruits, cashew nut, jackfruit, coconut, tea, rice, rubber
State Animal: Phayre's leaf monkey
State Bird: Green imperial pigeon

UTTAR PRADESH

Capital: Lucknow
Location: North
Area: 240,928 sq. km
Population: 199,812,341
History: Formed in 1950
Language: Hindi
Literacy Rate: 67.68%
Governor: Anandiben Mafatbhai Patel
Chief Minister: Yogi Adityanath
Major Rivers: Ganga, Gomti, Yamuna, Ghaghara, Ken, Betwa, Chambal, Son
Industries: Sugar, textiles, mining, automobiles, IT, cement, handloom, fruits, forestry, food processing
Agriculture: Rice, wheat, pulses, sugar cane, barley, millets, potatoes, cotton, tobacco
State Animal: Barasingha
State Bird: Sarus crane

UTTARAKHAND

Capital: Dehradun (winter); Bhararisain/ Gairsain (summer)
Location: North
Area: 53,483 sq. km
Population: 10,086,292
History: Formed in 2000
Languages: Kumaoni, Garhwali, Hindi
Literacy Rate: 78.82%
Governor: Lt Gen (Retd) Gurmit Singh
Chief Minister: Pushkar Singh Dhami
Major Rivers: Ganga, Yamuna, Alaknanda, Ramganga, Kali
Industries: Mining, forestry, hydel power projects, food processing, textiles, auto components
Agriculture: Rice, wheat, barley, millets, oilseeds, sugar cane, pulses
State Animal: Himalayan musk deer
State Bird: Himalayan monal

WEST BENGAL

Capital: Kolkata
Location: East
Area: 88,752 sq. km
Population: 91,276,115
History: Formed in 1947; reorganized in 1950 and 1956
Language: Bengali
Literacy Rate: 76.26%
Governor: Dr C.V. Ananda Bose
Chief Minister: Mamata Banerjee
Major Rivers: Hooghly, Teesta, Damodar, Rupnarayan
Industries: Steel, power, jute, tea, engineering, textiles, leather, aquaculture, coal mining
Agriculture: Rice, jute, maize, oilseeds, sugar cane, tea
State Animal: Fishing cat
State Bird: White-throated kingfisher

Background: West Bengal

UNION TERRITORIES

ANDAMAN AND NICOBAR ISLANDS

Capital: Port Blair
Location: Bay of Bengal
Area: 8,249 sq. km
Population: 380,581
History: Formed in 1947
Languages: Hindi, Bengali, Tamil, Telugu, Malayalam
Literacy Rate: 86.63%
Lt Governor: Admiral (Retd) Devendra Kumar Joshi
Industries: Handicrafts, fisheries, plastics, fibreglass, mild steel, tourism
Agriculture: Paddy, coconut, areca nuts, bananas, mangoes, pepper, clove, nutmeg, cinnamon
Official Animal: Dugong
Official Bird: Andaman wood pigeon

CHANDIGARH

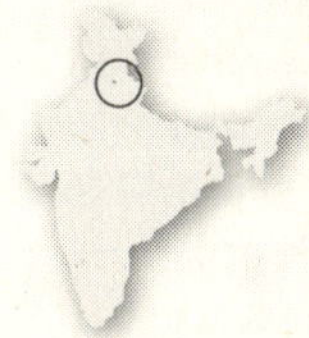

Location: Between Punjab and Haryana
Area: 114 sq. km
Population: 1,055,450
History: Formed in 1966
Languages: Hindi, Punjabi
Literacy Rate: 86.05%
Administrator: Gulab Chand Kataria
Industries: Light engineering, electrical/electronic items, machine tools, pharmaceuticals, plastics
Agriculture: Wheat, maize, rice
Official Animal: Indian grey mongoose
Official Bird: Indian grey hornbill

DADRA AND NAGAR HAVELI AND DAMAN AND DIU

Capital: Daman
Location: Between Maharashtra and Gujarat
Area: 603 sq. km
Population: 343,709
History: Formed in 2020 by combining two Union Territories
Languages: Marathi, Gujarati, Bhili, Hindi
Literacy Rate: 81.67%*
Administrator: Praful Khoda Patel
Major Rivers: Daman Ganga, Bhagwan, Kalem
Industries: Tiles, chemicals, rubber, forestry products, animal husbandry, textiles and yarns, plastic, metal-based units, tourism
Agriculture: Rice, mango, sapota (chikoo), coconut

* Taken as an average of the two former UTs

JAMMU AND KASHMIR

Capital: Srinagar
Location: North
Area: 42,241 sq. km
Population: 5,350,811
History: Formed in 2019*
Languages: Kashmiri, Dogri, Urdu, Hindi
Literacy Rate: 67.16%**
Lt Governor: Manoj Sinha
Major Rivers: Jhelum, Chenab
Industries: Machinery, sericulture, handicrafts, horticulture
Agriculture: Paddy, wheat, fruit, saffron, cumin, fruits
Official Animal: Hangul (earlier)
Official Bird: Black-necked crane (earlier)

* Official date of creation announced as 31 October 2019;
** Before the division

Background: Andaman and Nicobar Islands

UNION TERRITORIES

LADAKH

Capital: Leh
Location: North
Area: 59,146 sq. km
Population: 274,289
History: Formed in 2019*
Languages: Ladakhi (Bhoti), Purki, Shina, Tibetan, Balti, Urdu, Hindi
Literacy Rate: 77.20%
Lt Governor: Brig. (Dr) B.D. Mishra (Retd.)
Major Rivers: Indus, Zanskar, Shyok, Suru
Industries: Tourism, mountaineering
Agriculture: Barley, wheat, rice
Official Animal: Snow leopard
Official Bird: Black-necked crane

* Official date of creation announced as 31 October 2019

LAKSHADWEEP

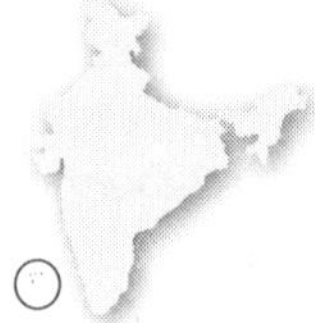

Capital: Kavaratti
Location: Arabian Sea
Area: 32 sq. km
Population: 64,473
History: Formed in 1956
Languages: Jeseri (Dweep Bhasha), Malayalam, Tamil, Urdu, Hindi
Literacy Rate: 91.85%
Administrator: Praful Khoda Patel
Industries: Coconut fibre, coir fibre, matting, fisheries
Agriculture: Coconut
Official Animal: Butterfly fish
Official Bird: Noddy tern

**WHAT ARE NCT AND NCR?

The NCT, a Union Territory of India, is administered by the Union Government and the elected government of NCT. It includes the metropolitan area of Delhi as well as nine districts, 59 census towns and 300 villages. NCR stands for National Capital Region and includes regions around Delhi, such as cities like Gurugram and Faridabad (Haryana), and Noida and Ghaziabad (Uttar Pradesh), which are parts of other states. The NCR has been expanded to embrace Sonepat, Bahadurgarh and Meerut. However, the NCR is not a legal or electoral entity.

PUDUCHERRY

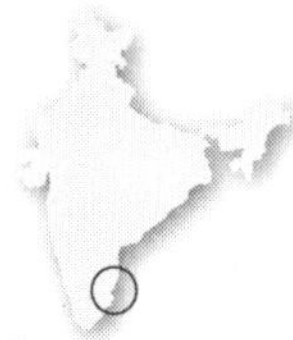

Capital: Puducherry
Location: South
Area: 483 sq. km
Population: 1,244,464
History: Formed in1954
Languages: Tamil, Telugu, Malayalam, French
Literacy Rate: 85.85%
Lt Governor: Kuniyil Kailashnathan
Chief Minister: N. Rangasamy
Major Rivers: Ponnaiyar, Koringa
Industries: Textiles, computer products, electronics, leather
Agriculture: Rice, pulses, groundnuts, coconuts, spices, chillies
Official Animal: Indian palm squirrel
Official Bird: Asian koel

NATIONAL CAPITAL TERRITORY OF DELHI**

Location: North
Area: 1,484 sq. km
Population: 16,753,235
History: The Union Territory of Delhi was officially renamed the National Capital Territory of Delhi in 1991 under the NCT Act of the same year
Languages: Hindi, Punjabi, Urdu
Literacy Rate: 86.21%
Lt Governor: Vinai Kumar Saxena
Chief Minister: Arvind Kejriwal
Major River: Yamuna
Industries: Light machines, textiles, automobile parts, bicycles, leather, sports and consumer goods, IT
Agriculture: Wheat, maize, millets vegetables, pulses
Official Animal: Nilgai
Official Bird: House sparrow

*All populations listed are from 2011 National Census

SUPERLATIVES

Fastest Animal Indian cheetah (speed: 112 km/h)

Largest Animal (land) Asian elephant (shoulder height: 2.4–2.75 m/ 7.8–9 ft; weight: 3,000–5,400 kg)

Largest Bird Great Indian bustard (length: 1.2 m/4 ft; weight: 15 kg)

Smallest Bird Pale-billed flowerpecker (length: 8 cm/3.1 in.; weight: 4–8 g)

Longest Bridge (railroad) Bogibeel Bridge, Assam (length: 4.94 km)

Tallest Building The 42, Kolkata, West Bengal (height: 268 m/879 ft)

Longest Canal Indira Gandhi Canal (length: 649 km)

Highest City Leh, Ladakh (altitude: 3,500 m/11,483 ft)

Largest City Delhi (area: 1,484 sq. km)

Largest Forest Cover (area-wise) Madhya Pradesh: 94,689 sq km, which constitutes 30.7% of the state's overall geographical expanse

Longest Corridor Ramanathaswamy Temple, Rameswaram, Tamil Nadu (corridor length: 1,220 m/4,002 ft)

Largest Dam Bhakra Nangal Dam, Himachal Pradesh and Punjab (height: 226m/ 741 ft; length: 520 m/1,706 ft – on the River Sutlej)

Longest Dam Hirakud Dam, Odisha (length: 25.79 km – on the River Mahanadi)

Highest Dam Tehri Dam, Uttarakhand (height: 260.5 m/854.6 ft – on the Rivers Bhagirathi and Bhilangana)

Largest Delta Ganga–Brahmaputra, Bay of Bengal (Total area: 105,641 sq. km; 35,213.6 sq. km in India and 70,427.3 sq. km in Bangladesh)

Largest Desert Thar Desert (area: approx. 200,000 sq. km)

Biggest Dome (new architecture) World Peace Monument Dome, Pune, Maharashtra (diameter: 48.77 m/160 ft)

Biggest Dome (old architecture) Gol Gumbaz, Vijayapura, Karnataka (diameter: 43.89 m/144 ft)

Largest Island Great Nicobar Island, Bay of Bengal (area: 921 sq. km)

INDIA

Deepest Lake
Manasbal Lake, Jammu and Kashmir (average depth: 4.5 m/15 ft)

Highest Lake
Gurudongmar Lake, Sikkim (altitude: 5,425 m/17,800 ft)

Largest Lake (artificial)
Govind Ballabh Pant Sagar, Uttar Pradesh (active capacity: 8.9 billion cubic m)

Largest Lake (freshwater)
Kolleru Lake, Andhra Pradesh (area: 245 sq. km)

Tallest Minaret (freestanding)
Qutub Minar, Delhi (height: 72.5 m/238 ft)

Largest Lake (saltwater)
Chilika Lake, Odisha (maximum surface area – monsoon: 1,165 sq. km)

Largest National Park
Hemis National Park, Leh, Ladakh (area: 3,350 sq. km)

Coldest Place (region)
Siachen, Ladakh (average temp: –50°C)

Hottest Place
Mungeshpur, Delhi (maximum recorded temperature: 52.9°C

Largest Port
Deendayal Port, by cargo handling capacity: 267.10 MTPA* (2020–21)

Longest Platform (railway)
Gorakhpur railway station, Uttar Pradesh (length: 1,366.33 m/4,482.7 ft)

Longest Railway Route
Vivek Express: Dibrugarh to Kanyakumari (length: 4,286 km)

Longest River
Ganga (length: 2,525 km)

Longest National Highway
NH-44 (length: 3,745 km)

Rainiest Spot
Mawsynram, Meghalaya (average annual rainfall: 11,873 mm/467 in.)

Largest Stadium
Narendra Modi Stadium, Ahmedabad, Gujarat (spread across 63 acres/25.5 hectares; seating capacity: 132,000)

Tallest Statue
Statue of Unity, Gujarat, (height: 182 m/597 ft)

Longest Tunnel (railway)
Pir Panjal Railway Tunnel, Jammu and Kashmir (length: 11.21 km)

Longest Tunnel (road)
Dr Syama Prasad Mookerjee Tunnel, Jammu and Kashmir (length: 9.2 km)

Longest Wall
Kumbhalgarh Fort, Rajasthan (length: 1,100 m/3,600 ft)

Highest Waterfall
Kunchikal Falls, Karnataka (height: 455 m/1,493 ft)

* Metric tonnes per annum

9 SCIENCE AND TECHNOLOGY

MAJOR BREAKTHROUGHS FROM INDIA

EARLY PERIOD

- **900** BCE – earliest Indian astronomical text, *Vedanga Jyotisa* is believed to have originated
- **800** BCE – The *Shulba Sutras* believed to be written by Baudhayana are from this time
- **6th–2nd century** BCE – Earliest atomistic theory is brought forward by Kanada in the *Vaisheshika Sutra*

- **3rd–2nd century** BCE – Pingala described the system of binary numbers in his book *Chandahsastra*
- **5th century** CE – Aryabhata uses trigonometric functions of sine and versine
- **15th century** CE – The Kerala School of Astronomy and Mathematics worked on the expansion of trigonometric functions
- **448** CE – Inscriptions found from the Gupta Empire indicate the usage of decimals
- **598–668** CE – Bhramagupta was one of the first mathematicians to treat 'zero' as a number

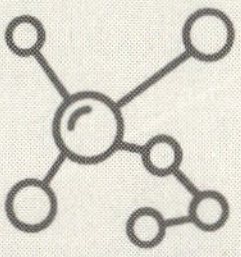

20TH CENTURY

- **1930** – C.V. Raman wins the Nobel Prize in Physics
- **1954** – Homi J. Bhabha sets up Trombay, the atomic energy establishment
- **1963** – Vikram Sarabhai establishes the country's first rocket launching station at Thumba
- **1969** – Indian Space Research Organization (ISRO) is established
- **1972** – The Space Commission and Department of Space is set up
- **1974** – First nuclear test is conducted
- **1975** – First satellite, Aryabhata, is launched
- **1981** – Indian Antarctic Programme is kickstarted
- **1984** – First Indian man in space, Rakesh Sharma spends seven days in space as part of the Intercosmos programme

- **1988** – Centre for Cellular and Molecular Biology sets up DNA fingerprinting technology
- **1991** – PARAM, the first indigeneous supercomputer is developed

21ST CENTURY

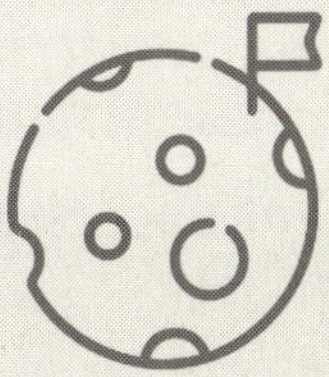

- **2009** – Venkatraman Ramakrishnan wins the Nobel Prize in Chemistry
- **2013** – Mars Orbiter Mission launched
- **2023** – Chandrayaan 3 lands near the lunar South Pole
- **2024** – Aditya-L1 completes its first halo orbit around the Sun-Earth L1 point

BRANCHES OF SCIENCE

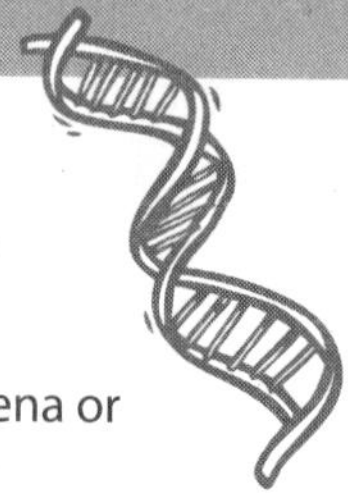

Science is divided into four main branches: Natural Sciences, Social Sciences, Applied Sciences and Formal Sciences.

NATURAL SCIENCES involve the study of natural phenomena or the laws of the physical world.

- **BIOLOGY** is the study of living things, including their structure, origin, growth, evolution, function and distribution. **Botany** deals with plants, **zoology** with animals and **microbiology** with microscopic organisms.
- **CHEMISTRY** deals with the composition of substances as well as their properties and reactions. **Organic chemistry** is the study of carbon and its compounds. **Inorganic chemistry** is the study of the structure, properties and reactions of chemical elements and their compounds. **Biochemistry** studies chemical processes that occur inside living organisms.
- **EARTH SCIENCES** study the Earth, its composition and structure. **Geology** is about the Earth's inner rock formation. **Geography** is the study of the Earth's terrain. **Oceanography** focuses on ocean currents and habitats. **Meteorology** studies the weather, and **astronomy** is the study of objects and matter outside Earth's atmosphere.
- **ENVIRONMENTAL SCIENCES** are concerned with the relationship between organisms and their environment.
- **PHYSICS** is associated with the study of properties and interactions of time, space, energy and matter.

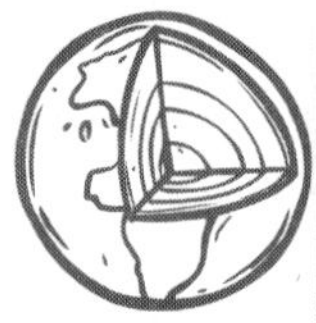

SOCIAL SCIENCES study human behaviour.

- **ANTHROPOLOGY** studies human physical traits, cultures and languages.
- **ECONOMICS** is the study of how money, goods and businesses affect people.
- **LAW** focuses on the rules of society, communities and nations.
- **POLITICAL SCIENCE** studies governmental processes and institutions.
- **PSYCHOLOGY** focuses on how the human mind functions.
- **SOCIOLOGY** analyses how humans behave in groups.

APPLIED SCIENCES involve the practical use of scientific knowledge.

- **BIOTECHNOLOGY** applies biological processes to make medicines and vaccines, and to enhance the quality of food and crops.
- **COMPUTER SCIENCE** focuses on computers and their functions.
- **ENGINEERING** is about the construction of machines and systems.

FORMAL SCIENCES form the category under which mathematics, statistics, logic and theoretical computer science fall. These disciplines, also called the 'formal' systems, have formal languages, based on logical reasoning, that contain strings of symbols and follow fixed sets of rules.

PHYSICS

Physics is the science that studies force, motion, heat, light, sound, electricity, magnetism, and changes that happen to these phenomena, not pertaining to chemical or biological changes.

MECHANICS AND MOTION

Mechanics is the field of physics dealing with the action of forces on solids, liquids and gases at rest or in motion. When forces act upon an object to make it change position with respect to time, it is known as motion. One of the ways to measure motion is to find out how much distance an object moves in one unit of time. This is known as speed, while velocity is speed in a definite direction. Velocities could increase or decrease in a given time period. The acceleration of an object is defined as its rate of change of velocity in one unit of time (usually measured in seconds).

NEWTON'S LAWS OF MOTION

In the 1680s, **Sir Isaac Newton**, an English physicist, worked on the idea of motion and formulated the three fundamental laws of motion.

THE FIRST LAW: This states that an object continues in its state of rest or of uniform motion unless an external force is applied to it.

THE SECOND LAW: The second law states that the acceleration of an object is dependent upon two variables – the force acting upon the object and the mass of the object.

THE THIRD LAW: The third law of motion states that for every action, there is an equal and opposite reaction. So if object A exerts a force on object B, then object B also exerts the same amount of force on object A.

HEAT

Heat is a form of energy caused by the motion of atoms and molecules in a body. When you increase the heat of a body, you are, in effect, increasing the amount of energy in its molecular system. When heat moves from one area to another, it is because millions of atoms and molecules are working together. The effect of heat on any atom leads to an increase in temperature and an expansion of volume (for example, railway tracks have expansion joints that let them expand and contract with temperature changes), or a possible change of physical state, like a solid turning to liquid, and a liquid turning to gas (as seen in the three states of ice, water and steam/vapour). This is known as a physical change.

LIGHT

Light is a form of energy that acts on the eye, illuminating objects. Light consists of electromagnetic (EM) waves that travel in straight lines. If you pass a ray of light through a glass prism, the colours split up into the 'spectrum' – the rainbow of colours in visible light when separated. What we call 'light' indicates only the light waves visible to us as human beings. There are different colours of light because of light waves that have different wavelengths: red light has the longest wavelength while violet light has the shortest. As far as we know, all types of light move at the same speed in a vacuum. The speed of light in a vacuum is 299,792.458 km/s. Funnily enough, light is used to measure really long distances, using a unit called a 'light year'. A light year is a unit of length equal to the distance light travels in a vacuum in one year. This distance is calculated to be 9,460,700,000,000 km (9.4607×10^{12} km).

> **At least 18 per cent of humans respond to bright lights by sneezing. This is called the photic sneeze reflex. It was first medically described in 1978. Initially, it was thought to be a reaction to heat. The disorder is actually caused by confused signalling from the trigeminal nerve, which is responsible for sensation in the face.**

ELECTRICITY

Electricity is a form of energy that produces heat, light, magnetic force and chemical changes. Objects around us contain billions of atoms, and each atom contains protons (carrying a positive charge) and electrons (carrying a negative charge). The protons are located in the centre of the atom, trapped in the nucleus. The electrons are in motion outside of the nucleus, and move to a positively-charged area. Currents are created when electrons move. We use chemicals to create an environment in which the electrons get charged enough to move, creating an electric current; this is how batteries can power electrical appliances.

MAGNETISM

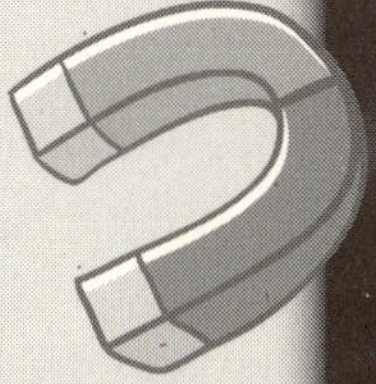

Magnetism is the force by which a material attracts or repels other materials. The space around a magnet, in which its power of attraction can have an effect on other objects, is known as its magnetic field. Magnetic poles are where the magnetic field lines begin, end and converge, at each end of the magnet. These poles have negative or positive charges. Positive poles attract the negative end of other particles and negative poles attract the positive end. Any object, small or large, may have magnetic fields. Earth, for example, has a huge magnetic field. Due to the high levels of iron in Earth's core, the magnetic field of our planet is very powerful. The North and South Poles are the magnetic poles of the Earth.

SOUND

Sound is a travelling wave that is an oscillation of pressure transmitted through a solid, liquid or gas, made up of frequencies within the range that can be heard. All matter is made up of molecules. Molecules can be tightly packed together as in a solid, or loosely packed as in a liquid or gas. When energy strikes molecules, it causes them to vibrate back and forth, producing a wave that transmits sound energy. It moves molecules in order to travel; that's why it's impossible for sound to move through outer space, where there are very few molecules. But sound does not have to move only through air – it can just as easily move through water or through metal.

SOUND AND LIGHT

Sound moves much more slowly than light. While light travels at 299,792.458 km/s, sound only goes at 1,220 km/h. That's why the Concorde airliner, with an average cruise speed of 2,140 km/h, was called 'supersonic' or 'faster than sound'. The difference in the speed at which light and sound travel is the reason why you often hear things long after you see them. For instance, you hear thunder several seconds after you see lightning in a storm, even though they may occur simultaneously.

TERMS THAT MATTER IN PHYSICS

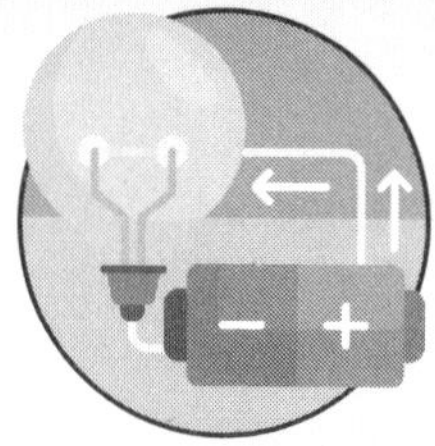

DENSITY: The density of a material is defined as its mass per unit volume. The symbol of density is ρ (the Greek letter *rho*).

ENERGY: In physics, energy is a physical quantity that describes the amount of work that can be performed by a force. Different forms of energy explain natural phenomena. These forms include (but are not limited to) kinetic, potential, thermal, gravitational, sound, light, elastic and electromagnetic energy.

ELASTICITY: It is the property of a substance that enables it to recover its original shape and size after an external force is applied to it.

FORCE: In physics, a force is that which can cause an object with mass to change its velocity. It has both magnitude and direction. A force acting on a three-dimensional object may also cause it to rotate or deform.

FRICTION: Friction is the force resisting the relative motion of solid surfaces, fluid layers or material elements in contact.

INERTIA: The property of a body to resist a change in its state of rest or of uniform motion is called inertia.

MASS: This is the quantity of matter that a body contains. A body of lower mass is accelerated less by the same force than a body of higher mass, if there is appreciable air resistance. Commonly, mass is used synonymously with weight. But, in physics and engineering, weight is the strength of the gravitational pull on the object. M (mass) = v (volume) x d (density).

MATTER: Matter is anything that has both mass and volume; it takes up space. Matter exists in five main states (or phases): solid, liquid, gas, plasma and the Bose–Einstein condensates.

MOMENTUM: The product of the mass and the velocity of a body, momentum is a measure of the quantity of motion in a body.

POWER: It is the measure of the rate of doing work.

VELOCITY: In physics, velocity is defined as the rate of change of position (or movement); both speed and direction are required to define it.

VOLUME: The quantity of three-dimensional space occupied by a liquid, solid or gas.

WAVE: A wave is a physical disturbance that transfers energy through time and space.

WEIGHT: Weight is a measure of the gravitational force acting on an object. Near the Earth's surface, the acceleration due to gravity is nearly constant, making an object's weight roughly proportional to its mass.
W (weight) = m (mass) x g (acceleration due to gravity).

BIOLOGY

Biology is the study of living things. Every form of life belongs to one of the five biological kingdoms:

A living thing is called an organism. All living organisms are made up of microscopic units called cells, which hold and carry all the biological equipment needed to keep an organism alive.

MONERA: This kingdom consists of very small, single-celled bacteria that don't have a nucleus. Some of these are able to move; others are not. Some of them can make their own food to live on, while others need to feed on things outside themselves.

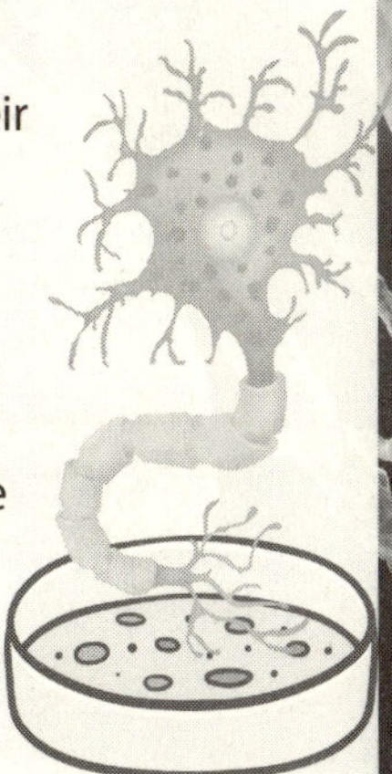

FUNGI: These creatures have more than one cell, and their cells have nuclei. Fungi generally can't move. They must depend on a source outside themselves for food. This kingdom includes mushrooms, moulds and yeast.

PROTISTA: The one-celled creatures of this kingdom share the same characteristics as those that belong to the Monera kingdom, except for the fact that they have a nucleus. Examples of protista are amoebas, paramecia and some one-celled algae.

PLANTAE: The plant kingdom consists of multicellular organisms that have nuclei, and remain in one place. They use sunlight and a substance called chlorophyll to produce their own food in a process called photosynthesis. Some plants produce flowers and fruit, while others don't. Examples of the plant kingdom are multicelled algae, ferns, mosses, shrubs, wildflowers, trees, fruits and vegetables.

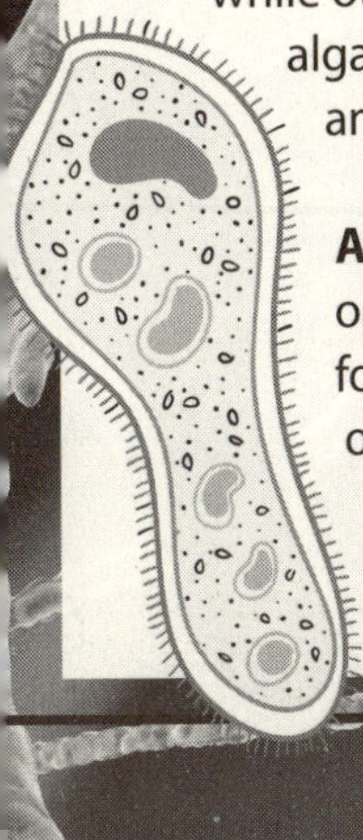

ANIMALIA: The animal kingdom comprises multicellular organisms that move and depend on outside sources for food. In general, they are the most complex creatures on Earth, and many members form social groups and communicate. Examples of animals include sponges, jellyfish, insects, amphibians, fish, mammals (including humans) and so on.

THE CLASSIFICATION OF LIVING THINGS

Scientists have divided and named every known living organism by a set of rules, called biological taxonomy. These names are called scientific names. For instance, scientists may say '*Canis familiaris*' for what you would call a 'dog'. The popular standard classification of living things is of seven groups. Each group has the characteristics of the level above it, but also has some of its own distinguishing features.

Kingdom: There are five main kingdoms: Animalia, which is made up of animals; Plantae, which is made up of plants; Protista, which is made up of protists (single-celled creatures invisible to the human eye); Fungi, which is made up of mushrooms, moulds, yeast and so on; and Monera, which is made up of bacteria.

Phylum: In the plant kingdom, phyla are often called 'divisions'. In the animal kingdom, the phylum Chordata, for example, refers to any animal with a backbone (fish, birds, mammals, reptiles, amphibians). Other phyla include Arthropoda (insects, spiders, crustaceans), Mollusca (snails, squid, clam), Annelida (segmented worms), Echinodermata (starfish, sea urchins) and many more.

Class: Phyla are further broken down into classes. The phylum Chordata includes classes like Aves (birds), Reptilia (reptiles), Amphibia (amphibians), Mammalia (mammals) and several others.

Order: Each class is made up of one or more orders. Mammalia is divided into Rodentia (mice, rats), Primates (Old- and New-world monkeys), Chiroptera (bats), Insectivora (shrews, moles), Carnivora (dogs, wolves, cats and weasels), Perissodactyla (horses, zebras), Artiodactyla (cows), Proboscidea (elephants) and many more.

Family: Orders are divided into families. The order Carnivora, for example, is broken down into *Canidae* (dogs), *Felidae* (cats), *Ursidae* (bears), *Hyaenidae* (hyenas, aardwolves), *Mustelidae* (weasels) and more.

Genus: The next division is the genus. The family *Felidae* (cats), for example, is divided into *Acinonyx* (cheetah), *Panthera* (lion, tiger), *Neofelis* (clouded leopard), *Felis* (domestic cats) and more.

Species: The next division is the species. The genus *Panthera* can be broken down to include *Panthera leo* (lion) and *Panthera tigris* (tiger). Subspecies, which differ slightly from each other, have evolved mostly due to geographical distribution or isolation: for example, *Panthera tigris sumatrae* is the Sumatran tiger. Usually, a species is called by its genus name (capitalized) followed by its species name (in small letters). A human being, for instance, is called *Homo sapiens* ('wise man' in Latin!).

Here's how these groupings apply to the animal called 'man':

Kingdom: Animalia
Phylum: Chordata
Class: Mammalia
Order: Primates
Family: *Hominidae*
Genus: *Homo*
Species: *sapiens*
Subspecies: *sapiens*

CHEMISTRY

Chemistry is the science concerned with the composition, behaviour, structure and properties of matter, as well as the changes it undergoes during chemical reactions.

WHAT IS MATTER?

Everything around you is matter, made of very tiny atoms and molecules. Anything that has mass, or takes up space, is known as matter. To date only five forms of matter have been found, though the possibility of there being more exists. The ones currently known are: solid, liquid, gas, plasma and Bose–Einstein condensates.

Changing States of Matter

Matter is constantly changing its form, depending on external forces acting upon it. Water is a common and good example of this. Whatever form it may be in, the compound is always two atoms of hydrogen and one of oxygen. The molecular structure of water will never change, whatever its state: gas, liquid or solid; or in other words: vapour, water or ice. Thus the physical state of a compound may change, but the chemical state always remains the same.

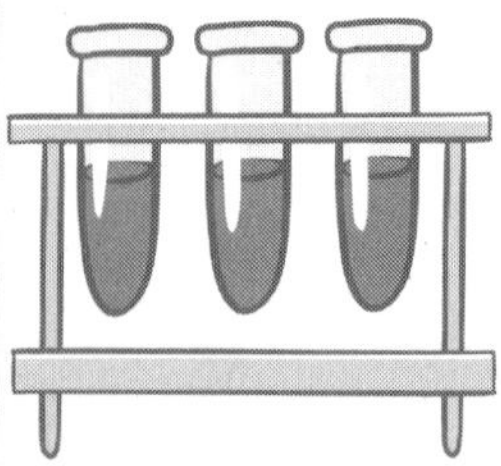

However, if you were to add an oxygen atom to water, that would constitute a chemical change, making hydrogen peroxide. Physical changes of a compound are about changing density, pressure, temperature and other physical properties, but the basic chemical structure does not change.

Solids, liquids, gases, plasmas and Bose–Einstein condensates are the different states of matter; all elements and compounds can move from one state to another state when special physical forces, such as increasing and decreasing temperatures, are introduced. Thus, when water reaches freezing point, it turns to ice, and when it reaches boiling point, it turns into steam. There are some other physical changes that may help cause a change in state, such as the application of pressure.

Physical changes are about energy and states of matter. Chemical changes happen at a

"Tungsten has the second highest melting point (3,422°C), after carbon (3,550°C), of all the known elements."

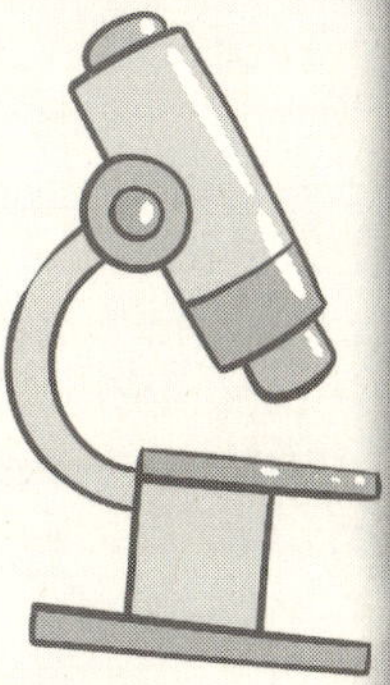

molecular level. When you step on a plastic bottle and crush it, you have forced a physical change. Chemical changes may happen on 'smaller' scales. While in some cases you can observe chemical changes such as a change in colour, most chemical changes occur at the molecular level, unseen to the naked eye. You can, for instance, see the chemical change in iron when it rusts over a long period of time; in fact, the change has occurred much earlier, but its visible manifestation happens later. Melting a sugar cube is a physical change, as you have not changed the chemical composition. However, when you burn it, the chemical bonds that held the sugar together are broken, making it a chemical change.

SOLIDS: Solids are hard as their molecules are tightly bound to each other. The tighter this bond, the harder the solid will be. This is not to say that the atoms and molecules of a solid are not always in motion. They may spin or rotate, but rarely change their positions.

LIQUIDS: Liquids are an in-between state of matter, found between solids and gases. When molecules of a gas, solid or liquid are dispersed and mixed with those of a liquid, the homogeneous mixture is called a liquid solution. A liquid has no shape of its own, and will fill up the shape of a container. Thus, if you pour water in a glass, a cup and a saucepan, the water will take the shape of each.

GAS: We are surrounded by gases. Our atmosphere is completely made up of gases. Gases are random groups of atoms. Their atoms and molecules are full of energy. Gases are used in various ways commercially, specifically because they fill a container of any size or shape. When you press down a bottle of deodorant, or open a bottle of cola, gases gush out. This is because gases are made up of free atoms and molecules, but in these cases they are packed under pressure in small spaces.

TERMS THAT MATTER IN CHEMISTRY

ACID: An acid is a chemical substance that donates protons or hydrogen ions and/or accepts electrons. Any chemical compound that, when dissolved in water, gives a solution with a hydrogen ion concentration greater than in pure water, that is, a **pH** value less than 7, is called an acid. The word 'acid' comes from the Latin words *acidus* or *acere*, which mean 'sour', since one of the characteristics of diluted acids is a sour taste – vinegar or lemon juice, for example.

ATOM: An atom is the basic unit of chemistry. It consists of a positively charged nucleus or core, containing protons and neutrons, and has a number of negatively charged electrons orbiting the nucleus.

BASE: Commonly speaking, bases are chemical compounds that, when dissolved in water, give a solution with a hydrogen ion concentration lower than that of pure water, that is, a pH value higher than 7. A soluble base is referred to as an alkali. Commonly, bases can be thought of as the chemical opposites of acids.

CATALYST: A substance that speeds up a chemical reaction without being used up in the reaction is called a catalyst.

COMPOUND: A compound is a substance that is formed by the union of two or more elements, in a definite ratio. Water, for example, is a compound with two atoms of hydrogen and one atom of oxygen.

ION: This is an atom or group of atoms that carries a positive or negative electric charge due to having lost or gained one or more electrons.

ISOTOPE: When an element has more than one possibility for the number of neutrons, it is called an isotope.

MOLECULE: A molecule is the smallest part of a compound, besides the atom. It has unique chemical properties, and undergoes certain well-defined reactions with other substances.

pH: This is a measure of the acidity or basicity of a solution, calculated on the basis of dissolved hydrogen ions, on a scale of 0 to 14, with 0 being the value of the strongest acids, and 14 being the value of the strongest bases. Distilled water is at 7, right in the middle, and, therefore, neutral.

SALTS: Salts are ionic compounds made of **cations** (positively charged ions) and **anions** (negative ions) so that the product is neutral. When acids and bases react with each other, they can form a salt and (usually) water. This is called a **neutralization** reaction.

SOLUTE: The substance (solid, liquid or gas) that dissolves in a solvent to produce a homogeneous mixture.

SOLVENT: The substance (solid, liquid or gas) in which a **solute** dissolves to produce a homogeneous mixture.

The Periodic Table of Elements

- Hydrogen
- Alkali metals
- Alkaline earth metals
- Transition metals
- Poor metals
- Non-metals
- Noble gases
- Rare earth elements

1	2	3	4	5	6	7	8	9	10	11	12	13	14	15	16	17	18
1 H																	2 He
3 Li	4 Be											5 B	6 C	7 N	8 O	9 F	10 Ne
11 Na	12 Mg											13 Al	14 Si	15 P	16 S	17 Cl	18 Ar
19 K	20 Ca	21 Sc	22 Ti	23 V	24 Cr	25 Mn	26 Fe	27 Co	28 Ni	29 Cu	30 Zn	31 Ga	32 Ge	33 As	34 Se	35 Br	36 Kr
37 Rb	38 Sr	39 Y	40 Zr	41 Nb	42 Mo	43 Tc	44 Ru	45 Rh	46 Pd	47 Ag	48 Cd	49 In	50 Sn	51 Sb	52 Te	53 I	54 Xe
55 Cs	56 Ba	La*–Lu*	72 Hf	73 Ta	74 W	75 Re	76 Os	77 Ir	78 Pt	79 Au	80 Hg	81 Ti	82 Pb	83 Bi	84 Po	85 At	86 Rn
87 Fr	88 Ra	Ac*–Lr**	104 Rf	105 Db	106 Sg	107 Bh	108 Hs	109 Mt	110 Ds	111 Rg	112 Cn	113 Nh	114 Fl	115 Mc	116 Lv	117 Ts	118 Og

*Lanthanides	58 Ce	59 Pr	60 Nd	61 Pm	62 Sm	63 Eu	64 Gd	65 Tb	66 Dy	67 Ho	68 Er	69 Tm	70 Yb	71 Lu
**Actinides	90 Th	91 Pa	92 U	93 Np	94 Pu	95 Am	96 Cm	97 Bk	98 Cf	99 Es	100 Fm	101 Md	102 No	103 Lr

A chemical **element** is a pure chemical substance consisting of one type of atom distinguished by its atomic number, which is the number of protons in its nucleus. Elements cannot be broken up into simpler substances, and in essence are the building blocks of everything around us. Common examples of elements are iron, copper, silver, gold, hydrogen, carbon, nitrogen and oxygen. In all, 118 elements have been observed as of 2012, of which 98 occur naturally on Earth.

The periodic table of chemical elements is a tabular method of displaying these elements. Although such tables existed earlier (including those by pioneering German chemist Lothar Meyer), the periodic table is usually credited to the Russian chemist Dmitri Mendeleev in 1869. He used the table to illustrate recurring ('periodic') trends in the properties of the elements.

The layout of the periodic table has been refined and expanded over the years as new elements have been discovered and added, and new theories presented to explain their chemical behaviour.

> **The only letter that doesn't appear in the periodic table is 'J'.**

ARTIFICIAL INTELLIGENCE TIMELINE

1642–1644
- Blaise Pascal invents the first calculation machine.

1843
- Ada Lovelace publishes the first computer program.

1943
- Warren McCulloch and Walter Pitts introduce the first neural network.

1950
- Alan Turing proposes the Turing Test to test a machine's ability to demonstrate human-like intelligence.

1956
- John McCarthy coins the term 'Artificial Intelligence'.

1958
- John McCarthy develops LISP, a ListProcessing computer language at MIT.

2005
- iRobot launches the most-awaited robot – a floor-cleaning, obstacle-avoiding, self-directing, battery-operated little helper called Roomba.

2009
- Stanford Racing Team's autonomous vehicle 'Stanley' wins the DARPA grand challenge by successfully driving across 211 km in under seven hours without human intervention.

2010
- Google introduces the first self-driving car for commercial services, thus launching Waymo.

2011
- IBM's Watson beat Jeopardy's top two contenders in a $1M match.
- The first virtual assistant, Siri, says hello as an app for iOS.

2012
- Without ever being told what a cat is, Google's neural network cluster discovers what cats are within a week-long exposure to YouTube videos, exhibiting near-accurate, self-taught recognition skills.

2013
- Boston Dynamics, maker of the four-legged robot BigDog, creates Atlas, a bipedal humanoid robot.
- Google introduces a beta test version of Google Glass, a brand of smart glasses.

2014
- Eugene Goostman, a chatbot that simulates a thirteen-year-old Ukrainian boy, is deemed to have passed the Turing Test.
- Amazon releases a virtual assitant, Alexa, that is capable of shopping via voice interactions.

2015
- Elon Musk and Stephen Hawking are among the 3,000 people to sign an open letter requesting a ban on the development and adoption of autonomous weapons for war purposes.

2016
- Google DeepMind's AlphaGo beats legendary Go champion Lee Sedol by 4–1.
- Microsoft releases AI chatbot 'Tay'. It was designed to learn from and respond to Twitter conversations and had to be shut down within sixteen hours because it began posting inflammatory and offensive tweets.

2017
- Nvidia debuts an AI that creates convincing fake photos of celebrities that do not exist.
- Google introduces AutoML, an AI designed to learn and create more AIs.
- Saudi Arabia grants citizenship to a social AI-based robot called Sophia.
- Mark Zuckerberg and Musk feud on Twitter about the pros and cons of a future ruled by AI.
- Robot Xiaoyi clears the Chinese National Medical Licensing Exam.
- iPhone X is launched with a neural engine.

2018
- Duplex by Google gets in trouble for being too convincing at its debut.
- Major companies like Amazon and Google suffer severe public and academic scrutiny for using AI in facial recognition and defence projects.
- OpenAI loses to professional Dota 2 players.

2019

1961

◆ First industrial programmable robot 'UNIMATE' – an electronic arm that performs sequential actions – lifts hot metal parts at the General Motors factory.

1964

◆ Joseph Weizenbaum creates ELIZA, a prototype chatbot that holds convincing therapy consultations with humans by focusing on keywords.

1966

◆ A robot that parses commands and decides subsequent actions, SHAKEY, is introduced by SRI.

1972

◆ Stanford University works on MYCIN, an early AI programme that provides a probable diagnosis with reasoning comparable to those of medical practitioners.

1974 TO EARLY 1980s

◆ AI winter as both interest and funding for R&D wanes because of excessive hype, slow results and low commercial viability.

1980

◆ XCON (eXpert CONfigurer) is successful in automatically selecting computer system components based on customer requirements.

1982

◆ ACE, a system for Automatic Cable Expertise, is used to provide troubleshooting reports and management analyses using a conventional database management system.

1984

◆ A panel called 'The Dark Ages of AI — Can we avoid or survive them?' is held at the 1984 AAAI conference.

1997

◆ DeepBlue, IBM's chess-playing supercomputer, is the first machine to defeat grandmaster with a score of 3.5 to 2.5.

1998

◆ Cynthia Breazeal's Kismet, a robot that interacts socially like a child with a caretaker, is able to identify and respond to emotions.

1999

◆ With over 3,000 sales in under twenty minutes, Sony launches its Artificial Intelligence roBOt dog (aibo) that grows from a puppy to a dog and interacts with its human. You can still order one today!

2002

2020

◆ OpenAI releases GPT-2, an AI that generates readable content based on a few lines fed into it intially.

◆ DeepMind trains AI to consider future consequences of decisions.

◆ CovidScholar – a search engine that compiles and classifies all available studies on COVID-19 – launches.

◆ The first AI university, Mohamed bin Zayed University of Artificial Intelligence, is established in Abu Dhabi.

2021

◆ OpenAI launches DALL-E which generates images based on text.

◆ Facebook and NYU release an AI that predicts a COVID-19 patient's condition over the next four days.

◆ The European Commission poses restrictions over the use of AI.

◆ AI predicts the onset of Alzheimer's in patients with 97 per cent accuracy.

◆ AI helps identify hundreds of exoplanets.

◆ Google launches its pilot flood prediction system in India.

2022

◆ OpenAI introduces ChatGPT – an AI that answers queries and executes instructions given in prompts – for free use.

◆ Google DeepMind releases AlphaCode, a system that autonomously codes at competitive levels.

◆ DeepMind introduces GATO that performs various tasks, such as holding conversations, captioning images, playing video games and even moving robotic arms!

2023

◆ Amazon CodeWhisperer, a generative AI that suggests and completes codes in nearly fifteen languages, is live and free for use.

◆ Google Bard is available for conversations and coding in over forty natural languages.

◆ Gen AI and 'AI for all' are on the rise. AI will be integrated into most fields, ushering in the age of augmented working.

2024

◆ More laws and regulations are being developed to set frameworks and standards for AI governance to protect people from misinformation, privacy issues and bias.

◆ Meta releases MetaAI on several of its applications like WhatsApp, Messenger, Instagram and Facebook, which allows users to to create content, deep dive into topics and get things done, all without leaving the app.

◆ GenerativeAI sees massive increase in funding and investment to help with rapid its development.

FROM 1G TO 6G: EVOLUTION OF MOBILE COMMUNICATION NETWORKS

When Dr Martin Cooper, along with his team at Motorola, made the first wireless phone call using the newly invented Motorola DynaTAC 8000X in 1973, they knew they were making a historic move in the telecommunications industry. Similarly, the introduction of First-Generation mobile networks in Japan, in 1979, brought in a new age of handheld phones unrestricted by wires. Fast-forward 50 years, and we are ready to welcome the Sixth Generation of mobile networks.

The First Generation: The inception of wireless cellular technology 1G in the 1980s allowed for communication between supported devices through a wireless network. It primarily facilitated calls, albeit limited due to roaming capabilities. It did not provide any internet access and limited communication to only voice calls.

The Second Generation: In 1990s, transitioning from analogue to digital technology, 2G introduced services like Short Message Service (SMS) and Multimedia Messaging Service (MMS). It had better roaming features and even provided internet support, though it was limited to text-based messaging like emails and simple internet browsing.

The Third Generation: The early 2000s brought to the world high-speed internet, thus paving the way for smartphones and mobile application ecosystems. 3G facilitated mobile televisions, online radio services and emails on phones, and its defining features included video calling and mobile phone applications. It had significantly faster internet speeds, allowing for improved web browsing and basic video streaming.

The Fourth Generation: The year 2010 witnessed a giant leap for mobile communications with 4G providing significantly faster data speeds, low latency i.e., ability of a network to provide responses with minimum delay, and the ability to handle high-definition video streaming, online gaming and other data-intensive applications. It also introduced technologies such as Long-Term Evolution (LTE) and WiMAX that facilitated the same. It gave rise to the app economy, enabling increased levels of content consumption and communications.

The Fifth Generation: 5G was only introduced in early 2020, promising high internet speeds and enabling technologies like the metaverse, leveraging Orthogonal Frequency-Division Multiplexing (OFDM) and millimetre wireless for enhanced data rates and low-latency communication. It not only connected individuals but also machines, objects and devices. Its features and applications were almost futuristic, opening doors for Virtual Reality (VR), Augmented Reality (AR), remote control and even autonomous vehicles. Out of all mobile network developments till now, 5G provided the fastest internet speeds, enabling a virtually lag-free experience. However, a major drawback for it was that the signal range was comparatively shorter to previous generations, requiring more infrastructural support such as cell towers.

THE BIG G: Introducing the new 6G technology

Four of Japan's major telecom companies, NTT Docomo, Inc., NTT Corporation, NEC Corporation and Fujitsu Limited, came together to release the first prototype of a 6G device in April 2024. The technology is stated to be 500 times faster than the existing 5G model. Testing for the same was successfully completed on 11 April 2024.

So, what are the features of this highly awaited communication technology?

6G aims to work on terahertz (THz) frequencies, allowing for data transfer over hundreds of gigahertz (GHz). It is expected to be significantly faster and have lower latency. It will integrate artificial intelligence to optimize managing traffic, ensure reliable data delivery and enhance network efficiency and adaptability. 6G will ensure safety by employing various security measures such as encryption and authentication.

The significance of 6G

Sustainability: 6G aims to promote sustainability by supporting data collection and closed-loop control of numerous appliances by enabling faster and lower cost-per-bit connectivity.

Energy efficiency: This technology is capable of turning off components and reducing capacity during low demand, thus conserving energy.
Security: Through various measures, 6G is being made to withstand threats such as jamming.

Applications of this new technology

6G can be applied in various sectors to meet the needs of individuals and businesses.
Healthcare: Improvements in responding to emergencies, access and meeting growing demands.
Agriculture: Creation of intelligent, predictive systems to anticipate yield, irrigation schedule, pesticide schedule and crop health information.
Transport: Various developments for air travel have been predicted to improve Urban Air Mobility.
Education: The technology may help in integrating the virtual to physical classroom spaces, as well as access to higher quality educational resources.
Space exploration: With 6G, there is a possibility of controlling space robots in real time, as well access to higher resolution pictures of planets and stars.

So, when is 6G coming to India? The Department of Telecommunications (DoT) has established a Technology Innovation Group on 6G (TIG-6G) to create the Bharat 6G Vision, a strategy to develop 6G technology in India by 2030. India also played a huge role in the creation of the 6G Vision Framework set by the International Telecommunication Union.

The Bharat 6G Vision is proposed to be implemented in two phases. Phase One (2023–25) aims to support explorative ideas, risky pathways and proof-of-concept tests. In Phase Two (2025–30), the aim is to back concepts with global potential, leading to eventual commercialization.

Apprehensions regarding 6G in India: The recent 5G mobile technology was launched in India in late 2022. The number of users of 5G are still comparatively less when compared to the population. While patents have been secured for 6G to be commercially deployed in India, there are still many apprehensions with regards to its implementation.

The main challenges include lack of infrastructure to support 6G, security concerns and overall difficulties that researchers may face during developing and implementing this complex technology. Another concern is the environmental impact, since most 6G-supporting devices are battery-powered, thus having a significant carbon footprint.

Nonetheless, the DoT and the Government of India are investing a lot into research and development of 6G technology to establish India as one of the front-line contributors at a global level.

SCIENCE AND TECH NEWS

India's first home-grown gene therapy for cancer

In 2015, a type of immunotherapy in which a person's T-cells are modified in a laboratory to selectively kill cancer cells, called CAR T-cell therapies, were being tested in clinical trials in the United States. Although CAR T-cell therapies seemed promising for certain blood cancers, they would be very expensive.

Alka Dwivedi, then a graduate student at the Indian Institute of Technology (IIT) Bombay, felt that the therapies wouldn't really be an option for many people in low- and middle-income countries like India. Dr Dwivedi and her colleagues wanted to design a different CAR T-cell therapy, one that could be made in India and accessible to the people of the country. Over the next several years, Dr Dwivedi worked on it with colleagues from IIT Bombay and Tata Memorial Centre in Mumbai.

On 4 April 2024, President of India Droupadi Murmu launched the first CAR T-cell therapy developed in India. She praised the treatment as a 'major breakthrough' that offers 'new hope for the humankind' in the fight against the illness.

Google's DeepMind Genie

DeepMind, an AI subsidiary of Google, has introduced Genie, a model that can be prompted to generate action-controllable virtual worlds described through text, images, photographs and even sketches. It was trained 'in an unsupervised manner from unlabelled Internet videos'. This nonetheless opens new ways of creating and stepping into virtual worlds. With Genie, people will be able to create their own entirely imagined virtual worlds.

Deepfakes

'Deepfake' is a combination of the terms 'deep learning' and 'fake.' The word signifies sound or visual media that has been altered or created using AI deep learning. The technology can change faces, control facial expressions and synthesize faces and speech. Most deepfake videos are created on high-end desktops with powerful graphics cards or with computing abilities in the cloud. A significant danger of deepfakes is that the manipulation is so well done that it is almost impossible to differentiate them from real videos. This is highly dangerous and the governments have issued an advisory that people should be beware of such malpractices.

AI brain implant helps a stroke survivor

Pancho, at age twenty, became severely paralysed from an earlier stroke. He could moan and grunt but not articulate clear words. Scientists at the University of California have developed a brain implant

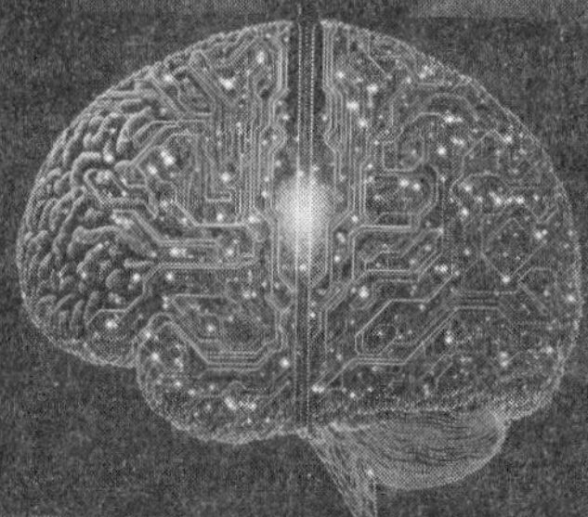

that uses artificial intelligence to help the native Spanish speaker who learned English as an adult communicate in both languages. Scientists from the university's Centre for Neural Engineering and Prostheses have worked for several years to design a decoding system that turns the man's brain activity into sentences in both languages and displays them on a screen. It shows the feasibility of 'a bilingual speech neuroprosthesis (a medical device that can enhance the input and output of a neural system), or bilingual brain implant'.

10 SPORTS

A JOURNEY OF SPORTS IN INDIA

EARLY PERIOD

3rd MILLENNIUM BCE Dholavira, Gujarat, shows traces of a stadium with terraced stands.

4th CENTURY BCE Origins of Kabaddi are attributed to this period.

13th CENTURY Indigenous forms of wrestling, such as 'malla yudha', come into existence. These later developed into 'dangals' and eventually modern-day wrestling in India.

19th CENTURY Snooker originates in India among the British Army officers stationed here. Modern polo evolved from existing games such as Kanjei-bazee or Pulu that was played in Assam.

20TH CENTURY

1900 Norman Pritchard represents India in the Paris Olympics and wins two silver medals.

1920 India sends an official contingent to the 1920 Antwerp Olympics.

1924 The National Games of India are held for the first time.

1927 The Indian Olympic Association is formed.

1928 India wins its first gold medal at the Olympics (Hockey); The Board of Control for Cricket in India (BCCI) is formed.

1934 India makes its debut at the Commonwealth Games.

1951 The first-ever Asian Games are held in New Delhi.

1952 Wrestler K.D. Jadhav wins independent India's first individual Olympic medal in 1952.

1958 Milkha Singh, the 'Flying Sikh', wins three gold medals (athletics) at the Asian Games.

1962 India wins its first gold medal in football at the Asian Games.

1968 India makes its debut at the Olympic Paralympic Games.

1981 India participates in the inaugural World Games.

MILKHA SINGH

VISWANATHAN ANAND

1983 India wins its first Cricket World Cup under the captaincy of Kapil Dev.

1984 India participates in the South Asian Games.

1986 P.T. Usha wins four gold medals (athletics) at the Asian Games.

1988 Viswanathan Anand becomes the first grandmaster from India.

1999 Leander Paes and Mahesh Bhupathi become the first all-Indian pair to win a Grand Slam title, bagging the French Open and Wimbledon.

21ST CENTURY

2008 Abhinav Bindra wins the first individual gold medal (shooting) at the Beijing Olympics.

2010 India hosts the Commonwealth Games.

SAINA NEHWAL

2011 India wins the Cricket World Cup under the captaincy of Mahendra Singh Dhoni.

2012 Saina Nehwal wins a bronze medal at the London Olympics 2012, marking India's first Olympic medal for Badminton.

2012 M.C. Mary Kom wins a bronze medal at the London Olympics, becoming the first Indian female boxer to win an Olympic medal.

2019 P.V. Sindhu becomes the first Indian winner of the Badminton World Championships; Mary Kom becomes the first boxer in the world to win eight World Championship medals.

2020 Neeraj Chopra wins India's first gold medal in Athletics at the Olympics; Motera Stadium, the largest in the world, is completed.

2023 India crosses the 100-medal mark at the Asian Games.

2024 India wins the ICC Men's T20 World Cup.

GENERAL NEWS

- The **Kansas City Chiefs** defeated the **San Francisco 49ers** 25–22 in the 2023 Super Bowl, securing their third Super Bowl victory in five years. The event had an average viewership of 123.4 million in the USA, making it the most-watched broadcast since the 1969 Moon landing.
- **Virat Kohli, Rohit Sharma** and **Ravindra Jadeja** decided to retire from the T20 International after winning the World Cup in Barbados.

- The **2024 Olympics** took place from 26 July to 11 August, and the **Paralympics** were held from 28 August to 8 September in Paris, France. The **2028 Olympics** are scheduled to occur in Los Angeles.
- **Gautam Gambhir** was named the head coach of the Indian **men's cricket team**.
- **Haryana** won its first ever **Vijay Hazare Trophy** after beating Rajasthan by 30 runs in the final.
- India finished fourth and fifth at the **2022 Asian Games** and **Asian Para Games,** respectively.
- **Neeraj Chopra** landed a best throw of 83.80m to secure the second position at the **Diamond League finals** in Eugene.
- The **2024 Tour de France** was the 111th edition of the race. It commenced in Florence, Italy, on 29 June and concluded in Nice, France, on 21 July.

ARCHERY

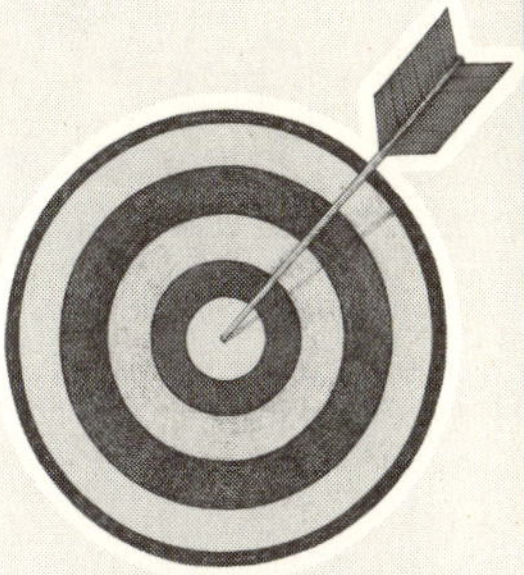

- The **2024 Archery World Cup** marks the eighteenth edition of the global archery series held each year by World Archery. This year's World Cup includes four events and is scheduled from 23 April to 20 October 2024.
- **Dhiraj Bommadevara** and **Ankita Bhakat** clinched the bronze medal by defeating Mexico in the recurve mixed team event at the Archery World Cup Stage 3 in Antalya, Turkey.

Archery comes from the Latin word 'arcus', which means bow.

- **Dhiraj Bommadevara** defeated **Mohammed Sagor Islam** from Bangladesh 6–0, **Riau Salsabilla** from Indonesia 7–1, **Santiago Arango** from Colombia 6–4, and **Jonathan Vetter** from Germany 7–3 to advance to the semi-finals, where he defeated Italy's **Mauro Nespoli**, a multiple-time Olympic medal winner, to win the bronze in the men's recurve event.
- The Indian team of **Jyothi Surekha Vennam**, **Parneet Kaur** and **Aditi Swami** secured their third straight gold medal in the compound women's team event at the Archery World Cup Stage 3.
- Archer **Bhajan Kaur**, who won a bronze medal at the 2022 Asian Games, bagged a gold medal at the Final Olympic Qualifier, securing India a quota spot for the women's individual recurve archery event at the Olympics.

ASIAN GAMES

- The **2022 Asian Games**, officially referred to as the **19th Asian Games,** and commonly known as **Hangzhou 2022**, took place from 23 September to 8 October 2023, in Hangzhou, China.
- The event was scheduled to take place from 11–25 September 2022 but had to be postponed because of increasing COVID-19 cases in China.
- India concluded their 2022 Asian Games journey with a remarkable total of 107 medals: 28 gold, 38 silver and 41 bronze, surpassing their previous record from the 2018 Jakarta edition where they secured 70 medals: 16 gold, 23 silver and 31 bronze.
- In athletics, India secured six gold medals, along with 14 silver and nine bronze medals, contributing to a total of 29 medals for the country.
- The cricket and kabaddi teams both won two gold medals each, while the men's hockey team won gold. Additionally, the women's hockey team clinched a bronze medal.
- Both the women and men's cricket teams, captained by **Harmanpreet Kaur** and **Ruturaj Gaikwad** respectively, won gold medals.
- In squash, India secured a total of five medals, with two of them being gold.
- India also clinched their inaugural Asian Games Badminton gold medal, thanks to the men's doubles duo of Chirag Shetty and Satwiksairaj Rankireddy.

HARMANPREET KAUR

BADMINTON

- The Indian women's team won a gold medal at the 2024 Badminton Asia Team Championships after beating Thailand 3–2 in the final in Shah Alam, Malaysia.
- Denmark mixed doubles badminton player **Mathias Christiansen** pulled out of the Paris Olympics. His national federation stated that this decision was due to several unintentional mistakes in reporting his location, as required by anti-doping rules.

PRAKASH PADUKONE co-founded the Olympic Gold Quest, a non-profit to support the dreams of Indian athletes and help them work towards Olympic gold medals.

- A seventeen-year-old badminton player from China tragically passed away after experiencing a cardiac arrest while playing in a match in Yogyakarta, Indonesia. **Zhang Zhijie** was facing off against Japan's **Kazuma Kawano** in the Asia Junior Championships when he collapsed on the court during the first game of their match.

P. V. SINDHU

- India's run at the Australian Open 2024 badminton competition concluded after **H.S. Prannoy** was defeated in the men's singles quarter-finals by Japan's **Kodai Naraoka** in Sydney.
- Indian badminton player **P.V. Sindhu** was defeated by **Carolina Marín** in the women's singles pre-quarterfinals at the Singapore Open.

Men's Singles Rankings

RANK	NAME	CHANGE	POINTS
1.	Chou Tien Chen	0	64,520
2.	Shi Yuqi	0	61,800
3.	Lee Zii Jia	0	58,900
4.	Anders Antonsen	+1	58,870
5.	Lin Chun-Yi	-1	57,860

(Last updated on 9 July 2024)

Women's Singles Rankings

RANK	NAME	CHANGE	POINTS
1.	Wang Zhi Yi	0	60,890
2.	An Se Young	0	58,650
3.	Busanan Ongbamrungphan	+8	57,530
4.	Nozomi Okuhara	+4	56,230
5.	Hsu Wen Chi	+1	55,220

(Last updated on 9 July 2024)

BOXING

- Six-time world champion boxer **M.C. Mary Kom** stepped down as India's chef-de-mission for the Paris Olympics.
- **Mohammad Hussamuddin** from India, who won a bronze medal at the 2023 World Boxing Championships, got eliminated from the World Qualification Tournament for the Paris 2024 Olympics. He lost his round of 32 match in Busto Arsizio, Italy.
- **Nick Ball** defeated **Raymond Ford** to claim the World Boxing Association Featherweight World Champion title in Riyadh, Saudi Arabia.

- **Oleksandr Usyk** defeated **Tyson Fury** by split decision to secure the world's first undisputed heavyweight champions title in twenty-five years, marking an extraordinary accomplishment in boxing's four-belt era.

OLEKSANDR USYK

CHESS

- The **World Chess Championship 2024** will be a chess match between the reigning world champion **Ding Liren** and the challenger **Dommaraju Gukesh** to determine the World Chess Champion. The match is provisionally scheduled between 20 November and 15 December 2024, with Singapore hosting the match.

DING LIREN DOMMARAJU GUKESH

- GM **Daniel Dardha** won the 2024 **Belgian Championship**, securing his fourth national title.
- GM **Vitaly Sivuk** won the **Swedish Championship** 2024, defending his national champion title.
- A nine-year-old chess prodigy is on track to create a historic moment by becoming the youngest individual to represent England at an international level in any sport. **Bodhana Sivanandan**, hailing from Harrow in north-west London, will be part of the English women's team at the Chess Olympiad in Hungary.
- **Magnus Carlsen** and **Ju Wenjun** were crowned champions at the Norway Chess tournament. Carlsen secured victory in the open section with 17.5 points, while Ju triumphed in the women's section with 19 points. **Praggnanandhaa** finished third.
- **Koneru Humpy**, the former world rapid chess champion, has chosen not to participate in the Chess Olympiad scheduled for September 2024 in Budapest, Hungary. She feels she is unable to compete in consecutive tournaments.
- The 18th **ICCD World Individual Deaf Chess Championship** took place from 25 June to

VISWANATHAN ANAND was the first player to win the Tata Steel Chess Tournament five times.

6 July 2024. **Yehuda Gruenfeld** and **Pawel Piekielny** scored 7/9 and shared the first position. Gruenfeld secured the victory based on a superior Buchholz tie-break.

Men's Ratings

RANK	PLAYER	RATING
1	Magnus Carlsen	2,832
2	Hikaru Nakamura	2,802
3	Fabiano Caruana	2,796
4	Arjun Erigaisi	2,778
5	Ian Nepomniachtchi	2,770
6	Nodirbek Abdusattorov	2,769
7	Dommaraju Gukesh	2,763
8	R. Praggnanandhaa	2,757
9	Wesley So	2,757
10	Wei Yi	2,755

(Updated as of July 2024)

Women's Ratings

RANK	PLAYER	RATING
1	Hou Yifan	2,632
2	Ju Wenjun	2,566
3	Lei Tingjie	2,548
4	Tan Zhongyi	2,545
5	Aleksandra Goryachkina	2,545
6	Kateryna Lagno	2,532
7	Koneru Humpy	2,530
8	Anna Muzychuk	2,521
9	Mariya Muzychuk	2,508
10	Nana Dzagnidze	2,505

(Updated as of July 2024)

CRICKET

- The 2024 Indian Premier League season started on 22 March and ended on 26 May. The Kolkata Knight Riders secured their third IPL championship by beating Sunrisers Hyderabad with an 8-wicket victory in Chennai.
- Sunil Narine became the first player to win the Most Valuable Player award in the IPL thrice. He first won the award in 2012, then in 2018 and now in 2024.
- The ICC Cricket World Cup 2023 was held from 5 October to 9 November.
- Australia secured their sixth World Cup trophy after beating India by 6 wickets in the finals on 19 November 2023.
- The ICC Men's T20 World Cup was held from 1 June to 29 June in the United States and the West Indies. India beat South Africa by 7 runs in the finals held on 29 June in Barbados.
- India defeated Pakistan by 5 wickets in the final of the World Championship of Legends 2024, held in Birmingham on 13 July.

- India made history by becoming the first team to win the **ICC Men's T20 World Cup** undefeated.

ICC MEN'S T20 WORLD CUP TEAM

- Rohit Sharma, Ravindra Jadeja and Virat Kohli announced their retirement from T20s shortly after the win.
- The ICC Women's T20 World Cup is scheduled between 3–20 October 2024 in the UAE. The tournament will have twenty-three matches featuring the top ten women's teams in the world.

DID YOU KNOW?
Mitchell Starc made history in the Indian Premier League by becoming the priciest signing ever, securing a deal worth ₹24.75 crore with Kolkata Knight Riders.

INDIAN PREMIER LEAGUE 2024

The 2024 Indian Premier League was the seventeenth season of the popular T20 cricket league in India, managed by the Board of Control for Cricket in India.

Ten teams competed in seventy-four matches from 22 March to 26 May 2024, in thirteen cities across India. Chennai was the host city for both the opening ceremony and the final of the tournament.

Kolkata Knight Riders won their third IPL title by defeating Sunrisers Hyderabad with an impressive 8-wicket victory in the finals.

Virat Kohli scored 741 runs and won the IPL Orange Cap.

Harshal Patel took 24 wickets and won the IPL Purple Cap.

Sunil Narine won the Most Valuable Player award.

Abhishek Sharma scored the highest number of sixes (42).

A new bowling rule was announced. Under this rule, bowlers could bowl up to two bouncers (fast short-pitched deliveries) per over. In previous seasons, only one bouncer was permitted per over.

- The ninth edition of ICC Champions Trophy is set to happen in February 2025 in Pakistan.

Men's ODI Team Rankings

RANK	TEAM	MATCHES	POINTS	RATING
1.	India	42	5,117	122
2.	Australia	34	3,936	116
3.	South Africa	30	3,357	112
4.	New Zealand	26	2,762	106
5.	England	33	3,349	101

(Last updated on 2 May 2024)

Men's T20 Team Rankings

RANK	TEAM	MATCHES	POINTS	RATING
1.	India	60	15,996	267
2.	Australia	40	10,241	256
3.	England	39	9,876	253
4.	West Indies	46	11,604	252
5.	South Africa	35	8,777	251

(Last updated on 17 July 2024)

Women's ODI Team Rankings

RANK	TEAM	MATCHES	POINTS	RATING
1.	Australia	30	4,889	163
2.	England	31	4,035	130
3.	South Africa	32	3,454	108
4.	India	24	2,490	104
5.	Sri Lanka	14	1,368	98

(Last updated on 3 July 2024)

Women's T20 Team Rankings

RANK	TEAM	MATCHES	POINTS	RATING
1.	Australia	34	9,982	294
2.	England	42	11,968	285
3.	India	50	13,099	262
4.	New Zealand	36	9,099	253
5.	South Africa	34	8,260	243

(Last updated on 14 July 2024)

FOOTBALL

- Argentina emerged victorious over Colombia in the **Copa América 2024**, securing their sixteenth championship title and solidifying their position as the most successful team in the tournament's history.
- **Lionel Messi** had to leave the field due to a visible injury to his right ankle during the final. He was replaced by Nicolás González.
- Spain emerged as the champions of **UEFA Euro 2024** after defeating England 2–1 in the final held in Germany.
- **Gareth Southgate** stepped down from his position with England following the team's loss in the Euro 2024 final. The fifty-three-year-old, who took on the role of head coach of the national team in 2016, departed after overseeing 102 matches.
- **Kylian Mbappé** left Paris St-Germain and joined Real Madrid.

KYLIAN MBAPPÉ

- **Rodrigo Hernández Cascante** (Rodri) was named the best player of Euro 2024 after helping Spain win the competition for the fourth time.
- The 2024–25 **Premier League** season kicked off on the weekend of 17–18 August, with the final set of matches to take place on 25 May 2025.

FORMULA F1

- **Max Verstappen**'s fifty-fourth victory moves him ahead of **Sebastian Vettel** into third place on the all-time win list, trailing only **Michael Schumacher** with 91 wins and **Lewis Hamilton** with 103 wins.
- **Enrico Cardile**, the ex-technical director of Ferrari, is set to become Aston Martin's chief technical officer in 2025.

LEWIS HAMILTON

- **Lewis Hamilton** secured victory after an intense battle with Max Verstappen and Lando Norris at the British Grand Prix, bagging his first win since December 2021.
- **George Russell** claimed victory at the **Austrian Grand Prix** following a crash involving **Max Verstappen** and **Lando Norris** as they battled for the lead. Verstappen received a ten-second penalty for the incident, where he squeezed the McLaren driver off track while Norris was attempting to overtake, leading to Norris's retirement from the race.
- The FIA and Formula 1 have revealed the schedule for the **2025 FIA Formula One World Championship**, featuring a twenty-four-round season to celebrate the championship's seventy-fifth anniversary. Starting with the Australian Grand Prix on 14–16 March and wrapping up with the Abu Dhabi Grand Prix on the weekend of 5–7 December, the season will span five continents.

POSITION	DRIVER	POINTS	WINS	PODIUMS
1	Max Verstappen	255	7	9
2	Lando Norris	171	1	7
3	Charles Leclerc	150	1	5
4	Carlos Sainz	146	1	5
5	Oscar Piastri	124	0	2
6	Sergio Pérez	118	0	4
7	George Russell	111	1	2
8	Lewis Hamilton	110	1	2
9	Fernando Alonso	45	0	0
10	Lance Stroll	23	0	0

TENNIS

BARBORA KREJČÍKOVÁ

- **Carlos Alcaraz** retained his Wimbledon championship by beating Novak Djokovic with a score of 6–2, 6–2, 7–6 in the 2024 final that took place on 14 July 2024.
- **Barbora Krejčíková** beat Jasmine Paolini 6–2, 2–6, 6–4 in the 2024 Wimbledon women's singles final to claim her second Grand Slam title.
- **Henry Patten** and **Harri Heliövaara** clinched a superb 6–7(7), 7–6(8), 7–6(11–9) victory against Max Purcell and Jordan Thompson in the 2024 Wimbledon men's doubles final.
- **Taylor Townsend** and **Kateřina Siniaková** beat **Gabriela Dabrowski** and **Erin Routliffe** 7–6(5), 7–6(1) in the 2024 Wimbledon women's doubles final. This marks Townsend's first Grand Slam title.
- **Carlos Alcaraz** won the men's singles tennis title at the 2024 French Open by beating Alexander Zverev in the final with a score of 6–3, 2–6, 5–7, 6–1, 6–2.
- **Iga Świątek** beat **Jasmine Paolini** 6–2, 6–1 in the French Open final at Roland Garros, Paris.
- **Jannik Sinner** beat **Daniil Medvedev** 3–6, 3–6, 6–4, 6–4, 6–3 to win the Australian Open men's singles title.
- **Aryna Sabalenka** beat **Zheng Qinwen** 6–3, 6–2 in the Australian Open women's single finals.
- The **2024 US Open** is scheduled between 26 August–8 September 2024.
- **Novak Djokovic** and **Coco Gauff** are the men's and women's defending champions respectively.
- The **2025 Australian Open** is set for 12–26 January 2025.

Men's Rankings

RANK	PLAYER	POINTS
1.	Jannik Sinner	9,570
2.	Novak Djokovic	8,460
3.	Carlos Alcaraz	8,130
4.	Alexander Zverev	7,015
5.	Daniil Medvedev	6,525
6.	Alex de Minaur	4,185
7.	Hubert Hurkacz	4,105
8.	Andrey Rublev	4,070
9.	Casper Ruud	4,030
10	Grigor Dimitrov	3,770

(Updated on 17 July 2024)

Women's Rankings

RANK	PLAYER	POINTS
1.	Iga Świątek	11,285
2.	Coco Gauff	8,173
3.	Aryna Sabalenka	7,061
4.	Elena Rybakina	6,376
5.	Jasmine Paolini	5,518
6.	Jessica Pegula	4,665
7.	Qinwen Zheng	4,055
8.	Maria Sakkari	3,925
9.	Danielle Collins	3,702
10.	Barbora Krejčíková	3,573

(Updated on 15 July 2024)

SPORTS NEWSMAKERS

CARLOS ALCARAZ

CARLOS ALCARAZ **In the news for:** Becoming the youngest man to win Grand Slam titles on all three types of tennis court surfaces. **Where:** Paris, France ▸▸ At only twenty-one years old, Alcaraz made history by becoming the youngest man to win Grand Slam titles on all three surfaces. Additionally, he has also become the youngest man to win three different Grand Slam events, surpassing Jimmy Connors's previous record set at twenty-two years and seven days.

RAMESHBABU PRAGGNANANDHAA

RAMESHBABU PRAGGNANANDHAA
In the news for: Beating world no. 1 Magnus Carlsen in classical chess. **Where:** Stavanger, Norway ▸▸ Rameshbabu Praggnanandhaa achieved a significant milestone by beating Magnus Carlsen, the top-ranked player globally, in classical chess at the third round of Norway Chess 2024. This win marks Praggnanandhaa's first classical victory over Carlsen. Carlsen won the top spot in the tournament with 17.5 points, with Praggnanandhaa securing the third rank with 14.5 points and Hikaru Nakamura at second place with 15.5 points.

RODRIGO HERNÁNDEZ CASCANTE **In the news for:** Being named UEFA Euro Player of the Tournament. **Where:** Berlin, Germany ▸▸ Spain midfielder Rodrigo Hernández Cascante (Rodri) was awarded the title of UEFA Euro 2024 Player of the Tournament after his significant contributions that led to La Roja's 2–1 victory over England in the final held in Berlin on 1 June. This victory also marks Spain's fourth win in the competition.

AVINASH SABLE

AVINASH SABLE **In the news for:** Improving his national record in 3000m steeplechase in Paris Diamond League 2024; **Where:** Paris, France ▸▸ Indian runner Avinash Sable set a new national record in the men's 3000m steeplechase event at the 2024 Paris Diamond League on 7 July. The Asian Games champion finished with a time of 8:09.91, improving his previous national record by over a second. He secured the sixth position in the event at the Charléty Stadium. The previous national record of 8:11.20 was achieved by Sable when he won silver at the Commonwealth Games in Birmingham two years ago.

ROHAN BOPANNA In the news for: Becoming the oldest player to win a Grand Slam. **Where:** Melbourne, Australia ▸▸ Rohan Bopanna made history by becoming the oldest player ever to win a Grand Slam at forty-three when he and Matthew Ebden defeated the Italian duo of Simone Bolelli and Andrea Vavassori 7–6(0), 7–5 in the men's doubles final at the 2024 Australian Open. Bopanna broke the record set by Jean-Julien Rojer, who claimed the French Open men's doubles championship in 2022 at the age of forty alongside Marcelo Arévalo.

LIONEL MESSI In the news for: Becoming the player with the most titles in football history. **Where:** Miami, USA ▸▸ Lionel Messi broke the record for the most collective titles in football history by winning the 2024 Copa América trophy. Messi now holds forty-five titles, surpassing Dani Alves. Messi's accomplishments consist of six titles with Argentina, thirty-five with Barcelona, three with PSG, and a Leagues Cup with Inter Miami.

VIRAT KOHLI In the news for: Becoming the first cricketer to achieve fifty ODI centuries. **Where:** Mumbai, India ▸▸ Virat Kohli surpassed Sachin Tendulkar by becoming the first cricketer to achieve fifty ODI centuries. Kohli has also exceeded Tendulkar's record for the most runs in a single ODI World Cup campaign, which Tendulkar set during the 2003 edition in South Africa.

NEERAJ CHOPRA In the news for: Winning a gold medal for javelin throw in the 2022 Asian Games. **Where:** Hangzhou, China ▸▸ Neeraj Chopra, the Indian javelin thrower, clinched the gold medal at the Asian Games with a huge throw of 88.88m, while Kishore Jena secured the silver medal with a distance of 87.45m. In 2021, Chopra grabbed the gold medal in Tokyo Olympics with a throw of 87.58m, making him the first track and field athlete from India to achieve Olympic gold.

LEWIS HAMILTON In the news for: Winning the British Grand Prix for the ninth time. **Where:** Northamptonshire, England ▸▸ Lewis Hamilton defeated Max Verstappen to secure his first victory since 2021, achieving a record-breaking ninth win at the British Grand Prix on 7 July. Hamilton secured the top spot with 25 points. Verstappen and Norris secured the second and the third place with 18 and 15 points, respectively.

RAVI DAHIYA In the news for: Being unable to compete in the Paris Olympics. **Where:** India ▸▸ Ravi Dahiya's hopes for the Paris Olympics were shattered on 21 May when the Wrestling Federation of India (WFI) opted not to conduct a final trial. The WFI decided that the six wrestlers who earned quotas by winning the previous trials in March 2024 would be the ones to compete. Dahiya was anticipating another opportunity in the men's 57 kg category.

SHEETAL DEVI **In the news for:** Indian archer who became a Para archery sensation against all odds. **Where:** Hangzhou, China ▸▸ World Archery Para Championships silver and Asian Para Games gold medalist Sheetal Devi was awarded the 'Best Para Woman Archer of the Year' award at the World Archery Awards. The sixteen-year-old made history by becoming the first Indian archer to receive this recognition. She also holds the title for the world's first armless archer to compete internationally.

VAISHALI RAMESHBABU

VAISHALI RAMESHBABU **In the news for:** Becoming the third Indian female grandmaster. **Where:** Spain ▸▸ Indian chess prodigy Vaishali Rameshbabu surpassed 2,500 International Chess Federation (FIDE) ranking points and secured her grandmaster title during the IV Elllobregat Open in Spain. This makes her the third Indian female grandmaster after Koneru Humpy and Harika Dronavalli. The victory also makes Vaishali and her brother Praggnanandhaa the world's first-ever brother–sister duo to become grandmasters.

SUNIL CHHETRI **In the news for:** Retiring. **Where:** New Delhi, India ▸▸ Indian footballer Sunil Chhetri retired from international football. The thirty-nine-year-old announced on social media that the FIFA World Cup qualifying match against Kuwait in Kolkata on 6 June would be his last. This signifies the end of a remarkable nineteen-year journey during which he became India's top goal scorer with a tally of ninety-four goals. Chhetri is also the fourth highest goal scorer in international matches after Cristiano Ronaldo, Ali Daei and Lionel Messi.

THOMAS MÜLLER **In the news for:** Retiring. **Where:** Munich, Germany ▸▸ German footballer Thomas Müller announced his retirement from international football. His final match was as a substitute in the eightieth minute during Germany's loss to Spain in the European Championship quarter-finals, marking his eighth major tournament appearance. Over a span of fourteen years, Müller earned 131 caps and netted forty-five goals. In 2010 World Cup, he scored five goals, which led to him receiving both the Golden Boot and the FIFA Young Player Award.

IMAGE COPYRIGHT INFORMATION

WIKIPEDIA COMMONS GODL-INDIA: 6 RAM JANMABHOOMI MANDIR: PIB on behalf of Prime Minister's Office; **7** RLV-TD LEX-02 Landing Experiment: ISRO; **9, 212** PMO MEETING T20 TEAM: PIB on behalf of Prime Minster's Office; **10** GAUTAM GAMBHIR: PIB on behalf of President's Secretariat; **17** SHEIKH HASINA: PIB on behalf of Prime Minster's Office; **56** MANU BHAKER: PIB on behalf of Prime Minster's Office; **151** RAKESH SHARMA: India/Indian Air Force; **156** GAGANYAAN CREW AT RUSSIA: ISRO; **203** CAR-T CELL THERAPY: PIB on behalf of President's Secretariat; **208** HARMANPREET KAUR: PIB on behalf of President's Secretariat; **209** P.V. SINDHU: PIB on behalf of Prime Minister's office; **WIKIMEDIA COMMONS PUBLIC DOMAIN/FREE TO USE/ OTHER LICENCES: 8** SONAM WANGCHUK: CC BY-SA 2.0 Generic: Sonam Wangchuk; **10** SUNITA WILLIAMS: NASA: http://www.jsc.nasa.gov/Bios/htmlbios/williams-s.html; **12** JAISHANKAR: CC BY-SA 4.0 International: Author: Department of Foreign Affairs and Trade (DFAT)/Michael Godfrey; AI: openclipart.org; **14** SOLAR STORM: CC BY-SA 2.0 Generic: Author: Markus Trienke; DONALD TRUMP: DOD photo by U.S. Air Force Staff Sgt. Jette Carr; **15** EBRAHIM RAISI: CC BY-SA 4.0 International: Author: Duma.gov.ru; **16** KEIR STARMER: Official Portrait: Picture by Simon Dawson/ No 10 Downing Street; **17** KAMALA HARRIS: Official Portrait: Picture by Lawrence Jackson; **34** AMRITA SHER-GIL: PD, JULES VERNE: Published by Goupil: Author: Étienne Carjat ; **35** MALCOM X: Author: Ed Ford, World Telegram staff photographer, WB YEATS: PD: Author: Alice Boughton; **36** HELEN KELLER: PD: Author: Whitman Studio; **37** MARIE ANTOINETTE: PD: Portrait by Élisabeth Louise Vigée Le Brun; **38** RUDYARD KIPLING: PD: Author: Bain News Service; **44** BERNARD BOSANQUET: PD, VIRENDER SEHWAG: CC BY-SA 2.0 Generic: Source: Flickr: Indian Cricket Team; **45** INDELIBLE INK: CC BY-SA 4.0 license: Author: AbhiSuryawanshi; **55** ARSHAD NADEEM: GNU Free Documentation License: Attribution: Erik van Leeuwen, SIMONE BILES: PD; **56** NEERAJ CHOPRA: CC BY-SA 4.0 International license: Author: DD News; **57** MANIKA BATRA: CC BY-SA 4.0 International license: Author: Government of Odisa; **142** LOKICERATOPS: CC BY-SA 2.0 Generic: Author: Mark Loewen; **146** PRZEWALSKI HORSE: CC BY-SA 2.0 Generic: Lawrence; **151** KALPANA CHAWLA: free licensed image catalogued by Johnson Space Centre, NASA, Photo ID: JS2002-E-25323; **152** ARTIMIS 2: Nasa Photo Credit: NASA/Kim Shiflett; **155** SOLAR SAIL BOOM: NASA/Aero Animation/Ben Schweighart; **200** CELLPHONE SPEED: openclipart by j4p4n; **206** VISWANATHAN ANAND: CC BY-SA 2.0 Generic/GFHund, SAINA NEHWAL: CCA-SA 3.0 Unported/Bollywood Hungama; **210** OLEKSANDR USYK: CC BY-SA 2.0 Generic: Author: Web Summit, DING LIREN: CC BY-SA 2.0 Generic: Author: Frans Peeters, GUKESH D.: CC BY-SA 2.0 Generic: Author: Frans Peeters; **214** LEWIS HAMILTON: CC BY-SA 2.0 Generic: Author: Agência Senado; **215** KREJCIKOVA: CC BY-SA 2.0 Generic: Author: si.robi; **216** CARLOS ALCARAZ: CC BY-SA 2.0 Generic: Author: si.robi, RAMESHBABU PRAGGNANANDHAA: CC BY-SA 2.0 Generic: Author: Frans Peeters, AVINASH SABLE: CC BY-SA 2.0 Generic: Author: U.S. Army; **217** NEERAJ CHOPRA: CC BY-SA 4.0 International license: Author: Anass Sedrati; **218** RAMESHBABU VAISHALI: CC BY-SA 3.0 Unported license: Stefan64; **PIXABAY:** 5, 11, 13, 141-146, 172, 204; **SHUTTERSTOCK: 9** IPL logo: Satheesh Sankaran / Shutterstock.com; **10, 56** VINESH PHOGAT: Attribution: Azamat; **47** NARENDER MODI: Exposure Visuals / Shutterstock.com **52** ELECTION: Saikat Paul / Shutterstock.com; **53** PEOPLE IN FRONT OF POLLING BOOTH: Sansad Bhavan: Shutterstock.com; **205** MILKHA SINGH: cameranest/Shutterstock.com; **213** MBAPPE: ph.FAB / Shutterstock.com; **217** LIONEL MESSI: Ringo Chiu / Shutterstock.com; MAPS: (Pictorial representations): Syed Salahaddin [Please see disclaimer on copyright page (2)]; **ALL OTHER PHOTOGRAPHS AND ILLUSTRATIONS SOURCED FROM THE PUBLIC DOMAIN.**